THE WARREN COURT

IN HISTORICAL AND

POLITICAL PERSPECTIVE

THE WARREN COURT

IN HISTORICAL AND

POLITICAL PERSPECTIVE

EDITED BY

MARK TUSHNET

UNIVERSITY PRESS OF VIRGINIA

Charlottesville and London

THE UNIVERSITY PRESS OF VIRGINIA

FIRST PUBLISHED 1993

Library of Congress Cataloging-in-Publication Data
The Warren court in historical and political perspective/edited by
 Mark Tushnet.
  p. cm.—(Constitutionalism and democracy)
  Based on papers presented at a symposium held at Georgetown
University, Jan. 27, 1990.
  Includes bibliographical references and index.
  ISBM 0-8139-1459-0
  1. United States. Supreme Court—History. 2. Judges—United
States—Biography. 3. Warren, Earl, 1891-1974. I. Tushnet, Mark
V., 1945- . II. Series.
KF8742.A5W37 1993
347.73'26'09—dc20
[347.3073509]   93-12626
                                                                 CIP

PRINTED IN THE UNITED STATES OF AMERICA

To the memory of Arthur Goldberg

CONTENTS

Earl Warren served as chief justice from 1953 to 1969, and "the Warren Court" stands as a distinct period in the history of the Supreme Court. Although the influence of the Warren Court remains important—its activism continues to affect discussions of the Supreme Court, and its decisions in many areas remain unimpaired—the period is now a fruitful topic for historical investigation. Archives containing material dealing with the appointments of the members of the Warren Court and, perhaps more important, with the internal deliberations of the Court are now available. Sufficient time has passed for historians to be in a position to locate the activism of the Warren Court in its historical context—the flourishing of the New Deal political coalition that culminated in Lyndon Johnson's Great Society programs. And, perhaps, we can now see more clearly the ways in which the co-existence of the New Deal coalition and the Warren Court's activism masked the possibility that the Warren Court's activism was a historical aberration for a Court more accustomed to letting legislatures have their way. A historical retrospective on the Warren Court, in short, seems appropriate even though that Court has continuing influence on public and academic perceptions of the activity of a Court now very differently constituted.

The essays in this volume offer biographical, historical, and legal perspectives, in varying combinations, on the Warren Court. The authors ask how individual justices contributed to the operation of the collective body we call the Warren Court. Some, like Justice Felix Frankfurter, helped constitute the Warren Court by voicing deep opposition to the way in which the Court was carrying out its work. Others, like Justice William Brennan, constituted the Court not only by playing an important role in coordinating the actions of the liberal justices but, as Robert Post argues, by articulating the central themes animating the Court's decisions. The interplay among biographical, historical, and legal perspectives offers important insights into the place of the Warren Court—and perhaps by implication the place of the Supreme Court—in United States history.

The collection of essays is divided, somewhat arbitrarily, into three sections. If only because it was the Warren Court, Professor G. Edward White's analysis of the influence of Earl Warren on the Court, and of the concept of "influence" itself, deserves first place. Yet, the Warren Court was in many ways the culmination of the jurisprudence of the New Deal, and it is therefore appropriate to reach back to the "first generation" of participants in the Warren Court, the appointees of Franklin Roosevelt who sat through much of Warren's tenure on the Court. The composition of the Court changes with some regularity, of course, and as the Warren Court proceeded, two justices became the focal points of the Court's activity. The second section deals with these justices, John Marshall Harlan, the conservative, and William Brennan, the liberal.

The final section deals with another group of justices, who can be described in at least two ways. Compared to Black, Harlan, or Brennan, Justice Byron White—despite the length of his service—is a relatively minor figure in the history of the Supreme Court, and Justice Abe Fortas served for such a short period that he too cannot be considered central to the composition of the Warren Court. The essays on these justices might be understood, therefore, as portraits of some of the workers in the vineyards of the law, laboring away while larger battles are being fought around them and having some influence on the outcome of those battles if only because they have votes to be cast one way or the other. Yet, seen in another way, these justices may appear rather more interesting. Unlike the more central figures, they accepted the assumptions of the Warren Court's activism without serious question, and their work can illustrate what might be thought of as the "normal science" of the law in the midst of contesting paradigms. In many ways it is only when a Court's assumptions are accepted almost unreflectively that we can understand precisely what those assumptions and their implications are, and the essays on Justices White and Fortas offer us that understanding.

Most of the chapters in this volume were presented in shorter versions at a symposium at the Georgetown University Law Center held on January 27, 1990. I am grateful to the Law Center and the following sponsors of the conference for their financial support: Covington & Burling; Hogan & Hartson; Miller, Cassidy, Larroca & Lewin; E. Barrett Prettyman, Jr.; and Wilmer, Cutler & Pickering. In addition I would like to thank former Assistant Dean June Jones for her help in putting the conference on and for the superb performance of her job throughout her tenure at the Law Center.

Chapter Four (by Melvin I. Urofsky), entitled "William O. Douglas as Common Law Judge," first appeared under the same title in *Duke Law Journal* 41 (Spring 1991): 133-59. Chapter Six (by Norman Dorsen), entitled "John Marshall Harlan and the Warren Court," first appeared under the same title in the 1991 *Journal of Supreme Court History*, pp. 50-62, and in an earlier version under the title "John Marshall Harlan, Civil Liberties, and the Warren Court" in *New York Law School Law Review* 36 (1991): 81-107. Chapter Seven (by Robert C. Post), entitled "William J. Brennan and the Warren Court," first appeared under the same title in *Constitutional Commentary* 8 (Winter 1991): 11-25.

THE WARREN COURT

IN HISTORICAL AND

POLITICAL PERSPECTIVE

1 *MARK TUSHNET*

The Warren Court as History

An Interpretation

Earl Warren was chief justice of the United States Supreme Court from 1954 to 1969, and "the Warren Court" is an established fixture in the public's understanding of the Supreme Court's role in government. The Warren Court's influence extended beyond Earl Warren's tenure, however, and that poses a problem for historians attempting to analyze the Warren Court. Ordinarily we gain historical insight on events and institutions only when we have enough distance from them to see them less as objects of current political controversy and more as subjects located within a broader sweep of historical events. The Warren Court's definition of the Supreme Court's role in government remains prominent in contemporary political discussion: liberals today yearn for a return to the Warren Court's true course, just as conservatives take the Warren Court to represent everything a Supreme Court should not be.

Perhaps the Warren Court remains too close for historical analysis, and perhaps the most we can hope for is a scorecard toting up decisions the analyst likes and dislikes. Nonetheless, at least a speculative beginning at a historical analysis of the Warren Court seems possible now. Twenty years have passed since Warren's retirement. Materials from within the Court have become available for scholars to study,[1] and at least some of the Warren Court's decisions can be seen in perspective. At the same time, though, the Warren Court is in important ways still with us, and the inevitable present-mindedness of historians means that some parts of what follows may be more affected by contemporary issues than a mature analysis will be.[2]

To understand the Warren Court, we must first define it. After a preliminary attempt to identify "the Warren Court" as a period in the Court's history, this chapter treats the Warren Court as an actor in 1960s politics. An examination of some Warren Court principles of constitutional adjudication identifies some aspects of that Court's liberalism that may have been overlooked in previous discussions of the Warren Court's liberalism.[3] The following section sketches differences between the Warren Court's personnel and deliberative processes and those of its predecessors and successors and speculates on the reasons for those differences. The final section returns to the question of periodization, examining the argument—alluded to in the later chapters on justices Warren and Brennan—that the best way to understand the recent history of the Supreme Court is to discuss not "the Warren Court" but "the Brennan Court."

I

By now the resonances are clear when one talks about the Warren Court to a knowledgeable audience. The Warren Court implemented the modern liberal agenda, enforcing norms of fair treatment and racial equality that, in their core meanings, are no longer substantially contested in American society. Yet, if the Warren Court's image in contemporary culture is clear, the congruence between that image and the Supreme Court's behavior during Earl Warren's tenure is less clear. The difficulties arise both during the years of his tenure and after. The Supreme Court's abortion decisions of 1973 generally are seen as products of "the Warren Court," and, in some sense, properly so. Yet the decisions were issued by a Court that Warren had left several years before, and indeed by a Court with four members appointed by Richard Nixon, who had pledged to change the Court's direction away from the liberal activism that to Nixon characterized the Warren Court.

The Warren Court's cultural image as modern liberalism's instrument, then, overlaps imperfectly with the reality of the Supreme

Court's actions. The reason may be that the rhythms of change on the Supreme Court are coordinated only imperfectly with the rhythms of change in society and culture. In the grand sweep of things, the Supreme Court—as a part of "the government"—is unlikely to stay out of line with views that prevail elsewhere in the government.

Those views, however, can take several forms. They may be the positions taken by the political tendency in control of Congress or the presidency. Structurally, life-tenured appointments to the Supreme Court mean that, on this level, the views that prevail on the Court may well differ substantially, and for a decade or more, from those that prevail elsewhere. With a broader time frame—a generation rather than a decade—the differences are likely to disappear. Prevailing views may take another, more general form—"ideologies" like the acceptance of large-scale government that followed the New Deal and is still with us. These ideologies have a life span long enough that after a transitional period the ones that prevail on the Supreme Court are quite unlikely to differ from those that prevail elsewhere.

The Supreme Court, in short, is unlikely to be an aberrational institution in the United States political system. And, indeed, the Supreme Court under Earl Warren was not aberrational, either in its broad ideology or in its particular positions. On the ideological level the Warren Court fully participated in the grand sweep of political liberalism that pervaded the political system, in various guises, from the New Deal to the Reagan Revolution and perhaps beyond. Like the political branches, the Warren Court accepted large government as necessary. Building on doctrinal developments during Fred Vinson's tenure and on political developments rooted most directly in the administrations of Harry Truman and Franklin Roosevelt, the Warren Court accepted and then elaborated the proposition that in our constitutional system all Americans are entitled to the benefits of formal equality.

Many observers sense, though, that the Warren Court was quite unusual in United States history. That sense may derive from two sources. First, the Warren Court was a liberal Court, in that its decisions were compatible with the policy agenda of political liberals during the 1960s and 1970s. Perhaps because political liberalism in the contemporary sense had never been a dominant force in national politics before, no Supreme Court had been liberal in that sense either. Second, for reasons discussed in more detail below, the "Warren Court"—as a cultural phenomenon—probably came into existence in the early 1960s. The Court's actions between 1954 and 1962 do not, on the whole and with the large exception of *Brown v. Board of Education,* play a major role in the public or historical perception of the "Warren Court." When that Warren Court was created, it was fully compatible with the dominant political coalition. Yet, some of the Warren Court's impulses persisted through the 1970s and into the 1980s, as the final section of this chapter suggests. By then, the political picture had changed, and the residue of the Warren Court was indeed in tension with the dominant political coalition. What remained of the Warren Court after the retirement of Earl Warren was aberrational, in lacking coordination with dominant political forces, in just the way that the Supreme Court from 1935 to 1937 was aberrational.

The foregoing argument rests on the proposition that the Warren Court came into existence in 1962. Before that, the image of a "liberal" Warren Court corresponds only imperfectly with the reality. Issues of race and McCarthyism dominated the national political scene during the first years of Warren's tenure. The Warren Court's image arose in part from the drama of *Brown v. Board of Education* at the outset of Warren's tenure.[4] The Court had postponed deciding *Brown* when Fred Vinson was chief justice, and the decision invalidating segregation, culminating the first term that Warren headed the Court, established the Warren Court as a symbol of modern liberalism. Had the justices sitting with Vinson been pushed to decide, a majority probably would have voted to invalidate segregation.[5] But with Vinson in charge, no one was pressing for a decision. Warren's arrival crystallized what was probably a latent majority, and his persuasive abilities eliminated the risk that Justice Stanley Reed would dissent.

The justices thought unanimity important because they believed that the South would more readily accept a unanimous decision. That belief turned out to be mistaken. The Court overturned segregation because the Justices all agreed that desegregation should occur gradually. As Armstead Robinson and Patricia Sullivan put it, "Southern whites interpreted the Supreme Court's 'with all deliberate speed' proviso . . . as a license to resist."[6] The justices had no real sense of what gradual desegregation was, and they were willing to let the lower federal courts work out the contours of acceptable desegregation plans. The early Warren Court generally took a hands-off approach to *Brown's* implementation. Still, the Little Rock school crisis reinforced the Court's image as a vigorous defender of racial equality. In *Cooper v.*

Aaron the Court sharply criticized violent resistance to *Brown* and vigorously insisted that the basic desegregation ruling was the law of the land.[7] Even though the Supreme Court itself contributed little to accomplishing desegregation before 1964, *Cooper v. Aaron* demonstrated the Court's continuing commitment to *Brown*'s vision of racial equality.

Close observers of the Court understood the limits of the Court's commitment. The limits were reached in *Naim v. Naim,* a challenge to a Virginia statute barring racial intermarriage.[8] The justices knew that they could not uphold the statute without undermining *Brown*'s moral force, yet they knew as well that they could not invalidate the statute, which represented the heart of the white South's emotional commitment to segregation, without exacerbating an already difficult situation.[9] On entirely specious grounds the Court refused to consider the constitutional challenge. The Court invoked technical grounds to explain its refusal, and only an insider could appreciate that on the facts of *Naim,* those grounds were quite ridiculous. Thus, even *Naim* could not seriously impair the Warren Court's liberal image in race-related cases.

The Warren Court's early confrontations with McCarthyism and associated issues of national security during the Cold War also suggested that the Warren Court would be reliably liberal. In 1951 the Vinson Court affirmed the convictions of leading Communists for violating the federal Smith Act, which prohibited subversive advocacy.[10] Six years later the Warren Court reversed the Smith Act convictions of second-rank Communist leaders. In an opinion by Justice John Marshall Harlan—hardly at the liberal core of the later Warren Court—the Court held that the statute, read in light of First Amendment values, required the government to prove that the defendants advocated unlawful action, not merely that they advocated doctrines that if followed would lead people to violate the law.[11]

McCarthy-inspired investigations of subversive activity also came before the Warren Court in 1957, and again the Court limited the legislatures' ability to examine the activities of Communists and their associates.[12] The Court skirted direct rulings on fundamental constitutional issues in most of these cases. Instead of finding that the First Amendment limited a legislature's ability to investigate, for example, the Court said that, if an investigation touched on free expression concerns, the legislature itself had to authorize its committee in quite clear terms to ask sensitive questions. In *Jencks v. United States,* a Smith Act case, the Court developed a general rule requiring prosecutors to disclose certain evidence to defendants, limiting the government's ability to use confidential sources of information.[13] Although the rule applied to all federal criminal prosecutions, observers took it as another example of the Warren Court's suspicion of McCarthyite prosecutions.

These decisions provoked an outpouring of adverse commentary.[14] Some members of Congress resented the Court's efforts to limit their ability to investigate whatever and however they chose; others saw the decisions as part of a sustained challenge to the nation's ability to combat subversion. Although most legislative attempts to overturn the Court's decisions failed, Congress did enact a statute, commonly known as the Jencks Act, imposing some procedural limits on how defendants could get evidence from the prosecutor.

In the face of this response, the Court retreated—or so it seemed. From 1959 to 1961 the Court decided a number of national security cases. It upheld legislative investigations and affirmed a Smith Act conviction.[15] In each case the Court's majority insisted that it had not changed course but said that the earlier cases were distinguishable on various grounds. From a careful lawyer's viewpoint, the cases were indeed distinguishable. Nonetheless, many commentators were skeptical of the majority's claims, particularly because the later cases were decided over strong dissents by the liberal core of the Warren Court—Warren himself and justices Black, Douglas, and Brennan—who insisted that the Court was effectively repudiating the precedents.[16] Further, when the Court overturned convictions on technical grounds, it could avoid deciding basic First Amendment questions, but when it affirmed convictions, it had to rule as well that the First Amendment did not protect the defendants. In that sense the later cases went further than the earlier ones and departed from the liberal position. Perhaps the most dramatic example was the Court's decision in 1961 sustaining the McCarren Subversive Activities Control Act of 1950 against a First Amendment challenge. By a five-to-four vote the Court held that Congress could require the Communist party to register with the government as a subversive organization.[17]

By 1961, then, the liberal image of the Warren Court was somewhat blurred. It had decided *Brown* and *Cooper v. Aaron* but otherwise had done little in the area of race, and *Naim* suggested that the Court had its limits. After an early foray to defend civil liberties against McCarthyite assaults, the Court retreated. The divisions on the Court, and its changes in direction, show that the Warren Court had not yet truly come into being.

The situation changed dramatically in 1962, however, and the change can be dated quite precisely.[18] Justice Charles Whittaker, a relatively conservative Republican who had served only since 1957, retired on April 1, 1962, psychologically overwhelmed by the difficulty he had in deciding the Court's hard cases. Justice Frankfurter, the most articulate proponent of judicial restraint on the Court, suffered a severe stroke on April 6; he resigned from the Court in August.

President John Kennedy appointed Byron White to replace Whittaker. White, the deputy attorney general, had played a prominent role in Kennedy's election campaign and, as William Nelson shows in his chapter, was strongly committed to using national legislative power to advance racial equality. To replace Frankfurter, Kennedy nominated Arthur Goldberg, his secretary of labor. Goldberg was a particularly valuable addition to the liberal core of the Warren Court, and his arrival created a solid liberal majority. Three years later President Lyndon Johnson persuaded Goldberg to resign to become ambassador to the United Nations where, Johnson said, Goldberg, a skilled mediator, could help resolve the Vietnam War and other international controversies. Abe Fortas, Goldberg's replacement, was just as reliable a liberal. When Johnson named Thurgood Marshall to the Court in 1967 to replace Tom Clark, the liberals were firmly in control. The "real" Warren Court, then, lasted from 1962 to 1969, when Warren retired.

The shift from the ambiguously liberal early Warren Court to the solidly liberal later one was illustrated dramatically in two cases first argued before Whittaker and Frankfurter resigned but decided after they left the Court. Both involved aspects of the southern attack on the National Association for the Advancement of Colored People, the organization that had guided the attack on segregation.[19] As part of a package of laws aimed at preventing desegregation, Virginia amended its statutes regulating the practice of law. One new rule barred private lawyers, like the ones who cooperated with the NAACP, from accepting referrals from nonlawyers, like NAACP staff members. Another modified the state's traditional prohibition of barratry—a long-established ban on stirring up litigation—by making it a misdemeanor for one person to pay another's litigation expenses. Enforcing these statutes would, as Chief Justice Warren noted during one of the Court discussions of the cases, have put the NAACP "out of business." After a fair amount of procedural wrangling, the NAACP's challenge to these statutes reached the Supreme Court in 1961.

At the same time the Court took up a Florida case linking the issues of race and national security. Southern legislatures tried to undermine the NAACP by treating it as a Communist front. In 1956 Florida created an investigating committee charged with probing connections between the NAACP and the Communists. By early 1958 the committee was looking at the Miami NAACP branch. After hearing testimony that two Communist party members had been NAACP members as well, the committee asked the branch president to turn over the branch membership list. He refused, and the case made its way to the Supreme Court. By the time the case got to the Court, the issue was whether the branch president had to answer questions about specific individuals after consulting the membership lists as a basis for his answer.

After the Virginia and Florida cases were first argued, the Court divided five to four in both, with the majority voting to uphold the states' actions. Frankfurter drafted a typically elaborate opinion in the Virginia case arguing that the state had adopted a reasonable reform of traditional rules regulating legal practice. Black and Douglas circulated proposed dissents emphasizing the connection between the new barratry statute and Virginia's resistance to desegregation; Black's draft said that the statute "could more accurately be labeled 'An Act to make it difficult and dangerous for the [NAACP] and Virginia lawyers to assert the constitutional rights of Negroes in state and federal courts.'" Harlan drafted the proposed majority opinion in the Florida case. He believed that the states "must have the power to ferret out communists," and that Florida had acted "responsibly" in requiring the branch president simply to use the membership lists to refresh his recollection about who was in the branch. His proposed opinion argued that the Court could not require the legislative committee to show "probable cause" for believing that there were Communists in the branch; that would be to ask the legislature "to prove in advance the very things it is trying to find out," as he put it later.[20]

The day after Whittaker announced his retirement, the Court, faced with a four-to-four division among the justices, ordered the cases reargued. Then, when Frankfurter resigned in August, the justices who had dealt with the cases found that a five-to-four majority against the NAACP's claims unexpectedly had become a four-to-three majority in their favor. After the cases were reargued with Goldberg and White on the bench, Goldberg added his vote to the new majority and was assigned to write the Court's opinion in the Florida case. His opinion stressed the importance of rights of association and concluded that Florida had failed to show "a substantial relation between the information sought and a subject of overriding and compelling state interest." He distinguished the early Warren Court's more conservative constitutional decisions dealing directly with the Communist party because they involved inquiries into membership in the party itself, "not an ordinary or legitimate political party, as known in this country."

Justice Brennan wrote the opinion for the new majority in the Virginia case. It is notable for two reasons. First, Brennan found it impossible to write an opinion invalidating the Virginia statute on classic First Amendment grounds. He could not show that regulating attorneys as Virginia did actually violate central free expression rights. He did find that litigation was "a form of political expression." But to invalidate the Virginia statute, he had to read it to bar "any arrangement by which prospective litigants are advised to seek the assistance of particular attorneys." This was a rather strained though defensible reading of the statute. Then, with the statute stretched to cover such activities, it was easy for Brennan to show that it cut too broadly into free expression rights. As Robert Post shows in his chapter, Brennan was attracted to the idea of overbreadth as ground of decision, here as elsewhere, because invalidating a statute as overbroad did not completely deny the state's ability to regulate the field; on its face it simply asked the state to go back and try again.

The second notable aspect of the Virginia decision arose from comments Frankfurter made during the Court's consideration of the case. Frankfurter was offended when Black suggested that the statute was aimed at the NAACP. He could not imagine "a worse disservice than to continue to being guardians of negroes," and he objected, in a related context, to "taking short cuts, to discriminate as partisans in favor of Negroes." Brennan's overbreadth analysis revived this issue, at least for Harlan. To show that "a vague and overbroad statute lends itself to selective enforcement against unpopular causes," Brennan included a two-page footnote listing NAACP cases showing that "the militant Negro civil rights movement has engendered the intense resentment and opposition of the politically dominant white community of Virginia." Harlan's dissent opened with a criticism of the cast of mind he thought the majority opinion reflected. The "same constitutional standards" must apply "whether or not racial problems are involved. No worse setback could befall the great principles established by *Brown* than to give fair-minded persons reason to think otherwise." Responding to Harlan's point, Brennan added "a final observation" to his opinion, saying that "the Constitution protects expression and association without regard to the race, creed, or political or religious affiliation of the members of the group which invokes its shield."

Brennan's use of overbreadth and his exchange with Harlan suggest an important dimension of the late Warren Court's liberalism. There was a certain willfulness to the Court's actions. The majority knew that the result was correct, and if one doctrinal approach would not get it there—if free speech theory was not quite satisfactory—some other approach—overbreadth, for instance—would have to do. A similar willfulness characterized the Warren Court's handling of the sit-in cases.[21] The cases came to the Court in 1962 and 1963. Doctrinally the cases were extremely difficult. The sit-ins occurred because private restaurants refused to serve African-Americans. Protesters sat in and were arrested for trespassing on private property or for causing a breach of the peace. The Warren Court regularly invalidated statutes and ordinances requiring segregation in private businesses, but the doctrinal tools to deal with private discrimination were not readily at hand. The fundamental difficulty was that the Constitution, as the Court interpreted it, prohibited only discriminatory state action, leaving private entities free to discriminate if they chose.

The Court might have said that although private owners can try to exclude African-Americans, as soon as they ask the police to enforce the discrimination by expelling protesters, there is state action. That theory, though, would have gone far to eliminate the state action requirement, and most of the justices were unwilling to do that. Instead, they searched for theories that would allow them to invalidate convictions of protesters without impairing the state action doctrine. Their search led them to a number of innovative results. Sometimes the Court found that although a city did not have an ordinance requiring segregation, statements by city officials effectively required restaurants to segregate their facilities.[22] Sometimes it strained to find that the protesters could not have known that their activities were unlawful.[23]

The Warren Court's willfulness is perhaps best illustrated in the

1963 sit-in cases. At the Court's conference the justices voted to decide the fundamental issue of whether private discrimination enforced through state trespass and breach of the peace laws violated the Constitution. A five-to-four majority voted that it did not. At a later conference Justice Goldberg tried to shake a vote loose from the majority but failed. Then justices Warren and Brennan switched to what Bernard Schwartz calls "a delaying tactic."[24] They persuaded Justice Stewart that so important an issue should not be decided without getting the views of the solicitor general, whose earlier amicus brief had not addressed the fundamental issue but instead urged the Court to reverse the convictions on narrow grounds.

The brief did not change any votes, though, and the justices began to circulate proposed opinions. As the cases had hung around the Court, most had been resolved without deciding the central issue. By the spring of 1963, the only vehicle left was a Maryland case. Brennan found a Maryland law, enacted after the sit-ins in Maryland, that prohibited discrimination in public accommodations, and he suggested that the case should be remanded to the Maryland courts for them to decide whether the new statute somehow invalidated the earlier convictions. When Black redrafted his proposed majority opinion to deal with Brennan's argument, Brennan insisted that the Court hold off from announcing the decision for two more weeks. At the Court's final conference before the decisions were to be released, Justice Clark announced that he had decided to go along with Brennan's position. At that point Black had only four votes to affirm the convictions, Brennan had his own vote and Clark's to remand the case to the Maryland courts, and Warren, Douglas, and Goldberg wanted to reverse the convictions completely.

Although Warren and Goldberg were willing to go along with Brennan's approach, Douglas refused, and another month was consumed in maneuvering over exactly how to dispose of the cases. Black made the most pointed argument: Six justices were prepared to decide whether it violated the Constitution to enforce private discrimination through trespass prosecutions, and four of them believed that the convictions should be affirmed. Realizing that the Court had reached an impasse, Justice Stewart decided to leave Black and join Brennan. At the end, five justices agreed to remand the case to the state court, but a total of six justices addressed the merits, dividing evenly.

What is most notable about these events is how insistently Brennan refused to lose. As the Court dealt with the cases, Congress was debating the statute that became the Civil Rights Act of 1964, and Brennan believed that a Court decision affirming sit-in convictions would only encourage those opposing the statute. So, though he was in the minority on the Court from the beginning to just before—and perhaps even through—the end, Brennan kept inventing reasons for holding a decision off. The delays increased the pressures on his colleagues, to the point that both Clark and Stewart defected from the majority.

Brennan insisted on securing the outcome he desired, but he did not willfully ignore the demands of legality. He was unwilling to abandon the state action doctrine simply to reverse the convictions and struggled to win within a rather constraining set of doctrinal limitations. More generally, the later Warren Court had a policy agenda that its members strove mightily to advance. They were not, however, lawless—certainly not lawless in the way that the *Naim* Court had been. In the Virginia barratry case, Brennan drew on some of his earlier cases suggesting a doctrine of overbreadth, and although the doctrine had not been fully developed by 1962, his opinion contributed to the doctrine's evolution into its mature form. Similarly, the remand to the Maryland courts to consider the implications of a more recent state law, while somewhat creative, was a good example of the Court's techniques for avoiding constitutional questions. The later Warren Court began to transform the law; as Professor Urofsky's chapter suggests, its steps, when evaluated according to the terms prevalent at the time, may have seemed awkward. Gradually, the legal changes became settled law, defining the terrain on which discussions would thereafter be held.

The later Warren Court is the Warren Court that has entered our culture. That Warren Court was created in 1962. Never monolithic, the Court remained divided. And as the liberalism of the early 1960s gave way to the liberalism for the 1970s, new tensions arose even among the core group of Warren Court's liberals. Before considering how long the Warren Court lasted, we should examine the political role and the nature of the Warren Court's liberalism.

II

The Warren Court was a liberal Court. After 1962 it was one institution in a unified government dominated in both Congress and the presidency by liberal Democrats. Martin Shapiro has emphasized the importance of seeing the Supreme Court as a political actor,[25] and the Warren Court's relation to liberal politics deserves special attention. Shapiro's approach must be handled delicately, though, because it is all too easy to slip between understanding the Court as a political actor and assuming that the justices understood themselves to be acting politically. Sometimes some did, of course, as Justice Frankfurter suggested when he told law clerks that the Court had delayed deciding *Brown* because the justices did not want "to come down with it in an election year."[26] Most of the time the Justices believed, simply, that they were interpreting the Constitution in the most sensible way. The justices on the Warren Court developed a way of thinking about constitutional adjudication in which the public could hardly discern the line between interpreting the Constitution, what the justices thought they were doing, and advancing the program of liberal politics, what the justices were also doing.

The modern Supreme Court was shaped by the New Deal experience, and the Court in the New Deal was in turn shaped by its reaction to the conservative Court that preceded it. After Franklin Roosevelt's effort to get Congress to pass legislation allowing him to pack the Supreme Court failed in 1937, Roosevelt proceeded to pack the Court by appointing justices who transformed it. As Shapiro puts it, the new justices came to occupy the last redoubt of the New Deal's opponents. They then had to choose what to do. Shapiro extends the military metaphor by pointing out that the New Deal Court had to choose between dismantling the weapons their opponents had used against them, by adopting a general theory of judicial restraint across the board, and turning those weapons against their former opponents, by developing a revised theory of judicial activism.

That choice preoccupied the Court for the next decade or so. As the New Deal justices considered their predecessors, they divided over what had gone wrong. For some the pre–New Deal Court was wrong because it was conservative and obstructed the adoption of progressive social programs. For those holding this view, there would be nothing wrong with a liberal Court that advanced progressive programs, even beyond what Congress and state legislatures wanted to do. For others the pre-New Deal Court was wrong because it invalidated legislation on grounds that had no support in the Constitution itself. These justices needed a theory to explain when and how the Court could properly find statutes unconstitutional. The early years of the New Deal Court were dominated by a search for theoretical bases to rest judicial review on; but by 1962, when the late Warren Court came into being, those disputes had played themselves out.

Led by Frankfurter, some justices articulated—and inconsistently applied—a theory of judicial restraint, arguing that the Court should be reluctant to override decisions made by legislatures because legislatures had a form of democratic legitimacy that the Court lacked. Other justices questioned the premise of judicial restraint that legislatures had democratic legitimacy in all that they did. Elaborating an insight first articulated in a passing footnote by Justice Harlan Fiske Stone,[27] they argued that the Court could identify situations where the democratic process malfunctioned—where some voters were kept from exercising the franchise, where some options were foreclosed when the legislature barred people from advocating them, or where prejudice meant that legislatures disregarded the interests of some voters. Less concerned with developing an overarching theory of constitutional adjudication, some New Deal justices like Frank Murphy and Wiley Rutledge believed that their commission was to ensure just outcomes in politics and law.

Frankfurter's judicial restraint was more a mood than a theory or doctrine. The Warren Court never found itself in that mood for long. The early Warren Court was the final stage in Frankfurter's ultimately unsuccessful struggle to induce the Court as a whole to adopt his stance. One reason for his failure lay in the New Deal coalition's successes. New Deal constitutional theory established that the Court should not interfere with the social welfare programs that legislatures adopted. The New Deal justices, though, had no desire to interfere with such programs. They could adopt the rhetoric of judicial restraint to explain why they accepted what legislatures did, but they hardly had to worry: refusing to invalidate social welfare programs was compatible with judicial restraint, the justices' sense of whether the democratic process had functioned properly, and their sense of just outcomes. Under these circumstances it began to seem less important to have a general theory of judicial restraint at hand to deal with the central problems that preoccupied New Deal constitutional theory.

When new problems emerged, the justices began to divide, and Frankfurter's opponents had the upper hand. Again, Shapiro's insights direct attention to the correct issues. Seeing the Court as an actor in politics, Shapiro considers the justices as allies of elements in the New Deal political coalition. The New Deal justices took labor unions and African-Americans as their particular constituencies. Like all politicians, the justices never fully satisfied the demands of their constituencies, as the Court's effective withdrawal from supervising desegregation between 1955 and 1964 shows. Further, the political positions of those constituencies went beyond the mere self-interest that often characterizes *interest groups* when the term is used as a pejorative. Many elements in the New Deal coalition understood that their own interests could be advanced best by adopting inclusive programs, which made them attentive to the concerns of people outside their particular constituencies. Whether characterized as extended self-interest, civic concern, or altruism, this attention to a broader public was part of the political position of the New Deal Court's constituencies.

Where those constituencies could not secure protection through the political process, the Court came to their aid. The New Deal Court's law of free expression was shaped by the union experience of labor picketing, on the one hand, and Communist influence within unions, on the other. Starting with *Hague v. CIO* in 1939 and *Thornhill v. Alabama* the next year, to *Giboney v. Empire Storage Co.* in 1949, the New Deal Court struggled to develop a law of free expression that provided sufficient scope for public regulation of disorder while allowing unions sufficient scope to organize. In 1950 the Court's decision in *American Communications Association v. Douds* upholding a statute denying unions with Communist leaders the benefits of the national collective bargaining system further elaborated the New Deal Court's First Amendment doctrine. The experience gained in the decade of the 1940s helped shape the justices' approach to the constitutional questions it faced in 1951 when leaders of the Communist party were convicted of violating the Smith Act. Although it was much more, *Brown v. Board of Education,* seen in this light, was a decision on behalf of its special constituencies: African-Americans and the political ideologists who took the elimination of segregation to be a core element in American liberalism.

By the middle of the 1950s, though, the political situation confronting the Court began to change. The New Deal had succeeded completely; although Dwight Eisenhower, a Republican, occupied the White House, the New Deal's fundamental principles were no longer controversial. If the reconstituted Roosevelt Court had to decide whether to use its weapons against the enemy, by the mid-1950s there were, in essence, no enemies to worry about, only problems to be cleared up.

In an important way the general acceptance of the New Deal program freed the Court from some constraints. In the presence of a real enemy, it had been important for the Court, seen as a political actor, to ensure that its actions were compatible with those of its allies in the New Deal coalition. With the enemy's disappearance, the Court could begin to act as an independent political force. Again *Brown* illustrates the Court's new position. The Democratic party coalition included southerners who tended to support—some wholeheartedly and some with misgivings—the social and economic agenda of the party, but who were adamantly opposed—either out of conviction or in response to political reality—to altering the southern system of race relations. Democratic party activists in the North, as well as liberal Republicans, believed that segregation had to go. Not only was it wrong, but it was an embarrassment to the nation in the international ideological competition with the Soviet Union. The Court's decision in *Brown* was, in the political sense, an act by one part of the governing coalition against another.

The Warren Court came into its own as an independent political actor after 1962. Frankfurter's retirement removed the Court's most forceful voice for a general theory of judicial restraint. Warren and his core liberal colleagues—Brennan, Fortas, Marshall—were unconcerned with general matters of constitutional theory. In part they relied implicitly on the assumption that the political process tended to work badly when issues associated with race were involved.[28] They tended to define *race issues* more broadly than their predecessors had. Criminal procedure cases had often been race-related: in the 1930s the principal cases involving coerced confessions and ineffective assistance of counsel were all race-related.[29] By the late 1960s the connection that liberals drew between race and criminal procedure was direct. Similarly, liberals came to see poverty as race-related. They were particularly concerned that widely accepted police practices led to discrimination in law enforcement. They also understood that the social welfare state made the correlation of poverty with race more problematic. Before the welfare state, poverty resulted from the market's operation. The market might produce racial discrimination, but that was not the government's responsibility. After the creation of the welfare state, it was much more difficult to deny that the government had some responsibility for the persistence of poverty and therefore for the association between poverty and race.

Race and the imperfections of the political process that the nation's treatment of race reflected were not all the late Warren Court worried about, however. Most notably, the Court's decision invalidating Connecticut's ban on the distribution of contraceptives cannot easily be justified by pointing to problems in the political process.[30] Nor did the Court's rhetoric in the contraceptive case focus on the political process. Rather, the concern was with the inherent right of the people to be free of intrusions on their private lives. The decision's forebears were justices Murphy and Rutledge, who had been similarly concerned with inherent (to Murphy, "natural") rights. Douglas's majority opinion and, even more clearly, Goldberg's concurring opinion dealt with the fundamental unfairness of such government intrusions on personal privacy.

Further, it seems likely that the justices themselves saw the race-related cases as far more closely connected to questions of basic fairness—how Americans ought to treat each other, acknowledging the dignity inherent in each person—than to questions about whether the political process was working fairly—whether African-Americans were unable to protect their interests because they were effectively denied the vote in the South.[31] For them, that is, the political process concerns were contained within their more fundamental concern with achieving just outcomes.

It is not clear that any of the justices who formed the core of the late Warren Court had well-developed conceptions about the proper role a justice should play in a roughly democratic political system. Rather, they found that they had been placed in a position where they had a fair amount of discretion to do what they believed right, and they believed that they were authorized, by virtue of their selection for that position, simply to do what they believed right. When they thought about majority rule, Warren and Marshall at least, and probably others, felt that they had been chosen for their positions because they had sound judgment and were expected to exercise that judgment.

This self-conception made the Warren Court justices quite confident that they could do what they thought right. They were relatively unconcerned about the theoretical bases of what they did or about the precise contours of the doctrines they developed to justify their actions. The "incorporation" controversy, or perhaps more precisely the lack of controversy over "incorporation," illustrates the point. The justices on the New Deal Court engaged in an extended controversy over whether the Fourteenth Amendment "incorporated" the provisions of the Bill of Rights and thereby imposed the same restrictions on the states that they placed on Congress.[32] The controversy had two dimensions, both connected to issues of constitutional theory. The first dimension was "original intent." Black argued that the framers of the Fourteenth Amendment intended to incorporate the Bill of Rights; Frankfurter disagreed. As an alternative, Frankfurter proposed that the Fourteenth Amendment meant that states had to act with "fundamental fairness." Black responded that Frankfurter's approach left too much to the justices' personal preferences. In the end Black prevailed, but not because the Warren Court accepted his, or any other, theoretical position on the question. Rather, one by one, the provisions of the Bill of Rights were "selectively incorporated" into the Fourteenth Amendment. No one bothered to come up with a decent theory supporting selective incorporation, because the Warren Court's members were not concerned with constitutional theory to any significant degree.

Because the Warren Court's justices were relatively unconcerned with theoretical issues, they were susceptible to the pressures of the particular case. Yet, they were also pressed by some of their colleagues—Frankfurter and Harlan on the right, Douglas and Black on the left—to go beyond the facts and the narrowest grounds available for decision. As a result, the Warren Court's doctrines often were inchoate, like Brennan's initial formulations of the overbreadth doctrine. The doctrines managed to reach results the justices found sensible in the case at hand, they were suggestive about other cases, and yet no one really knew where the doctrines would go. Just as Frankfurter's judicial restraint had been as much a mood as a theory, so too with the Warren Court's "activism": it set a tone rather than defining an agenda.

The Warren Court justices' self-conception also made them, more obviously than most judges, political actors who acted on their own— on behalf of interests specially protected by the Constitution, as the justices understood it, but not constrained by any of the formal mechanisms of representation. The Warren Court played an important part as the New Deal coalition transformed itself into the Great Society coalition. The Court's actions in support of African-Americans converged with Lyndon Johnson's interest in liberating the Democratic party from the grip of conservative southerners and with his populist leanings. The support that the Warren Court provided for civil liberties in general helped cement the "knowledge classes" associated with the expanding universities to the Great Society coalition. And after Warren left the Court, the reconstitution of the Great Society coalition to include the organized women's movement had its counterpart on the Supreme Court, which for the first time in 1971 held a statute unconstitutional because it discriminated against women and then in 1973 redefined the nation's abortion laws.[33]

The abortion decisions indicate another dimension of the consequences of the Warren Court's actions in the political arena. Unsurprisingly, as the Great Society coalition decayed, so did the coherence of the Warren Court. The election of Ronald Reagan in 1980 and the transformation of public policy that ensued of course led to changes on the Supreme Court, resulting in the dissipation of the Warren Court's legacy. But the Warren Court itself contributed to that dissipation. Its support of African-American claims opened the way for the Republican party to develop its long-hoped-for southern strategy: by strengthening the position of African-Americans within the Democratic coalition, the Warren Court made the Republican party relatively more attractive to southern whites. As Richard Nixon understood, the issue of "crime in the streets" was a convenient vehicle for mobilizing white urban fears of African-Americans; and by packaging the issue in the form of attacks on the Warren Court's criminal procedure decisions, Republicans could capitalize on those fears without openly appealing to racism.

Warren believed the reapportionment decisions to be his most important ones. Those decisions forced state legislatures to define district boundaries under the principle of "one person, one vote." For decades urban liberals had been attacking malapportionment because, as they saw things, it preserved the unjustified power of conservative rural areas in state legislatures. And, indeed, for the first few years after the reapportionment decisions, restructuring legislatures helped progressives in the cities. Reapportionment was, for that period, part of the agenda of New Deal liberals because they believed it would advance their political programs. It was also, and for longer, part of their agenda because it was consistent with their principled commitment to formal equality. In some ways it had taken liberals too long to win the reapportionment battle. By the mid-1960s suburbanization meant that the suburbs, typically more Republican than the cities, were reapportionment's primary beneficiaries. The principled commitment to equality came into conflict with the commitment to a particular political agenda. The Supreme Court followed the former rather than the latter. Notably, though, by the time reapportionment began to change the balance of political power dramatically, Earl Warren had retired. Adhering to the reapportionment decisions would no longer bring the Court into conflict with Republicans.

The Warren Court's school prayer decisions also contributed to the erosion of the Great Society coalition. Some of the justices were urban cosmopolitans, suspicious of the influence of religion on public policy. Others represented traditional anti-Catholic views about religion and politics, believing that allowing government aid to religion meant aiding the Catholic church. These quite different views on religion and government converged in the Court's decisions to invalidate school prayers and Bible reading. As a result, the decisions were uncontroversial within the Supreme Court. They were, however, wildly unpopular. Large segments of the public took the decisions to symbolize the Supreme Court's capture by forces entirely unsympathetic with the basic values of the nation's people. Again, Republican strategists were able to claim that the decisions showed how far the Great Society coalition, of which the Warren Court was an element, had departed from the country's most cherished values.

On the cultural level, social disorder in the 1960s and economic dislocation in the 1970s produced a widespread sense that people had lost control over their lives. The conservative critique of the Warren Court connected directly to that sense. When the Supreme Court invalidated laws that the public supported, it was, quite precisely, taking control over those decisions away from them.[34]

By the late 1960s the Great Society coalition had begun to decay. Its populist domestic agenda could not be disentangled from President Johnson's involvement in the Vietnam War. The Court's handling of antiwar protests indicates that the decay reached there as well. Over the lone dissent of Justice Douglas, the Court upheld a statute aimed at war protesters who burned their draft cards.[35] A year later Warren, Black, White, and Fortas dissented from a Harlan opinion voiding a conviction for flag burning;[36] although the case arose out of an African-American's protest at James Meredith's shooting, by 1969 flag burning was indelibly associated in the public mind with antiwar protests, as Professor Kalman points out in her chapter.

In the end the members of the Warren Court were happy with their understanding of the Constitution as a document that provided sensible solutions to pressing public policy questions. Understandably, they believed that the Constitution required the policy results they themselves found most sensible. Yet by presenting a version of constitutional adjudication that appeared to authorize the justices to advance what they understood to be the agenda of justice, the Court contributed to the dissolution of the Great Society coalition, which of course had large problems of its own. When that coalition dissolved, the period of liberal control of the Supreme Court was bound to end as well.

III

To say that the Warren Court was a "liberal, activist" Court is only to begin an analysis of the principles that animated the Court's decisions. Activism is a protean term. It can mean a judge's willingness to define the agenda for decision, willingness to decide cases on broad rather than narrow grounds, lack of reluctance at displacing the judgments made by legislatures, a generalized willingness to play a substantial role in making public policy, and much more.[37] Liberalism in the twentieth century is similarly protean. In part liberalism simply refers to the political programs of particular interest groups—African-Americans, labor unions, the organized women's movement in the 1970s and after—and it changes as those groups alter their programs. This is an important theme in the chapters by professors Nelson and Kalman. In part it refers broadly to the main lines of development of the modern social welfare state. To describe the Warren Court as liberal in this second sense simply restates the obvious proposition that the Supreme Court has been part of the government broadly defined.

Two other aspects of modern liberalism do lead to more insight. One dimension of liberalism has been the program of progressive bureaucrats, urging "clean government" programs and inclusive social welfare policies. The Warren Court's reapportionment decisions fit easily on this dimension. Another dimension has been a sustained discussion of the choice between structuring government on the basis of idealistic aspiration and structuring it on the basis of hard-nosed realism. These aspects of liberalism shed new light on some of the Warren Court's most important and interesting decisions.

Miranda v. Arizona directed that police officers give a specific set of warnings before they questioned suspects in their custody.[38] *Miranda* was the culmination of the Court's long struggle to define involuntary confessions, whose use was barred by the Fifth Amendment. Concerns about equality intersected with concerns about police practices, as the liberal justices became troubled by the anomaly that well-to-do and knowledgeable suspects were far more likely to refuse to answer police questions, as they were entitled to, than were poor suspects. They came to think that wealth was determining whether people actually exercised their constitutional rights. *Miranda,* on this account, was an effort to impose standards of fair conduct on the police.

In addition, the cases preceding *Miranda* had led the Court to an impasse. One set of cases created a doctrinal structure that strongly suggested that no confessions could ever be used, a conclusion incompatible with the realist strand of modern liberalism. Another set seemingly imposed on the courts the intractable task of assessing the facts and circumstances surrounding each police station confession, which seemed to exceed the courts' capacities. *Miranda,* on this account, provided a realistic method of allowing confessions without forcing the courts to supervise every interaction between a police officer and a suspect.[39]

These aspects of *Miranda* should not be minimized, but it is worth noting as well that the decision allowed progressive police chiefs to exert control over their officers. The rigidity of the *Miranda* warnings is a real advantage to bureaucratic administrators. They can instruct their subordinates precisely how to act, and they can monitor their performance by evaluating it against clear standards. From a progressive police chief's point of view, it is much more effective to say to officers, "Give the *Miranda* warnings," than it is to say, "Don't coerce confessions."

Seen in this way, *Miranda* rationalized the law in two ways. It advanced the program of progressive urban reform, which at least since the 1930s had been concerned about the corruption and violence associated with policing. Urban reformers wanted to substitute routine for discretion, believing that working-class police officers too often shaded their actions in light of their personal predilections. In addition, *Miranda* contributed to what a sociologist influenced by Max Weber might call the rationalization of criminal procedure. On the level of constitutional doctrine, the law before *Miranda* required the courts to assess all the circumstances—the length of detention, the precise police tactics used, the maturity of the suspect—to determine whether a confession was involuntary. *Miranda* substituted an apparently clear rule.

Many of the Warren Court's criminal procedure decisions can be understood as implementing this twofold system of rationalization. The decisions restricted the discretion of lower-level participants in the criminal justice system, and they gave courts clear rules to administer. But there was another dimension to the criminal procedure decisions as well: the "idealism-realism" dimension, perhaps best brought out by *Mapp v. Ohio*.[40] There the Court held that evidence discovered in an unconstitutional search could not be used in a criminal prosecution of the search's victim. *Mapp,* like *Miranda,* can be seen as a decision placing an instrument of control in the hands of superior officers. Indeed, on some level that is the modern understanding of the case: the exclusionary rule, it is argued, is the method of deterring unconstitutional searches. Yet although *Mapp* contained the deterrence theme, another was far more important. For Justice Clark, the author of the *Mapp* opinion, what mattered was that the exclusionary rule kept the courts free of the taint of unconstitutional conduct. It served, in his terms, the imperative of "judicial integrity."

That imperative is the form that idealism takes in the Warren Court's criminal procedure decisions. Some seem simultaneously to acknowledge that the criminal justice system in the real world is pervaded by discrimination and unfairness and to insist that the courts envision the system as perfectly fair.[41] The tension between idealism and realism was apparent in the very structure of Warren's opinion for the Court in *Terry v. Ohio,* which upheld the power of police to stop and frisk people engaged in suspicious activity.[42] After describing the "practical" necessity for such police activities, the opinion noted the tension between "stop and frisk" practices and "the heart of the Fourth Amendment" and suggested that approving the practices "would constitute an abdication of judicial control over . . . substantial interference with liberty and personal security by police officers." It then immediately mentioned "the limitations of the judicial function in controlling the myriad daily situations in which policemen and citizens confront each other on the street" and, after describing the judicial integrity argument for the exclusionary rule, discussed "its limitations . . . as a tool of judicial control." The rule might be "effective" when police officers wanted to obtain convictions, but "it is powerless to deter invasions of constitutionally guaranteed rights where the police have no interest in prosecuting." Then, having set up the problem in these terms, the opinion held that "stop and frisk" actions were permitted even without probable cause to believe the suspect was committing a crime.

As an analytic matter, Warren's discussion of the exclusionary rule's limits is peculiar. Perhaps the rule cannot control all police activity, but that does not imply that it is pointless to apply it when the police end up, perhaps to their own surprise, prosecuting a defendant. And, more broadly, if the Court said that evidence found in a stop could not be used at trial, police officers might stop fewer people, or use stops only to declare their presence and interrupt planned criminal activities. But the rhetorical impact of Warren's presentation is quite clear. His message is that this activity will occur, that as a practical matter the courts are unable to stop it from occurring, and therefore the courts, to avoid making meaningless statements about police behavior, must conclude that the activity is consistent with the Constitution. The idealistic view of the courts as the guardians of justice is bracketed on both sides by Warren's invocation of practical reality.

Powell v. Texas provides another example of the division within the Warren Court over idealism and realism.[43] It is particularly dramatic because the liberals divided down the middle. In *Powell* a defendant arrested for public drunkenness claimed that imprisoning him for a condition, alcoholism, over which he had no control violated the constitutional ban on cruel and unusual punishments. The Court tentatively voted to accept Powell's claim, and Justice Fortas drafted an opinion using phrases typical of professional reformers. It described alcoholism as a medical condition and argued that criminal punishment was an unsuitable way to deal with the problems of public order that drunkenness created. Shortly after Fortas circulated his draft, the tentative majority began to unravel.[44] Eventually the opinion was assigned to Justice Marshall, who ended up writing for a plurality that included Warren, Black, and Harlan—three "liberals" and one conservative. The dissenters were Fortas, Douglas, Brennan, and Stewart—

three "liberals" and one moderate. Justice White followed his own path and concurred in the result. Marshall's plurality opinion made a number of points—that the evidence showing that alcoholism was a disease was too limited, for example—but at its center was a practical point. "It would be tragic," Marshall wrote, "to return large numbers of helpless, sometimes dangerous and frequently unsanitary inebriates to the streets of our cities without even the opportunity to sober up adequately which a brief jail term provides." The nation simply had not devoted enough resources to alternative methods of dealing with public drunkenness, and, Marshall said, "before we condemn the present practice . . . , perhaps we ought be to able to point to some clear promise of a better world for these unfortunate people."

Finally, at the heart of the Warren Court's concern with race, there is *Swain v. Alabama*.[45] Justice White, writing for the Court, held that a defendant's constitutional rights were not violated when a prosecutor removed African-Americans from the jury simply because of their race. His opinion sounded the Warren Court's realist theme in stressing the practical difficulty of administering a rule that would bar racially motivated challenges and cautioned against making "a radical change in the nature and operation" of jury challenges.

Terry, Powell, and *Swain,* decided by the Warren Court in the full flush of its liberalism, show a side of that liberalism that is often overlooked. But the tension between idealism and realism was apparent to the Court from the start of Warren's tenure. After deciding in *Brown* that segregation in education was unconstitutional, the Court ordered reargument on the question of what the remedy ought to be. The discussions among the justices made it clear that they were concerned primarily about the possibility of violent southern resistance to desegregation, which within the Court was referred to as a problem arising from white "attitudes" in the South. To minimize resistance, the justices agreed that the remedy for segregation should be developed gradually. Yet they were faced with numerous decisions in which the Court had said that constitutional rights were personal and present; under these cases, any individual who showed that his or her rights were being violated was entitled to an immediate remedy for the violation, no matter what other people thought. Justices Black and Douglas believed that the Court could finesse this problem by declaring an immediate remedy, expecting all the time that only a few courageous African-Americans actually would claim their rights immediately.[46]

The rest of the Court, though, found a different way out. Relying on what Warren's opinion ended up calling "equitable principles," the Court decreed that segregation should be eliminated "with all deliberate speed."[47] The realism of this remedy was, in important ways, undercut by the Court's statement that "it should go without saying that the vitality of [the] constitutional principles [announced in *Brown I*] cannot be allowed to yield simply because of disagreement with them." Yet, if disagreement with *Brown* was irrelevant, there was no reason to delay desegregation.

From the beginning to the end, then, the Warren Court found itself torn between a liberal idealism that saw the Court as an engine for progressive social reform and a liberal realism that saw severe limits on the Court's ability to accomplish progressive reforms. The tension between idealism and realism on the Warren Court reproduced the divisions among liberals over foreign policy, represented by Reinhold Niebuhr's "realism" and Eleanor Roosevelt's "idealism," and over many aspects of domestic policy, represented by John Kennedy's peculiar combination of realism and idealism. Again, Warren's perception that the reapportionment cases were the most important he decided is accurate. By pursuing the idealistic program of formal equality through reapportionment, the Court could improve the political process enough that what resulted would be acceptable. The fact that the Court lacked effective capacity to accomplish progressive reforms would be less important if legislatures were themselves reformed.

IV

The Warren Court's processes of decision reflected the justices' understanding of their role. Although Justice Brandeis reportedly said that "the reason the public thinks so much of the Supreme Court is that they are almost the only people in Washington who do their own work," that had begun to change by the time Warren arrived at the Court. A number of the justices on the Vinson Court relied heavily on their law clerks to draft opinions, and by the end of the Warren Court virtually all of the justices did so. The justices varied in how closely they supervised the drafting and how carefully they edited the drafts their law clerks produced, but by 1969 it could no longer be said that the justices "did their own work" in the way Brandeis meant. Rather, as Justice Lewis Powell put it, the justices ran nine small and independent law firms, with one senior partner, the justice, and several junior associates, the law clerks. As in law firms, the senior partner did relatively little drafting, providing instead general guidance to the law clerks.[48]

In some respects the growth in the law clerks' role simply mirrored developments in the national political system. Staff support for members of Congress, and the president's staff as well, grew substantially between 1954 and 1969. Moving from one law clerk to two, then three and four, meant only that the Supreme Court, too, was participating in the modernization of the national government. After Warren left the Court, the process continued, as Chief Justice Burger began to add a number of support services, including an administrative assistant to the chief justice, to the Court.

The justices' increasing reliance on law clerks, though, probably had other sources as well. Using law clerks was compatible with many of the justices' prior experience. Warren, for example, had been the governor of California, and he used his law clerks much as a governor would use administrative assistants. Warren had to lead the Court's discussions of the cases it heard, and he frequently had his law clerks develop "talking points" that he used to guide his presentations at the conferences.[49]

More important, though, was the justices' understanding of their task. Many of them, including Warren, Fortas, and Marshall, believed that they had been appointed to the Supreme Court because of the quality of their judgment, their ability to penetrate to the heart of a problem and figure out what the right answer was. They exercised their judgment much more in making decisions than in writing opinions, and for many, the opinions simply worked out the details to support the judgments they had made.

This conception of a justice's work contributed as well to changes in the interactions among the justices. In the 1940s the Court's deliberations included a fair amount of personal contact among the justices once the conference reached a tentative decision. Interaction occurred, in part, simply because Justice Frankfurter insisted on dealing with his colleagues in a rather intense and personal way. It also occurred because the justices were part of the same social and political circles; in short, they knew each other because of their pre-Court activities. Over the course of Warren's tenure, the interactions among the justices became more bureaucratic. Although the conferences had not been forums for extended discussion of the merits of the Court's cases under Warren's immediate predecessors, they became, more than they had been, meetings where the justices simply stated their positions so that someone could add up the votes. After that, communications among the chambers on the cases occurred through relatively formal letters from one justice to another, and often the letters themselves were drafted by law clerks.

As the Warren Court began to dissolve in the 1970s and 1980s, some of these processes accelerated. Formal communications on Court work were an easy way to deal with the sharper ideological divisions within the Court.[50] And increasingly the justices came from backgrounds that provided little common ground. Immediately after Warren was appointed, the Court had on it a former governor and presidential contender (Warren), three former senators (Black, Burton, and Minton), two former attorneys general (Jackson and Clark), two former solicitors general (Jackson and Reed), and two of the nation's leading law professors (Frankfurter and Douglas, the latter of whom had also been chair of one of the New Deal's most important regulatory agencies, the Securities and Exchange Commission). They were not all personal friends, but as part of the national political elite they knew how each other approached the issues of public policy that came to the Court, refracted through the litigation process.

When Warren Burger joined the Court, its members had less substantial experience in the national political arena. Burger had been an assistant attorney general and then a federal judge. Potter Stewart was a politician in Ohio and then a federal judge. William Brennan was a relatively unknown state supreme court judge, although he was the protégé of Arthur Vanderbilt, one of the country's leading state judges in the 1950s. John Marshall Harlan was a leading member of the New York bar before he became, briefly, a federal judge. Only Byron White, who had been deputy attorney general; Abe Fortas, a private practitioner who was a close adviser to Lyndon Johnson; and Thurgood Marshall were large figures on the national political scene when they were appointed to the Supreme Court.

By 1992 the Court had been transformed in more than its political orientation. White was then the only justice who had played a major role in national politics. Chief Justice William Rehnquist and Justice Antonin Scalia had been assistant attorneys general, although Scalia also had been the chair of a relatively obscure federal oversight panel dealing with administrative law. It is an indication of the unimportance of assistant attorneys general that President Nixon stumbled over Rehnquist's name in a conversation shortly before he nominated Rehnquist to the Court.[51] Justices Harry Blackmun, John Paul Stevens, and Anthony Kennedy were federal judges when they were appointed to the Supreme Court; they had been private practitioners uninvolved in the national political scene before that. Justices Sandra Day O'Connor and David Souter were state court judges without any national reputation.[52] Of the justices recently appointed to the Court, only Clarence Thomas, who had served as chair of the federal Equal Employment Opportunity Commission and had been a prominent spokesman for conservative judicial positions, was a figure with some national stature before his appointment to the Court. Aside from Thomas, almost none of the justices on the Court in 1992 had been mentioned in national newspapers before their appointments to the Court, except in stories speculating about potential nominees.

This dramatic transformation in the kind of person appointed to the Supreme Court had its roots in the Warren Court's actions. By 1992 the justices, except for White, had been appointed by Republican presidents, most of whom had to have their nominees confirmed by Democratic Senates. The divided nature of the process imposed some limits on presidential choices and undoubtedly played a part in leading presidents to nominate sitting judges to the Supreme Court. Judges already had one obvious professional qualification for the position, and the fact that most Republican nominees had not been active in national politics meant that they did not have track records their opponents could take advantage of. The three failed Republican nominations, and the intensely controversial Thomas nomination, came when the nominees did have that kind of track record. In addition, Republican presidents sometimes saw the chance to nominate a justice as a political opportunity—to name the first woman to the Supreme Court, for example—but found it difficult to locate a distinguished nominee whose nomination satisfied all the political constraints on the choice.[53]

More important, though, Republicans had campaigned against the Warren Court on the ground that it had been enforcing the justices' personal political preferences rather than the law. The rhetoric was of "strict construction," of "applying the law, not making it." Republicans could dramatically differentiate their justices from the Democrats' by making judicial experience an important qualification for the Supreme

Court. The nominees' claim that they would apply the law—rather than act politically—might carry more credibility than the same claim made by someone who had just been engaged in substantial national political activity.

That might account for the prevalence of judges among the Republican appointees, but not for their relative lack of distinction. Justice Scalia is often offered as a counterexample to this assertion. In fact, however, before his appointment to the federal bench, he had been a second-rank faculty member at a first-rank law school, whose leading publications were articles on "The ALJ Fiasco—A Reprise," an article on an important administrative law decision by the Supreme Court, a co-authored article on "Procedural Aspects of the Consumer Products Safety Act," and an article on "The Hearing Examiner Loan Program." Compared to the preappointment scholarship of his academic predecessors on the Court, Frankfurter and Douglas, this is thin indeed.[54]

Although one can do no more than speculate, the Republicans' choices probably resulted from a complex strategy. The Democrats' nominees had substantial political experience on the national scene. After 1980 Republicans were interested in reducing the national government's role in public affairs. By appointing relatively undistinguished people to the Court, Republican presidents could diminish the public image of the Court as an important institution of government. Appointing people whose primary experience was outside Washington had the same effect. Further, the Warren Court justices were men who saw their service on the Supreme Court as just another job on the national political scene, like the others they had held. And to the degree that the job was like the others, they would behave as justices as they had in their other political jobs. In contrast, for the Republican nominees the appointment was not the culmination of a career of distinguished public service; it was a sharp jump up the scale. Under these circumstances some of the Republican appointees found their job a humbling experience. All accepted the principle that the Court should take a smaller role than the Warren Court had. This combination of experience, personal humility, and principle meant that they were unlikely to approach their work with a mind-set that commended aggressive participation in making public policy.

Did the change in the Court's processes and personnel matter? To some degree the differences were in rhetoric and self-conception, which need have little connection to the way judges actually behave.

And the experience of actually being a Supreme Court justice—and having one's name in the newspapers regularly—can change the way a person thinks about the job. Indeed, it seems difficult to identify effects of the changes in the Court since the Warren era, other than the obvious, the changed political orientation of the Court.

V

Many of the present Court's characteristics were reactions to the Warren Court experience. The New Deal / Great Society coalition reconstituted itself, lost control of the presidency, and became less important in Congress. The personnel of the Court changed, and the justices began to respond, in the principles they articulated and the policies they advanced, to the new array of power in the wider government. The changes on the Court occurred gradually, which raises two final questions: was there a "Warren Court," and paradoxically, is it still with us?

Dividing the history of the Supreme Court into periods is, like all tasks of periodization, difficult. Often we identify Courts with the chief justice who presided. The reason, though, is that such chief justices have been strong figures, both within the Court and in the public perception of the Court. When the chief justice did not provide those kinds of leadership, we give the Court a different name: the Court from 1937 to 1954 was the Roosevelt Court, not the Stone-Vinson Court. Roosevelt and the policies associated with the New Deal defined the agenda for the Court from 1937 to 1954. We have seen that there was an early Warren Court, from 1954 to 1962, which articulated themes of formal equality and rectifying imbalances in the political process but did not develop those themes in detail. There was also a later Warren Court, from 1962 to 1969, during which the Court elaborated and deepened those themes and added a concern for achieving results that the majority found substantively just without concern for rooting the results in a process-based theory.

What followed? First, there really was no Burger Court, because Warren Burger neither set the terms of discussion within the Court nor stood for a clear position with which the public could associate him and, through him, the Supreme Court. Rather, the period from 1969 to 1986 saw the Court slowly shifting from the premises of the Warren Court but never fully repudiating them. If *Miranda* was the symbol of

Warren Court activism in criminal procedure, the Court that followed did not overrule it. And where the Court under Warren had failed to regulate strictly the administration of the death penalty the Court under Burger first held the death penalty unconstitutional, and then allowed it, but only under what the Court considered substantial restrictions. If *Griswold* symbolizes Warren Court activism on behalf of the justices' vision of a just society, the Court extended the precedent to the far more controversial area of abortion in *Roe v. Wade.* During the 1970s the Supreme Court approved structural remedies aimed at altering the operation of schools and prisons in a way far more intrusive than any the Warren Court had endorsed.[55]

The Court under Warren Burger did not, of course, advance and refine the same agenda that the Warren Court had. Rather, it shifted emphasis in subtle but important ways. The inclusiveness of the New Deal/Great Society approach was replaced by an approach that advanced the interests of the Court's constituencies in a more self-interested way. Two cases decided in early 1973 provide a nice counterpoint.[56] In January the Court decided the abortion cases. In March it decided *San Antonio Independent School District v. Rodriguez,* rejecting a challenge to Texas's system of school finance.[57] If we consider the cases politically, we might see them as identifying a new set of constituencies for the Court: roughly, the middle class. That view of the cases is supported by the Court's decisions in 1977 and 1980 that the abortion decisions mean only that the government cannot place obstacles in the way of women who want abortions, not that the government must provide financial assistance for the abortions.[58] Some political liberals criticized the financing decisions as creating a two-tier system of abortion, one for the poor and a better one for the middle class; yet the decisions simply confirmed that two-tier systems, in health care, education, and elsewhere, were what the Constitution was all about, in the view of the post-Warren Court. That Court might have been called the Powell Court, a Court with the agenda of protecting the interests of the suburban middle class. Yet Lewis Powell never became the kind of figure outside the Court that would make it appropriate to define his tenure as a distinct period in the Court's history. And the Court's attention to constituencies at a disadvantage in the political process gradually withered away, but during Powell's tenure it did not disappear.

New Deal and Great Society programs strove for inclusiveness, but their accomplishments were necessarily politically vulnerable. Those who benefited from the inclusiveness of the programs were, almost by definition, less active politically, and it took relatively small shifts in the political and economic scene to induce the interest groups that supported inclusive programs to adopt a more narrowly self-interested perspective. Yet the vision of inclusiveness persisted on the Supreme Court to some extent well after Warren left it.

The continuities between the Court's actions while Warren was chief justice and what it did during Burger's tenure have suggested to some that it is misleading to discuss a "Warren" Court.[59] On this view, the "Warren Court" lasted beyond Warren's tenure, and the label is therefore misleading. If one needs a justice's name to label a period, they have contended, the best candidate is William Brennan. Brennan was on the Court when it decided all the cases that defined the "Warren" Court except for *Brown,* and he enthusiastically endorsed that decision. Indeed, Brennan was the primary author of the only Warren Court opinion on desegregation between 1955 and 1963, *Cooper v. Aaron,* which specifically stated that the justices who joined the Court since 1954 were "at one with the Justices still on the Court who participated in that basic decision as to its correctness."[60] In addition, most observers agree that Brennan's persuasive skills played a large part in keeping the Court from repudiating too much of the Warren legacy and, indeed, in leading the Court after 1969 to follow the course laid out from 1962 to 1969.[61]

That, however, makes too much of Brennan's role within the Court. Labeling Courts is an exercise in cultural analysis, and the real question is what the public understands about the Supreme Court and its history. Brennan was primarily a tactician, devising ways to implement a vision clearly and properly associated with Warren. In that sense there was a Warren Court, and not a Brennan Court.

Perhaps more interesting for the future, did the Warren Court ever end? In one sense, of course it did. The substantive political agenda associated with the Warren Court, as an expression of a changing modern liberalism, was almost completely irrelevant by the mid-1980s. Some residues of earlier decisions retained some vitality: the Court in 1992 refused to repudiate completely the 1973 abortion decisions, though it substantially modified the restrictions they placed on state authority, and it refused to undermine the law of the establishment clause as it had developed between 1949 and 1980, though it did not heartily endorse that law either. The Warren Court's commitment to formal equality continued to have generative impact: the Court overruled *Swain* and extended its reach, and more significantly, it invoked principles of formal equality to limit the scope of affirmative action. But on the whole a constitutional law that took the cases decided after 1985 as the starting point would look quite different from a constitutional law that took Warren Court decisions as its starting point.

And yet the present Supreme Court does not seem notably reluctant to play an important part in shaping public policy. Perhaps Frankfurter's mood of judicial restraint could never be disentangled from his views about how particular constitutional controversies ought to be resolved, but that seems even more true of today's Supreme Court. Justices sometimes use the language of judicial restraint, but the same justices sometimes hold practices unconstitutional in the face of decent arguments that the practices are constitutionally permissible. The Warren Court seems to have taught the justices that the Supreme Court could help shape public policy. In that sense the Warren Court does indeed seem likely to stay with us for quite a while.

PART I

THE FIRST

GENERATION

2 *G. EDWARD WHITE*

Earl Warren's Influence

on the Warren Court

The question of Earl Warren's influence on the Court of which he was chief justice is of course a treacherous one, calculated to encourage the kind of broad and vapid generalizations with which academics love to associate their colleagues (as distinguished from themselves). Moreover, the question is treacherous not simply because it affords an opportunity to posture but because it is intricate and complex. The influence of a Supreme Court justice is a composite of multiple factors that need to be sorted out but at the same time are difficult to weigh and to compare.

For example, what sort of influence is one addressing? Influence within a Court, that is, on the sitting justices that compose the Court during a chief justice's tenure? Or influence on constituencies of the Court, such as lower courts or litigators or other bodies who make a practice of paying close attention to the Court's opinions? Or influence on Court watchers in the media and in the academic community, the chief shapers of a judge's reputation? Or influence on history, in the sense of identification with momentous decisions or jurisprudential points of view ascribed great significance by later generations?

These sorts of influence seem rather different. A judge may be consistently effective—and thus influential—among his or her colleagues in ways that persons outside the inner circles of the Court might never perceive: Justice Willis VanDevanter, the solid, astute center of the "Four Horsemen" on the Taft and Hughes Courts, comes to mind. Another judge may be a maverick, a loner, even a marginal figure on his or her Court but hold a point of view that catches fire with time, as in the case of Justice John Harlan the Elder's views on racial discrimination. A justice may be well connected to communities that help shape the image of justices and may thus be ascribed a stature, even a reverence, that colleagues on the Court did not ascribe to him or her: the leading example here is Justice Felix Frankfurter. And a justice may possess all the characteristics conventionally associated with influence—intellectual ability, eloquence, charisma—and because of the vicissitudes of environment or temperament may end up a singularly uninfluential figure: a good example here is Justice Robert Jackson.[1]

An analysis of influence in a Supreme Court justice that reflected the complexity of the concept would need to speak in terms of different types of influence, the different constituencies of Supreme Court justices, and perhaps most centrally of the contingencies of time and place. This chapter puts those complexities aside to make a more straightforward argument for the significance of Earl Warren and, in the course of that argument, to respond to some of Warren's detractors. It should go without saying that the question of Warren's influence is far more complicated than what comes next may appear to assume.

I

If one uses the term *influence* in a rough and ready sense, stripping it of complexities, one can reduce its central tension to one issue: what really counts in determining influence, technical proficiency or result orientation? It has long been conventional wisdom in academic circles to insist that only the former counts, that the latter is ephemeral and even unbecoming to the image of a profession guided in its judgments by analytical reasoning. Recently this wisdom may have diminished in stature, but it is still powerful enough to exclude, for example, any consideration of Justice Frank Murphy as an influential Supreme Court justice, despite his consistent support for liberal positions that were vindicated after his tenure, because of his lack of interest or skill in professional techniques of legal analysis.

The Murphy example haunts discussions of Earl Warren's influence. What, after all, were the differences between Murphy and Warren? Murphy was occasionally an heroic dissenter in history's eyes, as in *Korematsu v. United States*,[2] where he alone explicitly labeled the incarceration of Japanese-Americans a racist policy. Warren never took a comparably isolated and retrospectively noble posture. To be sure, Murphy's dissents sometimes appear more eccentric than heroic, but consider Warren's position in *Marchetti v. United States*,[3] where his dissent reduces itself to the proposition that gamblers should not be accorded Fifth Amendment rights because they are gamblers. Murphy may have lost stature with a certain group of constituents for having been a politician rather than a judge before coming to the Court, for squiring women around Washington, and for occasionally confessing that he sometimes yearned to leave the Court to participate more fully in the world of politics.[4] But Warren had also been a politician before being named chief justice, read the sports pages and went to baseball games, and agreed to chair the Warren Commission when others thought the task unseemly or undignified.

The Murphy analogy, then, is part of the case against Warren, rather like the analogy one critic of Warren's once made in suggesting that Warren more resembled the chiefs who preceded and succeeded him, Vinson and Burger, than the great chiefs, Marshall and Hughes, with whom he had been compared.[5] The analogies aim at diminishing Warren's stature by associating him with justices whose lack of technical proficiency was apparent. And from one perspective the analogies are telling, because there is no gainsaying Warren's indifference to the approved analytical reasoning of his time. One commentator, in describing Warren's reasoning, said that he would put out a principle as big as all outdoors in one case, then take it back in the next one, announcing another equally encompassing principle. In an age still dominated by process theory, in which judges were expected to engage in "reasoned elaboration," duly acknowledging their sources and demonstrating their capacity at analytical reasoning, Warren's style of opinion writing was offensive; many called it inept.

Elsewhere I have argued at some length that Warren's jurisprudence, with its emphasis on the links between open-ended constitutional provisions and ethical propositions, was not inept but merely unconventional, revealing as much about the limitations of conventional professional definitions of legal analysis as about Warren.[6] That argument implies that Warren's subordination of reasoning to results is neither unusual nor wrongheaded in a judge, and that Warren's bottoming of results on extratextual ethical principles is not necessarily an inept way to engage in constitutional analysis.

So the first step in the case for Warren's influence is to attack the conventional platitude that result-oriented judging is to be condemned. The attack could begin by noting the truism that if Warren was result oriented, so were all his colleagues: so have been all members of the Court, whose business after all is to reach results in contested cases. Yet the platitude is not so easily dismissed, for even if all judges are result oriented in a narrow sense, technical proficiency might still be important. One could push the analysis to a deeper level and argue that while judicial reasoning is always in the service of results, perhaps some reasoning is nonetheless better than other reasoning, the better reasoning being that which makes credible and skillful use of the conventional sources of the judicial profession— precedents, texts, and the like—so as to persuade others that the result comes from those sources rather than the whims of the judge. The evil, then, is not result orientation but the unprincipled and unpersuasive substitution of personal whimsy for authoritative sources.

In this argument technical proficiency becomes a constraint on judges. Technically proficient judges convince us, through a skillful use of conventional sources and reasoning patterns, that they have used the common ground upon which legal issues are analyzed. By doing so they supposedly reassure us that they have not simply made decisions on the basis of personal preference. Yet all decisions are at bottom matters of personal preference, the preference for one result rather than another. Technical proficiency therefore seems to reassure us not so much about judicial motivation but about judges' willingness to track the conventional reasoning patterns and professional sources of their time.

Warren seemed singularly uninterested in carrying out this tracking. Consider the major Warren Court opinions he wrote: *Brown v. Board of Education*[7], *Reynolds v. Sims*,[8] *Miranda v. Arizona*.[9] In each conventional reasoning patterns and sources leaned heavily against Warren's position; in each he ignored them. In *Brown* he ignored precedent, legislative history (which clearly indicated that the Fourteenth Amendment could coexist with racially segregated public schools), and the canon of his time that barred the Court from substituting its judgment for legislatures' in the absence of an "overwhelming constitutional mandate." In *Reynolds* he not only ignored precedent, legislative history, and the language of the Constitution; he also violated the then predominant judicial canon of deference to the democratically elected branches of government in matters—denominated "political questions"—deemed to be peculiarly within their competence. And in *Miranda* he concluded that the sparse language of the Fifth and Sixth Amendments required an unprecedented and mandatory series of warnings for all persons in the setting of custodial interrogation, even though such warnings had never been part of the American criminal justice system.

What were Warren's patterns of reasoning in those cases? Did he not see that the Fourteenth Amendment was not intended to apply to public education and in any event had been held for over fifty years to permit racially separate schools if their physical facilities were substantially equal? Did he not think it of any constitutional importance that the Fifteenth Amendment said nothing about a constitutional right to vote, let alone a right to have one's vote counted equally, and that bicameral legislatures, with one house apportioned on a base other than population, were the norm when the Constitution was framed? Did he find it unimportant that the Fifth and Sixth Amendments said nothing about requiring lawyers in a criminal interrogation, or informing detainees of their right to remain silent in a custodial setting?

Of course Warren was aware of those analytical obstacles to the results he reached; they had been prominently emphasized in briefs and colloquies on the cases. Warren did not see the obstacles as decisive, though; implicitly he expanded the scope of his sources for each decision. In *Brown* he spoke of not "turn[ing] the clock back" to an age when racial inferiority was more widely assumed and when public education was less pervasive and vital. His principles in *Brown* were the inherent injustice of depriving a person of equal educational opportunities on the basis of skin color and the momentous consequences of that denial in modern America. He did not believe, given the political world that he knew, that physical equality in segregated schools was true equality, or that southern legislatures were likely to integrate their public schools, or that an 1896 precedent of the Court had much relevance to the 1950s. His principles in *Brown* were philosophical, political, and intuitive, not legal in the conventional technical sense.

A similar analysis can be made of *Reynolds* and *Miranda*. As a former governor of California and district attorney, Warren knew that mountain county voters had more political influence than urban voters and that police interrogators held all the psychological cards when interrogating suspects. He also knew that state legislators would no more vote to diminish their power than southern legislatures would integrate their schools, and he knew that neither lawyers nor the police would voluntarily ensure that custodial interrogation became a more evenhanded process. With this knowledge, and given the patent unfairness of having some residents' votes count more than others or of having persons detained for interrogation placed in situations where their ability to protect themselves from self-incrimination was markedly reduced, Warren did not hesitate because precedent or legislative history or literal readings of the constitutional text pointed in the other direction.

II

Warren was not alone in those decisions. In all three he was joined by Justice Black, despite the fact that none of the results had been part of the "original intent" of the framers, and none was compelled by the text of the Constitution; in *Brown* he was joined as well by Justice Frankfurter, despite Frankfurter's great deference to legislatures on "political" questions. If the analytical stakes were so one-sided, why did those justices, so interested in preserving the jurisprudential integrity of their theories of constitutional interpretation, sign on to Warren's opinions?

Internal histories of the Warren Court help explain why other justices subscribed to Warren's apparently eccentric reasoning.[10] Black and Frankfurter supported the result in *Brown,* but the latter was concerned about reasoning and the former about the importance of maintaining a united front among the justices. Warren addressed both those concerns in his treatment of the *Brown* case in internal deliberations. He first cast the arguments in *Brown* as arguments about white supremacy: to support *Plessy* and the system of separate but equal, he argued, was to affirm theories of racial superiority. One of the moral principles at stake in *Brown,* therefore, was the continued viability of racial supremacist theories. This put those who would defend *Plessy* on technical grounds on the defensive: technicalities became a way of defending white supremacy. Then, together with Frankfurter, Warren addressed the delicate problem of implementing *Brown,* which resulted, of course, in *Brown II,* the notorious "all deliberate speed" language, and Black's ultimate impatience with the Court's desegregation decisions.

The consequence of Warren's responses was unanimity, not only in *Brown* but in all subsequent Warren Court racial desegregation cases. Those cases went well beyond public education with almost no additional analytical discussion. They made it clear that a new source had been added to the Warren Court's corpus of reasoning: the antidiscrimination principle. That principle had not been present in the Constitution before; indeed the three-fifths clause had specifically built racial discrimination into the document. The principle was added because in Warren's judgment—and implicitly, the judgment of all his colleagues—the antidiscrimination principle made moral and thus legal sense in the race relations context.

Here we begin to get closer to the meaning of influence as it pertains to Warren. *Brown, Reynolds,* and *Miranda* were all cases in which prior experience contributed to his sense of what was at stake in each decision: the reluctance of legislators to vote in ways that would offend their constituents or undermine their own power; the ability of those implementing legal rules to do so to their advantage. In each case Warren converted his perception of the decision's practical context to a moral principle. Maintaining separate but equal schools became support for white supremacy; legislative inertia in the face of malapportionment became opposition to the democratic process; judicial deference to existing police practices in custodial interrogation became hostility to elemental fairness. And in each case that recasting of issues in moral terms was decisive because it swayed the views and votes of Warren's colleagues. Unanimity was secured in the segregation cases when a term before the Court had been fragmented. A major doctrinal obstacle to judicial intervention in "political" cases was abandoned with *Reynolds* and *Baker v. Carr.*[11] And a majority, consisting not only of activists but of justices such as Black who professed to hold to a more restrained view of constitutional interpretation, was secured for the proposition that the general language of the Bill of Rights permitted considerable judicial overseeing of police practices.

When one recalls that each of these decisions was not only politically controversial but doctrinally radical, at least in terms of the mid-twentieth-century canons of institutional competence and "neutral principles" of textual exposition, the nature of Warren's influence takes on a sharper focus. He was what might be called an antidoctrinal force on his Court, at least in the sense in which doctrinal analysis had been understood. His jurisprudence emphasized the practical context and moral implications of decisions and deemphasized doctrinal and institutional constraints on judicial decision making. The success of his perspective on the later Warren Court shows that his colleagues came to realize, if only implicitly, that doctrinal and institutional constraints on the Court are constructed rather than cast in stone. In Warren's hands textual literalism and institutional deference became pitted against the arguably more significant principles of antidiscrimination and elemental fairness. The confrontation revealed, at a minimum, that if the Constitution did not necessarily embody those principles, neither did it embody the canons of postwar process theory.

III

Warren's elevation of practical politics and morality to major components in the Court's decision making downgraded the significance of technical reasoning in the process of reaching decisions. The canons of textual fidelity and institutional deference, combined in the talisman of "neutral principles," had suggested that judicial professionalism and competence were linked to the use of canonized reasoning patterns in opinions. In *Brown, Reynolds,* and *Miranda,* Warren abandoned those patterns, which emphasized fidelity to precedent, a limited definition of the sphere of judicial competence in constitutional interpretation, and a careful extraction of the textual basis on which an opinion was bottomed. His success in marshaling support for his opinions despite their novel analytic character can be seen, then, not only as a reaffirmation of the role of practical and moral factors in constitutional interpretation but as a reevaluation of the contingent nature of "technical proficiency" as a guideline for evaluating judicial performance.

The Warren Court's significant cases revealed that technical proficiency had become, in the eyes of the Court's academic critics, the
equivalent of support for a series of twentieth-century canonized restraints on the Court. Those restraints, the Court's critics suggested,
were permanent features of constitutional interpretation, and thus the
Warren Court's decisions were flawed in not giving sufficient attention
to them. In that suggestion the critics were simply wrong. Activism,
expansive construction of constitutional language, severe scrutiny of
legislative activity, abandonment of precedent, and a keen sense of the
moral implications and the political ramifications of judicial decisions
were not novel features of the Supreme Court's decision-making process. Those features were only novel in the face of the established
canons of process theory, which had given a time-bound and insular
meaning to the technical proficiency of a Supreme Court justice.

The case for Warren's influence is necessarily a case against the influence of other justices on his Court who accepted the canons of process theory more completely. The list of such justices, given the character of the Warren Court, is not particularly long. Frankfurter surely
had a larger and more devoted following among academics than any
other Warren Court justice, but he retired in 1962 and was increasingly
in dissent from 1957 on; for him *influence* would require a particularis-
tic definition. Harlan wrote a number of eloquent opinions, but they
were primarily dissents, and Harlan's deep commitment to precedent
meant that he tended to accept doctrinal changes once they were in
place.

Moving from dissenters to supporters of the Warren Court majorities, one finds Black, who staked out a number of positions that, while
idiosyncratic to the point of eccentricity, had the effect of broadening
the boundaries of discourse, particularly in the area of applying Bill of
Rights protections against the states. Black was also a tireless proselytizer for his views and a stubborn adherent to positions he had once
expressed, whether in dissent or not. Still, a commentator who attempted to equate influence with adherence to the canons of technical
proficiency would be hard-pressed to defend Black, whose theory of
constitutional interpretation was both bizarrely rigid (as in his distinction between speech and expressive conduct) and mysteriously flexible
(as in the reapportionment cases, where he had no difficulty embracing
the one person–one vote principle despite its absence of support in the
literal text).

Warren's leading rival for influence has been William Brennan, whose high percentage of concordance with Warren Court majorities[12] and relatively greater interest in the orthodox analytics of mid-twentieth-century process theory has encouraged some commentators to claim that the Warren Court should more accurately be described as the "Brennan Court."[13] Brennan's stature has risen with the years, and on his retirement both supporters and detractors acknowledged that he can fairly be described as one of the major Supreme Court justices of the twentieth century. But one should not confuse Brennan's influence over the entire course of his career, which lasted for twenty years after Warren's retirement, with his influence on the Warren Court.

Brennan's jurisprudence had political and philosophical roots that were similar to Warren's, and the two justices were close friends and strong mutual supporters during Warren's tenure. Brennan, a Harvard Law School graduate and a former judge, was more interested in technical analytics than Warren and less inclined to invest his opinions with moral shibboleths or emotional admonitions. But he and Warren were both essentially concerned, on the Warren Court, with building majorities for results to which they were strongly committed.[14] Brennan's implicit task in majority building was often a technical one: rewriting draft opinions in response to difficulties raised by the overtones of language. Such difficulties, depending on one's perspective, could be seen as crucial factors in developing a consistent and principled constitutional jurisprudence for the Court, or they could be seen as ad hoc reactions to discrete justifications for a result in one case. The case for Brennan's influence on the Warren Court ultimately rests on the former perception of his technical efforts to preserve majority coalitions. That perception seems difficult to square with the ephemeral status of almost all Supreme Court majority opinions, whether perceived as principled or not. Opinions can never fully be disentangled from the results they seek to justify, and as results settle into the culture or decay with time, so do the opinions accompanying them.

In short, if the Supreme Court's task is essentially to make decisions in politically divisive and analytically complex cases, rather than to build a corpus of immutable constitutional principles, Brennan and Warren performed complementary functions on the Warren Court, functions that facilitated the achievement of majority decisions they supported. And Warren's part may well have been more elemental and thus more important. He articulated and pressed upon others the intuitive personal and philosophical convictions on which he felt a majority decision should rest. For him such convictions controlled the technical details; details never controlled convictions. The force generated by Warren's asserted convictions altered the meaning of technical debates on the Warren Court. Such debates, in that context, became matters of mere detail; what counted in decision making was the conviction that a result was right.

IV

Equating influence in a Supreme Court justice with technical proficiency presupposes a unilateral professional definition of *technically proficient* that, while it may once have been thought to exist, has collapsed in the last twenty-five years. Indeed, the Warren Court majorities for doctrinal innovations whose technical underpinnings were unorthodox may have been the first stages of the collapse of the idea of law as an autonomous profession, with its own distinctive methodologies and patterns of reasoning.

When the Warren Court came into being, a distinctive consensus existed within the legal profession's elite sectors, the leading law schools and the upper echelons of a stratified bar, about the appropriate materials for legal education, methods of scholarly analysis, and relationship of law to other professions and disciplines. That consensus identified the appropriate goals of the legal profession as the training of professional analytics through Socratic exchange; the parsing of appellate opinions; the writing of narrowly focused, tightly reasoned scholarly articles; and the compilation of professionally useful treatises and restatements on legal subjects. Law was implicitly defined as a distinctive subject, legal reasoning as distinctive reasoning, and the obligations of institutional actors within the legal profession as capable of distinctive definition.

Among the actors whose functions and obligations had been implicitly defined by this consensus was the Supreme Court of the United States. The consensus stressed the "countermajoritarian" role of the Court, whose members were not politically accountable in any direct fashion. It identified the reasoning process justifying Supreme Court decisions as the principal source of the Court's accountability. It stressed the importance of institutional and doctrinal constraints on the Court, such as the text of the Constitution, precedent, and the limited lawmaking powers of the judicial branch. And it made elite academic and practitioner critiques of Court decisions the means of holding the Court's members accountable by pointing out the deficiencies in the Court's analytical reasoning.

With the Warren Court's controversial cases, this consensus was explicitly and implicitly challenged. The explicit challenge came in the Court's defiance of the academic criticism of its opinions in *Brown*, *Bolling v. Sharpe*,[15] *Baker*, *Reynolds*, the school prayer cases, *Miranda*, and many others. Academic criticism only seemed to provoke the Court to greater activism, building on the precedents that elite commentators were attacking. The commentators did not appreciate this reminder that justices, not critics, determined the course of constitutional law, but the reminder was hardly unprecedented: criticism of the Court and judicial defiance in response can be traced back to John Marshall's tenure.[16]

In retrospect, the Warren Court's implicit challenge to the consensus was more significant. By deciding cases that orthodoxy suggested should be relegated to other branches of government and by justifying decisions in ways that abandoned or circumvented orthodox analytics, the Court was implicitly suggesting that there were limits on the capacity of a profession to isolate itself, through refined techniques of analytical reasoning, from the culture of which it was a part. When one recalls some of the criticisms leveled at the *Brown* decision—that the Court should not have substituted its judgment for that of legislators in closer touch with the problem of segregation in the South, that the Court should not have relied on sociological evidence about the impact of segregation on black children because that evidence was not legal in character—one is tempted to recall an incident involving Earl Warren when he was a law student at Berkeley.[17]

Warren had found irritating two practices at the law school: the convention that all students were to engage in classroom dialogue and the rule that students could not work for local law firms while they were enrolled. The second practice Warren simply chose to violate, working part-time during his law school career without informing the authorities at Boalt. Warren's refusal to speak in class came to the attention of the dean, who suggested that he might well not graduate. Warren responded that he knew of no rule requiring students to speak in class, that he thought it of no practical value and consequently a waste of time, and that he intended to pass his examinations and graduate.

In protesting against Boalt's practices, Warren was implicitly arguing that the definition of professional training embodied by those practices, emphasizing recitation and Socratic exchange and de-emphasizing practical apprenticeship, was unduly narrow. Likewise the Warren Court's decision to reject the analytical guidelines of the elite profession in making its controversial decisions was an implicit argument that those guidelines were too narrow in that they identified legal reasoning with a prescribed series of institutional and doctrinal obligations that were out of step with the practicalities of mid-twentieth-century American life. In *Brown* and in *Reynolds,* in particular, the Court's critics argued that professional guidelines suggested that certain areas of American life should remain outside the ambit of constitutional law; the Court responded that those areas were too vital not to be brought within that ambit. And if the orthodox analytics of the profession made such an undertaking unsound, the Court suggested that it would find new analytics, if not from legal orthodoxy then from somewhere else.

The Court's defiance of orthodox analytical reasoning in *Brown* and later cases marked the beginning of the collapse of an ideal of the elite legal profession as autonomous, internally self-fashioning, and methodologically integrated. It may be hard to think of the often-derided footnote 11 in *Brown* as the first stirrings of the "law and" movement, but *Brown* has always been the case that places the greatest amount of pressure on neutral principles, institutional deference, and the other analytical strictures of process theory. And we have now been told by no less an authority than Judge Richard Posner that it was the collapse of process theory that ushered in "law and" and the "decline of law as an autonomous discipline,"[18] so perhaps the Warren Court justices were greater deconstructionists than they imagined.

V

If Earl Warren has become something of an intuitive revolutionary in this account, perhaps the characterization is not as extreme as it might first appear. It seems more than accidental that a badly divided Court found a unanimous voice in *Brown* after Warren's succession to the chief justiceship. It seems more than accidental that Warren's principal guidelines for his opinion in *Brown* were that it be "non-rhetorical" and "non-accusatory," and short enough to be printed in full on the front pages of newspapers.[19] It seems more than accidental that in the opinion Warren violated every analytic canon of process theory, from fidelity to the text and the intent of the framers to the use of sociological evidence. And it seems more than accidental that *Brown* ushered practical politics and morality into the stable of legitimate justifications for Supreme Court decisions, thereby cracking the shell of process theory's image of legal reasoning as autonomous and professionally isolated. It is hard to think of contributions more influential than those. It may be, in fact, that we deign to attribute influence to Warren because his contribution threatens our image of ourselves as self-contained professionals. However threatening a figure Warren may be, he was surely an influential one, influential among the people and on the issues that really mattered. He had a significant effect on how his fellow justices voted in the cases that came before them. I know of no clearer evidence of influence in a Supreme Court justice.

3 *MICHAEL E. PARRISH*

Felix Frankfurter,

the Progressive Tradition,

and the Warren Court

$\mathbf{H}$is law clerks called him affectionately "The Little Judge." Most of them recalled Felix Frankfurter bouncing (he apparently never walked) down the corridors of the Supreme Court building while he whistled (usually off key) the sextet from *Lucia de Lammermoor* or the adagio from Mozart's Clarinet Quintet. Bursting into their office after conference with the other justices, he amused them with stories about his brethren on the nation's highest court: when Justice Reed, nicknamed "Dopey," said something especially ridiculous; when Justice Whittaker, unable to make up his mind, switched his vote for the fifth time; or how the chief justice, grappling with the problem of the foreseeability of lightning in a Federal Employers' Liability case, finally threw up his hands in despair and said: "Oh, hell, how can I know if it's foreseeable? I don't know that much about lightning. We don't have lightning in California."[1]

Dean Acheson, who walked to work with Justice Frankfurter in the early 1950s, spoke of "the general noisiness of the man," an opinion shared by Supreme Court staff and clerks who often heard his voice piercing above others from the justices' private conference room. Just being Felix Frankfurter, observed one journalist, "is in itself a violent form of exercise."[2]

He often tested his law clerks' intellectual mettle by goading them into fierce arguments about legal history, current events, and music: name ten milestones in Anglo-American law and defend your choices; did the due process clause of the Fourteenth Amendment incorporate the Bill of Rights? Who was home secretary in the Atlee government? And who was the greater composer, Bartok or Bruch? To win these debates, he did not hesitate to intimidate his younger opponents by invoking his seniority or his intimate knowledge of the persons and events under discussion. Sometimes sensing defeat, he would stalk out of the clerk's office in disgust. Next morning, Justice Frankfurter would tell his secretary within earshot of the wounded clerk: "Wasn't that a marvelous argument last night? Wasn't Al just great. Did you hear what he said to me? Wasn't he terrific?"[3]

With less affection, attorneys who appeared before the Supreme Court from the late 1930s to the early 1960s recalled how Frankfurter peppered them with vexing questions. Perched forward on his green high-backed chair, looking at times like a brittle, bespectacled, irritated sparrow, he turned the proceedings into a law school seminar. He could be especially brutal in his interrogation of former students and clerks such as Joe Rauh or Philip Elman, who often became targets for their mentor's display of judicial impartiality. "How," he asked one lawyer about a jurisdictional issue, "did you get to our Court this morning?" "I came in on the Baltimore & Ohio, Mr. Justice," was the befuddled reply.[4]

For nearly a quarter century on the bench, in chambers, and in conference, his judicial colleagues endured Frankfurter's wit, leering, arrogance, and fury. "If you had gone to the Harvard Law School," he once quipped to Justice Jackson, "there would be no stopping you."[5] Chief Justice Fred Vinson, he observed, made only two notable contributions to the rhetoric of jurisprudence: the expressions "for my money" and "in my book."[6] During one heated argument with Earl Warren, he shouted: "Be a judge, god damn it, be a judge." After another tense conference exchange, Justice Black told his son: "I thought Felix was going to hit me today, he got so mad." No doubt speaking for many, Warren told a friend, wearily: "All Frankfurter does is talk, talk, talk. He drives you crazy."[7]

For twenty years his suite of offices at the Supreme Court remained a beehive of activity, sometimes so crowded with visitors that one referred to it as "Felix's barbershop" and suggested that each caller, whether journalist, poet, diplomat, or lawyer, take a numbered slip and get in line. Another steady stream of friends and acquaintances poured through the Frankfurters' Georgetown home and summer retreat in Charlemont, Massachusetts. "Felix is everyone's contemporary," remarked drama critic Garson Kanin. "His subject is human beings; not in the abstract, nor in the mass, but one by one." Her husband, Marion Frankfurter once said, had "two thousand best friends."[8]

To the chagrin of even friends, this virtuoso of conversation loved the telephone and used it at all hours of the day or night. Shortly before Pearl Harbor, Frankfurter rang up his former student Archibald MacLeish, then Librarian of Congress, to read him Lawrence Lee's poem, "The Tomb of Thomas Jefferson." The hour was 1 A.M. Mac Leish was permitted to return to bed only after hearing all the stanzas and agreeing with the justice that Lee had written a beautiful poem.

Next to the *U.S. Reports,* he treasured most the *Oxford Unabridged Dictionary* and routinely criticized those who used words such as *impact, seminal,* and *semantic.* But he larded his own prose with *eschew, bifurcate,* and *eventuate,* and he could describe a draft opinion by Justice Tom Clark as "this farrago of irresponsible, uncritical admixture of far-reaching needlessly dangerous incongruities."[9]

From his appointment by Franklin Roosevelt in 1939 to his retirement in 1962, Felix Frankfurter stirred strong emotions, seldom neutral ones. Critics accused him of betraying an earlier progressive faith and capitulating to the forces of reaction. "What," asked one Washington pundit, "is the difference between Frankfurter and [George] Sutherland?" The answer: "They both wear whiskers, only Felix wears his on the inside of his head." Others branded him "an intellectual whore," who cultivated those in power but ignored the plight of the dispossessed, who spoke of the Court as "a monastery" but regularly dabbled in the politics of Congress and the executive branch. His admirers, at the same time, praised Frankfurter's stubborn independence, his consistency, and his willingness to stand against the fashions of the legal academy. "No judge, not even Brandeis," wrote one, "has faced the essential [judicial] task with greater valor or . . . greater rectitude."[10]

History has not been kind to Justice Frankfurter, despite frequent celebrations by former clerks and friends. Even they concede that the publication of his Court diaries and letters has revealed a man of enormous insecurities, one frequently consumed and crippled by rage, vanity, and self-pity. There is now almost a universal consensus that Frankfurter the justice was a failure, a judge who, in Joseph Lash's memorable phrase, became "uncoupled from the locomotive of history" during the Second World War, and who thereafter left little in the way of an enduring jurisprudential legacy. Like the "Four Horsemen" of the New Deal years, he watched as his own constitutional structures were demolished during his lifetime, principally in the case of the exclusionary rule[11] and legislative reapportionment.[12] And unlike many great dissenters in the past—Field, White, Holmes, Brandeis—his imprint on constitutional developments seemed to diminish over time.[13]

Frankfurter's retirement and replacement by Arthur Goldberg in the summer of 1962 gave Earl Warren a dependable fifth vote and opened the most militant chapter in the Court's defense of civil liberties and civil rights. His departure clearly altered the outcome in a number of controversial pending cases, notably *Kennedy v. Mendoza-Martinez*[14] and *Rusk v. Cort*[15] challenging the constitutionality of portions of the Immigration and Nationality Act and contempt cases involving the House Un-American Activities Committee[16] and the Florida chapter of the NAACP.[17] Frankfurter was prepared to sustain the government in each instance, but Goldberg's vote tipped the balance the other way.[18]

During and after the Warren years, judicial liberals spurned Frankfurter's views on justiciability, political questions, due process, and the First Amendment. New conservatives from Warren Burger to the present, on the other hand, could not take much comfort in his frequent defense of government economic regulation, his opposition to capital punishment, or his near-absolutist views on both the separation of church and state and the Fourth Amendment.[19]

In their efforts to reconstruct Frankfurter's judicial universe and the values that sustained it, scholars have utilized a range of tools. Conventional legal analysis usually emphasizes the intellectual tradition of judicial restraint which Frankfurter absorbed from James Bradley Thayer and Holmes.[20] Social-psychological and social-cultural explanations stress his humble immigrant background, unresolved identity crises, and quest for acceptance by a Protestant establishment symbolized by the Harvard Law School, Henry Stimson, FDR, and his wife,

Marion Denman Frankfurter, the daughter of a Congregational minister. He was, in Robert Burt's pungent description, the Jewish insider and parvenu who "struggled against acknowledging his outcast status . . . and . . . always remained homeless in spite of himself." By rejecting any hint that he remained an outsider, Burt concludes, "Frankfurter lost all sympathy for outsiders anywhere."[21]

Original and provocative, these explanations border on reductionism and fail to take account of instances in Frankfurter's personal and judicial life that do not fit the hypothesis. A man of many emotional and intellectual contradictions becomes one dimensional. The conclusion that as a justice, having reached the pinnacle of "insider" status, he "lost all sympathy for outsiders anywhere" must ignore Frankfurter's impressive opposition to capital punishment from *Chambers v. Florida*[22] in 1940 to *Culombe v. Connecticut*[23] two decades later. No one can read Frankfurter's opinion in *Culombe,* reversing the conviction of a thirty-three-year-old illiterate mental defective who had confessed to murder after five days of grilling by the police, without feeling his sympathy for Arthur Culombe, an adult with a mental age of nine who had been in trouble with the law since he was an adolescent.[24]

Of even greater significance in this regard is his dissenting opinion in *Fisher v. United States,*[25] a capital murder case from the District of Columbia in 1946. Fisher, an African-American janitor, had been convicted of first-degree murder for killing his white employer during a brawl. Speaking through Justice Reed, a majority of the Court affirmed the conviction and death sentence, despite defense arguments that Fisher had been provoked, acted in self-defense, and that the trial judge had failed to instruct the jury properly on the issue of premeditation. Frankfurter's scathing dissent not only took the trial judge to task and noted the long history of conflict between Fisher and his boss but emphasized that the fight had begun when the employer called Fisher "a black nigger." Virtually to a man, the other justices pleaded with Frankfurter to strike the phrase "black nigger" from his dissent. He refused. President Truman would not commute Fisher's death sentence, despite a personal appeal from Justice Frankfurter.

These examples could be multiplied by reference to Frankfurter's behavior in other capital cases over three decades, notably those involving Louis Lepke, a notorious enforcer for the New York mob; Julius and Ethel Rosenberg, convicted atomic spies; and Caryl Chessman, the alleged "red light" bandit in California. Outsiders all, they elicited Justice Frankfurter's sympathy because they faced execution under circumstances that suggested to him their accusers had not played according to the rules.

One should also note several cases during the Warren years involving resident aliens accused of subversion, where one might have expected the insider, parvenu justice to don his patriotic gown and defer to the will of Congress and the immigration bureaucracy. But in *Carlson v. Landon*,[26] Frankfurter dissented with Black, Douglas, and Burton against the proposition that Congress could deny bail to five alien Communists pending a final determination on their deportation. And in *Rowoldt v. Perfetto*,[27] he provided the fifth and decisive vote to reverse the deportation of an elderly Jewish alien who had been briefly a member of the Communist party in the 1930s. Earl Warren always liked to point to *Rowoldt* as an example of Frankfurter's failure to practice judicial restraint when his personal sympathies got the better of him. "I think Frankfurter is capable of a human instinct now and then," Warren told one of his clerks. "Frankfurter really obviously just felt sorry for this poor old immigrant. . . . I think Frankfurter may well have thought that there but for the grace of God go I."[28]

Finally, it should be recalled that Brandeis, who supposedly displayed "instinctive sympathy with oppressed outsiders," joined Holmes's 1927 opinion that sustained Virginia's effort to sterilize Carrie Buck, a mentally defective woman with a "feeble-minded" mother and a "feeble-minded" child. Frankfurter, on the contrary, endorsed Justice Douglas's opinion fifteen years later that effectively nullified the notorious ruling.[29]

No one who has read Frankfurter's opinions in the two *Flag Salute* cases,[30] the Illinois group libel case,[31] or those touching upon issues of expatriation[32] can seriously doubt that his immigrant roots and own Horatio Alger–like career profoundly colored his jurisprudence at many points. He could be as patriotic as the Fourth of July. He believed deeply in the public schools as nurseries of social cohesion and in the melting pot and assimilation as the only viable outcome for the nation's ethnic and religious diversity.

He broke the color barrier at the Supreme Court by becoming the first justice to employ an African-American law clerk, future cabinet secretary William Coleman. But he also wrote the Court's 1950 opinion in *Hughes v. Superior Court of California*,[33] upholding an injunction that banned picketing to force a grocer to hire a certain percentage of African-American clerks. No California law prohibited racial hiring quotas, but the state courts had nonetheless ruled such picketing inimical to the state's policy of nondiscrimination. Frankfurter, long a supporter of the NAACP's original program of nondiscrimination, would not move beyond that position during his judicial career. A decade after the *Hughes* case, following conference discussion of the first "sit-in" case, *Garner v. Louisiana*,[34] Frankfurter told Justice Black: "It will not advance the cause of constitutional equality for Negroes for the Court to be taking short cuts to discriminate as partisans in favor of Negroes or even to appear to do so."[35]

Despite extensive discussion of Frankfurter's psychological dramas and social-cultural roots, however, surprisingly little attention has been paid to how his long career in the progressive movement shaped his judicial values before and during the Warren era.[36] Yet with the exception of Brandeis and Charles Evans Hughes, no twentieth-century member of the Supreme Court was so deeply immersed in the legal, intellectual, and political battles of the era from Teddy Roosevelt to FDR. Frankfurter served as an assistant United States attorney under Stimson, charter member of the NAACP, founding father of the *New Republic* magazine, presidential adviser, government employment agent, and advocate before the Court in landmark wages and hours cases such as *Adkins v. Children's Hospital*.[37]

As historians from George Mowry to Daniel Rodgers have noted, progressivism was a many-faceted reform movement of diverse, frequently warring constituencies, whose participants often shared little in common except a belief that the conditions of social and economic life could be consciously improved through the tools of democratic self-government. Progressives, especially those from the urban Northeast like Frankfurter, believed in material and moral progress, the upward trajectory of human welfare, and enlightment through science and reason. Like their philosophical spokesman John Dewey, they believed that "constructive intelligence" and "constructive social engineering" ultimately would triumph in America over a chaotic, unjust economic system, racial and ethnic discrimination, religious fanaticism, and other irrational tribalisms. By harnessing the talents of experts to broad democratic participation and allowing maximum scope for experimentation, these Progressives affirmed, government could become an instrument of both moral education and social improvement.

Dewey, Herbert Croly, Jane Addams, Margaret Sanger, Walter Lippmann, Brandeis, and Frankfurter were by this measure clearly progressives. Just as clearly, people such as Henry Adams and Oliver Wendell Holmes were not. It was Holmes who observed to Brandeis shortly after the First World War: "Generally speaking, I agree with you in liking to see social experiments tried but I do so without enthusiasm because I believe it is merely shifting the pressure and that so long as we have free propagation Malthus is right in his general view."[38] It was Brandeis, to the contrary, who argued that "denial of the right to experiment may be fraught with serious consequences to the Nation. It is one of the happy incidents of the federal system that a single courageous State may, if its citizens choose, serve as a laboratory; and try novel social and economic experiments without risk to the rest of the country. This Court has the power to prevent an experiment. . . . But in the exercise of this high power, we must ever be on our guard, lest we erect our prejudices into legal principles."[39]

Frankfurter, a friend and admirer of both justices, cast his intellectual ballot ultimately with Brandeis rather than Holmes, both with respect to the virtues of decentralization and federalism and also on the more fundamental questions of experimentation and progress. "Government means experimentation," he declared in his 1930 Storrs Lectures at Yale; "opportunity must be allowed for vindicating reasonable belief by experience."[40]

Progressives could not agree, however, about the means to reach their goal. They fashioned contradictory tools of reform, both the modern administrative state, staffed by specialists, as well as devices such as the primary, the referendum, and the initiative, intended to broaden popular control over public policy. And among progressives, a sharp debate raged over the relationship between these experts, democracy, and progress. Two of Frankfurter's closest allies in the progressive movement, Lippmann and Croly, staked out the contrasting positions.

Believing the people to be generally ill-informed, irrational, and easily manipulated by symbols and stereotypes, Lippmann and those who thought like him spurned what he called the "mystical fallacy of democracy" in favor of government by experts, an intellectual elite who would seldom be obliged to consult the public on questions of real importance. Croly responded that Lippmann's approach would utterly destroy moral initiative, self-government, and progress, because only through the clash of values and interests was genuine political and social education possible as people "tested, adjusted, modified and transcended" their customary conduct and ideas. "The ultimate value to civilization of any social project such as a proposed war, a new or old party, or some radical reforming agitation," Croly concluded, "depends less upon the desirability of the particular end ... than upon the quality of the individual men and women which participation in it tends to bring to the surface."[41] In his Storrs Lectures, Frankfurter opted for Croly's path. "The expert," he told his audience, "must always be on tap, but never on top."[42]

Having labored in the progressive vineyards for three decades to empower government at all levels and permit experimentation, Justice Frankfurter was especially sensitive to judicial efforts to limit either. He eagerly embraced the nationalistic reforms of the New Deal. But among post–New Deal justices, he became something of a rarity in resisting the spirit of economic nationalism that would have swept away state regulatory power under the banner of the commerce clause. He did not believe, for example, that Congress intended to oust the states from their primary role in policing the insurance industry or managing the underwater resources of the outer continental shelf, views that most of his brethren scorned, but that Congress later confirmed in legislation.[43] He rejected the notion that the marketing of milk required a single, uniform national rule.[44] He sought to preserve the fiscal base of both the states and the federal government by demolishing the vast array of tax immunities erected by the federal courts.[45]

Frankfurter's commitment to the empowerment of state government was demonstrated vividly in cases touching the interpretation of state laws and state constitutions by local courts. "The state courts belong to the States," he wrote on one occasion.[46] "Not only do we not review a case from a state court that can rest on a purely state ground," he added, "but we do not even review state questions in a case that is properly here from a state court on a federal ground."[47] Civil libertarians and environmentalists who today look to state courts and state constitutional provisions to defend individual rights and save local resources under the banner of "independent state grounds" owe a great deal to Justice Brennan's opinions in the 1970s and 1980s. But they also owe a debt to that old Brandeisian progressive, Felix Frankfurter.

Civil libertarians during the Warren years and ever since had greater difficulty understanding or condoning Frankfurter's judicial endorsement of governmental powers that tread deeply upon individual rights. They point often to his general reluctance to curb the contempt power of legislative committees investigating alleged subversives during the McCarthy era[48] and his opinion sustaining the registration provisions of the McCarran Internal Security Act.[49]

Frankfurter had little doubt legislative committees such as HUAC could and would abuse their investigative powers. His personal loathing for McCarran, McCarthy, Mundt, Nixon, and Jenner was well known around Washington. Voting to reverse HUAC contempts in *Quinn v. United States*[50] and *Emspak v. United States*,[51] Frankfurter told Justice Harlan "it was right to charge those loose-mouthed, loose-mannered, and loose-headed men on Capitol Hill with a little more responsibility in the serious business of congressional investigations."[52]

But Frankfurter also recalled the Ballinger-Pinchot inquiry, Teapot Dome, the Pecora hearings, and the La Follette committee of the late 1930s where the legislature's probing had exposed malfeasance in government, educated public opinion, and promoted wholesome reforms. The investigative tools of Congress, he believed, should be kept largely intact for another day when they might again be needed on behalf of progressive causes. Who could have imagined that one of HUAC's leading stars, Congressman Richard Nixon, would one day be called to account by another congressional inquiry? A principal architect of the 1935 Public Utility Holding Company Act that required the registration of huge capitalist institutions with the SEC, Frankfurter did not see how the Court could deny Congress the same authority with respect to the Communist party, an avowed enemy of capitalism.[53]

Frankfurter's progressive faith played a contradictory role in his conception of judicial power and the Supreme Court's function in American life. He preached ad nauseam the virtues of judicial restraint and humility with respect to legislative policy choices and ultimate constitutional questions. At the same time he possessed the most exalted opinion of the judiciary's competence and usefulness of any justice in the modern era.

The justice who seldom voted to invalidate a legislative policy choice, whether compulsory flag salutes or reapportionment, also rarely reversed a judicial contempt order. The contempt power, he wrote in 1954, "is a mode of vindicating the majesty of law."[54] In conflicts between the press and the judiciary, pitting the First Amendment against the Fifth or Sixth Amendments, he invariably sided with the judges.[55] And he reserved his greatest scorn for judges—Webster Thayer in the Sacco-Vanzetti case, Harold Medina in the Smith Act prosecutions, Irving Kaufman in the Rosenberg trial—who openly dropped the veil of judicial impartiality and engaged in partisanship. They undermined "the majesty of law" as surely as irresponsible newspapers during a murder trial, John L. Lewis and his defiant mine workers, or civil rights demonstrators who engaged in civil disobedience.[56]

Shortly before his illness in 1962, Frankfurter attended a performance of Robert Bolt's play *A Man for All Seasons* with Sir Howard Beale, the Australian ambassador to the United States. At one point in the drama, Sir Thomas More warns his future son-in-law William Roper not to "cut a great road through the law to get after the Devil." When Roper insists that the ends justify the means, More snaps back: "Oh? And when the last law was down, and the Devil turned round on you—where would you hide, Roper, the laws being flat. . . . Yes, I'd give the Devil benefit of law, for my own safety's sake."[57] According to Beale, Frankfurter became so excited during this scene that he kept jabbing him in the ribs and muttering, "That's the point! That's it, that's it!"[58]

The Beale anecdote reminds us why Frankfurter never became a fan of Jerome Frank and the legal realists during the 1930s, despite his earlier endorsement of Roscoe Pound's "sociological jurisprudence." Felix Frankfurter truly believed in "the majesty of law." From his perspective, the justices were its high priests and greatest experts, as important in their sphere of responsibility as the other trained specialists who manned the Federal Reserve Board, the Forestry Service, or the SEC. But while "on tap," these experts in the law should seldom be "on top" when weighing the constitutionality of decisions reached by the popular branches of government. That form of judicial activism, Frankfurter believed, eroded participatory citizenship, self-government, and the possibility of social and moral education that arose when people were required to test, modify, and transcend their customary conduct and values in the political arena.

What kind of lesson did five or six justices, whose power was nearly absolute, teach when they struck down a piece of illiberal legislation? Was it tolerance? Restraint? The virtues of compromise? Frankfurter doubted it. He was fond of quoting Justice Jackson: the justices were not final because they were infallible, they were only infallible because they were final. The *Mapp* ruling was premature and ill-advised, he told Justice Clark, because a majority of the states had already adopted the exclusionary rule by statute or judicial ruling. Other states probably would follow this enlightened path, and the most serious forms of police misconduct could be dealt with through the due process clause on a case-by-case basis. Why substitute a Platonic guardianship for the deeper education possible on democracy's long march? Many of their brethren on the Court, he told Justice Harlan, were "the Lorelei voices of remaking the world according to one's own judicial heart's desire." [59]

With respect to the due process clause, however, Frankfurter believed that the justices had a special constitutional responsibility by virtue of their role as experts in the law. The due process clause was the vehicle through which the justices confirmed the moral progress of the society that arose from the people's education in democratic politics. Due process was therefore open-ended, ever evolving toward more civilized standards of conduct.

"Due process of law," he wrote in 1949, "conveys neither formal nor fixed nor narrow requirements. It is the compendious expression for all those rights which the courts must enforce because they are basic to our free society. But basic rights do not become petrified as of any one time, even though, as a matter of human experience, some may not too rhetorically be called eternal verities. It is of the very nature of a free society to advance in its standards of what is deemed reasonable and right. Representing as it does a living principle, due process is not confined within a permanent catalogue of what may at a given time be deemed the limits or the essentials of fundamental rights." [60]

On this constitutional issue, of course, Frankfurter became the true judicial activist and found himself engaged in a thirty-year war with Justice Black, the apostle of judicial restraint. A southerner and a populist, Black had a deep suspicion of judges and judicial power. In his experience, they had seldom been able to tame their own prejudices whether the issue had been race relations or economic justice.

An avid reader of Greek and Roman history, Black remained highly skeptical about human progress as well. The same calamities, misfortunes, and oppressions always seemed to plague societies from antiquity to the present. Only a fixed, immutable catalogue of rights could protect against these recurring follies; and only such a catalogue could truly limit judicial power. Through the doctrine of incorporation, Black hoped to tie down the judges with hoops of steel and to limit the content of due process to the specific guarantees of the Bill of Rights—no more, no less. He regularly denounced Frankfurter's approach as "this stretching-contracting meaning of due process" or "the accordion-like meaning of due process."[61]

As they set off boldly toward the Heavenly Constitutional City of Enlightenment, especially after Frankfurter's retirement in 1962, the Warren majority usually choose the route charted by Justice Black's incorporation theory. Through it, the Warren Court rapidly accomplished a major transformation in our law—*Mapp, Gideon,* and *Miranda*[62]—but ran aground when it came to vindicating rights not explicitly catalogued in the Bill of Rights, especially privacy. Here, Frankfurter's approach to due process, carried on by Justices Harlan and Blackmun, helped to extend the rights revolution.[63]

When he wrote his searching critique of the Warren Court at the end of the sixties, the late Alexander Bickel titled it *The Supreme Court and the Idea of Progress.*[64] It is ironic that Frankfurter's former clerk and perhaps his ablest academic protégé did not include his mentor among those on the Warren Court who traveled to the Heavenly City. Frankfurter did make that journey, but in an old progressive vehicle that many of his contemporaries rarely recognized.

William O. Douglas

as Common-Law Judge

Few members of the United States Supreme Court created as much controversy in their lifetimes as William O. Douglas. In his record thirty-six years on the bench, he spoke out openly and forcefully on issues as wide-ranging as American foreign affairs and the environment; traveled round the world, visiting strange lands and friendly people; wrote dozens of books and articles on a variety of topics aimed at the general public; and divorced and remarried three times. In addition, for over three decades he championed the most liberal position on nearly every issue before the Court.[1] During his lifetime his political and judicial liberalism as well as his idiosyncratic life-style infuriated conservatives, who, led by then Congressman Gerald R. Ford, tried to impeach him in 1970.[2]

A decade after his death in January 1980, Douglas remains a controversial figure, now less for his extrajudicial activities than for his jurisprudence—or lack of it. This chapter briefly examines some of that criticism and then suggests that one way of evaluating William O. Douglas's contributions to American constitutional development may be to see him as a common law judge.

Melvin Eisenberg describes two "social functions of the common law: One function faces toward the parties and the past, relying on precedent and hemmed in by institutional constraints; the other function faces toward the general society and the future. In adjudicating disputes, courts are often torn between these two functions, and it is that tension that makes the common law so creative. Those who favor the first function tend to take a more static view of the law, and are concerned by limits they believe inherent in the nature of a judicial system. Those who favor the latter function are less interested in limits and more concerned with questions of justice and morality." Moreover, according to Eisenberg, judges have to make determinations of moral norms as they apply to law, even though these "norms are not universally practiced."[3] That is, common-law courts sometimes have to be in front of the general will in identifying and applying changing moral norms.

One might well use these two sets of characteristics to describe some courts and some judges. Felix Frankfurter, for examnple, certainly fit the first category of a man more concerned with questions of set rules, precedents, and what he considered the institutional limits of the Court.[4] William O. Douglas, on the other hand, believed in the need to do justice and to write moral ideals into the law. While we do not normally consider Douglas a leader of the Warren Court, in the way that Hugo Black and William Brennan were, his common-law view of the Court as a means of doing justice informed the Warren Court in many of its most controversial and lasting accomplishments.

I

Criticism of Douglas and his activist colleagues on the Stone Court—notably Hugo Black and Frank Murphy—came early. Within the Court, Felix Frankfurter, the self-proclaimed inheritor of the mantle of judicial self-restraint from Holmes and Brandeis, attacked the "Axis," as he termed them, for their failure to follow his lead and adhere to strict standards of judicial decision making. The willingness of Douglas and the other activists to overturn prior decisions and to expand the reach of the Bill of Right also elicited complaints from some lower-court judges, such as Learned Hand, who shared much of Frankfurter's anger at the "Axis." They are sowing the wind, Hand wrote, "those reforming colleagues of yours. As soon as they convince the people that they can do what they want, the people will demand of them that they do what the people want. I wonder whether in times of bland reaction—[and] they are coming—Hillbilly Hugo [Black], Good Old Bill [Douglas] and Jesus lover of my Soul [Murphy] will like that."[5]

Thomas Reed Powell, a friend of both Douglas and Frankfurter, lamented, only partially in jest, that he was afraid to meet his classes on Monday until after the Court handed down its opinions, so he would know what Douglas and the activists had done, and whether or not what the law had been that morning still held true in the afternoon.[6]

Specific decisions of any justice are always open to criticism, when the cases are decided and for decades, even centuries later, and Douglas came in for his share of praise and damnation from the law reviews and the popular press. Even before his retirement from the Court in 1975, however, some scholars had begun to look at patterns in his opinions and found them wanting.

Yosal Rogat, in a 1964 review of two of Douglas's books, charged that Douglas, despite his avowed support of judicial restraint,[7] "rejects the austerity and detachment traditionally imposed upon a judge. Indeed, he has come to think of himself as no mere judge, but [as] a moralist, a political visionary, a universal philosopher." These traits, Rogat claimed, informed not only Douglas's books but his court opinions as well, in which the justice took a simplistic view of complex constitutional and moral issues: "A case does not present a tangle of competing principles, but a single transcendent principle—for instance, free speech or religious freedom—which need only be identified for the solution to be plain. In this way he avoids the task, so basic to legal analysis, of reconciling competing principles. Instead, he substitutes simple labels and lines: 'the abuse of speech can be punished but the right itself cannot be.' Unfortunately, few cases are so simple." Rogat went on to castigate Douglas for the carelessness of his opinions and an indifference to legal analysis, which Rogat attributed to Douglas's "exclusively political conception of the judicial role."[8]

Shortly after Douglas retired from the Court, Bernard Wolfman, professor of tax law at the University of Pennsylvania, weighed in with an analysis of Douglas's votes in the 278 federal tax cases decided during his tenure on the bench. In his early years on the Court, Douglas wrote many tax opinions sustaining the government's position. Then he began to dissent, usually in favor of the taxpayer: "And he often dissented alone, without opinion, or with only a few words. In the last decade and a half particularly, Douglas' positions in tax cases have been marked by a strong disposition in favor of taxpayers' positions, a lack of sympathy with the administration of the Internal Revenue Service . . . and an increasing failure to explain his votes in well-reasoned opinions." Again, one finds the claim that Douglas did not develop his opinions in a judicially acceptable manner, and that he failed to support his judgments with reasoned analysis.[9]

One of the most controversial cases decided during Douglas's tenure involved the Rosenbergs' appeal of their death sentences following conviction for espionage. The Court went through several twists and turns before finally refusing to hear the appeal,[10] leading Felix Frankfurter to call the episode "the most disturbing single experience I have had during my term of service on the Court."[11]

Douglas, in his autobiography, clearly tried to portray himself as a champion of the underdog, fighting against the McCarthyism rampant not only in the country but on the Court as well.[12] Subsequent studies, however, have showed that Douglas constantly changed his position on whether the Court should accept the appeal for a full hearing, and that in the end his decision to vote against accepting the appeal proved the decisive vote. James Simon, in his generally sympathetic biography of Douglas, agrees that his votes on this question "seemed so inconsistent with his whole judicial approach and philosophy. . . . Douglas seemed content to let the Rosenbergs go to their execution without even hearing a variety of legal arguments put to the Court by the Rosenberg attorneys."[13]

Douglas has not been without his champions. Upon his retirement from the Court, his former pupil, lifelong friend, and occasional colleague Abe Fortas declared that "throughout his life, Douglas has occupied high ground—the highest that life on this earth offers. He is, of course, an idealist; but, for him, ideals are not abstractions; they are objectives demanding present fulfillment."[14]

One of his favorite law clerks, Vern Countryman, wrote extensively on Douglas and the enduring impact his opinions and dissents have had on American constitutional development.[15] Another former law clerk defended Douglas's actions in the *Rosenberg* case, claiming that the justice acted consistent with his belief that the Court should only consider specific questions before it, and not reach out for issues. Douglas opposed granting review when there were no such questions, changed his mind when presented with new facts, and then retreated when it appeared these would not affect the results.[16] Other commentators have written more specifically on his contributions to the First Amendment freedoms of speech and religion, civil rights, and especially privacy.[17] The most sustained attack on Douglas's judicial record, from the pen of G. Edward White, deserves special consideration.[18]

II

White castigates Douglas for rejecting "both of the principal twentieth-century devices designed to constrain subjective judicial lawmaking: fidelity to constitutional text or doctrine, and institutional deference." White subjects Douglas's autobiographical writings, especially *Go East, Young Man* (1974), to an extensive psychological analysis, since he believes that the "compelling themes of Douglas's life have deep ramifications for his professional life, especially his career as a Supreme Court justice."[19]

The chief lesson that White would have us draw is that Douglas saw himself, from childhood on, as a loner, and that he self-consciously created a public image of himself as an individualist. Douglas the environmentalist, Douglas the iconoclast, Douglas the dissenter all built upon and in turn fostered the persona of the loner rejecting the rigid mores of middle class society. Yet, as White notes, much of the autobiographical writing is unreliable and contradictory. These writings set out "to present to us one description of a life—the triumph of a man who was true to his individuality—and ends up presenting us with quite another description, the trials of a man who could not escape his individual torment."[20]

Once on the Court, Douglas evidently found its work less than fulfilling and indeed described his appointment as "in a sense, an empty achievement." Although he worked very hard, he found time to engage in all sorts of extrajudicial activity, including lectures, travels, and crusades to save the environment. The work of the Court, he claimed, never took him more than four days a week, although clerks at the beginning and near the end of his tenure report that he worked five or six days, and long hours each day. How intellectually engaged he was is difficult to determine; certainly during the heyday of the Warren Court he seemed involved. In his last few years, however, some observers believed he had lost interest in the Court's work.[21]

Although the Court since John Marshall's time had operated under collegial patterns designed to develop a consensus among the judges and to present a unified appearance to the outside world, "Douglas seemed to have demonstrated an indifference to these norms almost from the beginning of his tenure."[22] White locates the origins of this attitude in two events Douglas described in his memoirs. In his first term on the bench, Douglas joined the seven-to-two majority in *O'Malley v. Woodrough* to sustain the constitutionality of a 1932 statute making the salaries of federal judges subject to federal income tax.[23] His vote in this case, Douglas later recalled, changed his entire outlook on what constituted appropriate judicial behavior. As he entered the vote in his docket book,

> I decided that I had just voted myself first-class citizenship. The tradition had been that Justices never even voted in public elections. . . . I took a different course. Since I would be paying as heavy an income tax as my neighbor, I decided to participate in local, state, and national affairs. . . . That meant I would register and vote; . . . that I would become immersed in conservation . . . ; that I would travel and speak out on foreign affairs. Many people assume that a Supreme Court Justice should be remote and aloof from life and should play no part even in community affairs. But if Justices are to enjoy First Amendment rights, they should not be relegated to the promotion of innocuous ideas.[24]

The second revelation, which Douglas characterized as "shattering but . . . true," came during a conversation with Chief Justice Charles Evans Hughes. "You must remember one thing," Hughes said. "At the constitutional level where we work, ninety percent of any decision is emotional. The rational part of us supplies the reasons for supporting our predilections." Before this conversation, Douglas claimed, "I had thought of the law in the terms of Moses—principles chiseled in granite." He had known that judges had predilections but had believed that they never allowed "gut reactions" to determine their decisions. Hughes's comment "destroyed in my mind some of the reverence for immutable principles."[25]

As Professor White notes, to take Douglas's account of these two episodes at face value "is to ignore his entire career as a legal academic."[26] While not a constitutional scholar, Douglas had been one of the leaders of the Realist movement at Yale[27] and certainly knew the ideas of men like Karl Llewellyn, Jerome Frank, and Benjamin N.

Cardozo, who had discussed the role of personal predilection in judicial decision making.[28]   Aside from the question of veracity, it appears that Douglas utilized these incidents as a post hoc rationalization of his later behavior. In fact, White asserts in the gravamen of his case:

> Douglas went on the Court with a rather different calculus, one that rested on the assumption that because law was, at bottom, a collection of the predilections of judges, the political ideology of a Justice was the most significant dimension of his service and should not be suppressed. The remainder of Douglas' career can be seen as consistent with that assumption. Because he believed that law was, fundamentally, nothing more than politics, he took no pains to avoid open participation in public affairs unless, as he put it, "a particular issue was likely to get into the Court, and unless the activity was plainly political or partisan." . . . The doctrinal dimensions of judging, for Douglas, were relatively insignificant; what counted were the results in cases and the political philosophies that those results signified. . . . That is why legions of commentators and the Justices with whom he served found him, although one of the most intellectually talented persons ever appointed to the Court, to be strangely uninterested in the doctrinal underpinnings of his opinions.[29]

It was not a question of whether Douglas could write a sustained analysis; he could.[30] Rather he did not consider such analysis necessary. If judges were, in fact, no different than legislators, then the bottom line of their decisions involved only a question of right or wrong, measured against whatever moral or political standards that particular judge held.

To support his charges, Professor White analyzes in some detail Douglas's record in the *Rosenberg* case, as well as his opinions in a few key cases expanding equal protection coverage. The *Rosenberg* case, according to White, illustrates the Douglas approach to judicial involvement in political questions. Where previous scholars had seen Douglas's actions as self-serving or even hypocritical, White sees them as consistent with his belief that Court deliberations should reflect and further politically conscious ideology.[31]

Certainly the most interesting sections of Professor White's article deal with his analysis of a few cases to illustrate his central point, Douglas's "unwillingness to buttress the results he reached in cases by resort to the common analytical techniques employed by twentieth-century Justices as justificatory devices."[32] White identifies three cases as illustrative of his point: *Harper v. Virginia Board of Elections*[33] ("a Douglas opinion not undertaking extensive doctrinal distinction or analogy"),[34] *Skinner v. Oklahoma*[35] and *Griswold v. Connecticut*[36] ("Douglas opinions undertaking novel doctrinal analysis without extensive justificatory effort").[37]

The most famous of these, *Griswold*, established privacy as a constitutionally guaranteed right, but according to White the Court faced an impasse because privacy seemed a right protected by substantive due process, a doctrine then still out of favor because of its abuse by economic conservatives during the 1920s and 1930s. So Douglas engaged in his "penumbral" analysis, pulling in various guarantees of the First, Third, Fourth, Fifth and Ninth Amendments to create a constitutionally protected zone of privacy. According to White, the "significance of Douglas' *Griswold* opinion was . . . that it responded to what appeared to be a doctrinal impasse by simply creating constitutional doctrine on the spot." Douglas did not engage in extended analysis or elaboration of the results; "the justification for the results was ultimately that they were overwhelmingly 'right.'"[38] Douglas realized that doctrinal barriers stood in the way of the "right" result, so he simply disregarded them.

In *Harper*, which outlawed poll taxes in state elections, Douglas again ignored doctrinal and analytical difficulties by sweeping them away in broad yet unfounded generalities. The fact that liberals for the most part agreed with the result did not prevent at least one of them from noting that the *Harper* opinion "expressly or impliedly repudiates every conventional guide to legal judgment," such as constitutional text and traditional judicial construction of constitutional clauses.[39]

Douglas, in sum, became what White terms an "anti-judge," one who ignored the essential doctrinal and jurisdictional constraints that separate law from politics. He became the most outspoken activist judge of this century, one who "regarded his task as a Supreme Court Justice to be that of translating his views of social policy into law, with 'law' being the thin veneer of doctrine that somehow made those views acceptable."[40]

III

Professor White's lament that Douglas ignored the principal modes of modern analysis recalls, in a reverse manner, complaints made nearly a century ago against jurists who adhered, blindly and devotedly, to the accepted legal lockstep of the time. In his classic analysis of reform thought at the end of the nineteenth century and in the early twentieth century, Morton White described the dominant form of social philosophy in general, including legal thinking, as "formalism." Formalism represented the triumph and stultification of the ideas of European philosophers such as Hegel, Kant, and Bentham, with their emphasis on rigid rules and an abstract interpretation of the real world. In jurisprudence, this meant viewing the law as an abstract entity, with fixed and immutable values, that a judge could discover by applying the correct rules of analysis. This view of law also assumed a strong correlation with ethics; the discovery of the correct legal principle to apply to a particular case would mean that the correct moral judgment had been made as well.[41] The only problem with this approach is that it bore no relation to reality, and its defects were exposed in the legal writings of Oliver Wendell Holmes, Jr., especially in *The Common Law*, first published in 1881.[42]

In an important essay on legal interpretation, written after sixteen years' experience as a judge on the Massachusetts Supreme Judicial Court, Holmes attacked the idea that "a given word or even a given collocation of words has one meaning and no other. A word generally has several meanings, even in the dictionary. You have to consider the sentence in which it stands in order to decide which of those meanings it bears in the particular case."[43] The "law" itself, therefore, could never be precisely defined, and Holmes declared that the study of law could do little more than point at certain outcomes. "The prophecies of what the courts will do in fact," he said, "and nothing more pretentious, are what I mean by the law."[44]

Holmes's realism, as Morton White suggested, consisted "in rejecting the view that law is an abstract entity present as *the* meaning of a given statute, waiting to be found by a judge. On the contrary it is, in great measure, *made* by the judge."[45] This is certainly clear in that famous battle cry against legal formalism with which Holmes began his Lowell Lectures:

> The life of the law has not been logic; it has been experience. The felt necessities of the time, the prevalent moral and political theories, intuitions of public policy, avowed or unconscious, even the prejudices which judges share with their fellow-men, have had a good deal more to do than the syllogism in determining the rules by which men should be governed. The law embodies the story of a nation's development through many centuries, and it cannot be dealt with as if it contained only the axioms and corollaries of a book of mathematics.[46]

Those lectures, of course, dealt with the common law, the means by which Anglo-American law has kept step with social and economic realities for the past several centuries. "The common law is not a codification of exact or inflexible rules for human conduct"; rather, it is "the embodiment of broad and comprehensive unwritten principles, inspired by natural reason and innate sense of justice. . . . The inherent capacity of the common law for growth and change is its most significant feature."[47]

While it has long been accepted that legislatures may statutorily amend or even abolish common-law rules, there has been ongoing debate over the extent to which courts themselves should make new law when confronted by competing principles of social policy. Those who advocate judicial restraint argue that in modern times it is the legislative and not the judicial branches that should determine new rules in areas such as tort reform.[48] The opposing, and what we might call the activist view, was well stated by Judge Marcus M. Kaufman of the Supreme Court of California: "The imposition of a tort duty is not contingent upon a consensus of so-called experts. The *courts* are the custodians of the common law—not the economists, or the legislators, or even the law professors. We abdicate that duty when we abjure decision of common law questions under the guise of 'deference' to the political branches."[49]

This view has also been urged by legal scholars, including Arthur Corbin, who wrote: "It is the function of our courts to keep the doctrines up to date with the mores by continual restatement and by giving them a continually new content. This is judicial legislation, and the judge legislates at his peril. Nevertheless, it is the necessity and duty of such legislation that gives to judicial office its highest honor, and no brave and honest judge shirks the duty or fears the peril."[50]

Certainly here is a description that seems to capture exactly the charges against Douglas; but instead of seeing them negatively, they allow us to see Douglas in a different and perhaps more favorable light, that of a common-law judge on the nation's highest court. By this view, it is the obligation of a judge to face policy issues squarely, to read moral norms into the law, even if at times discerning what those norms are is a difficult task. In short, it is the duty and the power of common-law courts as it is of the legislative branches to make law.

IV

One puzzling aspect of the criticism put forth by White and others is that they ignore an important fact. Douglas very often got it right, and in a way that won the support not only of his colleagues on the bench but of the American public as well. The last to fall in line have been the law school professors.

Erwin N. Griswold recalled that about a year after Douglas took his seat on the Court, he wrote the opinion in *Helvering v. Clifford*,[51] which Griswold describes as "surely one of the strongest pro-government tax cases in the books." But Griswold goes on to say,

> From an Olympian point of view, the result may well have seemed desirable. But there was little, if anything, in the statute to support it. Nor was it the culmination of a series of decisions, slowly etching out a new ground in the law. Even today, it seems to have been a rather strong case of judicial law-making. Ultimately, it has, on the whole, worked out quite well. However, there was at first an enormous amount of litigation. Several years later, the Treasury undertook to clarify the situation with comprehensive regulations. Finally, in 1954, fourteen years after the *Clifford* decision, Congress enacted detailed statutory provisions. . . . It may well be that this result never would have been reached without the bold action of the Supreme Court in the *Clifford* case.[52]

Professor White uses two cases to illustrate Douglas undertaking "novel doctrinal analysis without extensive justificatory effort." According to White, both *Skinner v. Oklahoma*[53] and *Griswold v. Connecti-*

cut[54] "were doctrinally audacious opinions whose innovativeness was cryptically, even assertively presented; both involved end runs around apparently insurmountable analytical barriers; and both touched upon a theme—the decision to procreate and thus to pass on one's legacy of individuality to one's progeny and hence to posterity—that touched deep currents in Douglas' life."[55]

Skinner involved an Oklahoma statute mandating sterilization for "compulsory criminals." Holmes, in an earlier opinion supporting a Virginia sterilization law for persons with hereditary imbecility or insanity, seemingly had cut off any equal protection argument by deriding it as "the usual last resort of constitutional arguments."[56] The abuse of substantive due process in the 1920s and 1930s had made that avenue equally unattractive, especially after the Court, in *West Coast Hotel v. Parrish*,[57] abjured using the Fourteenth Amendment to second-guess legislative judgments.

As White points out, faced by a jurisprudential environment which apparently negated both due process and equal protection arguments, Douglas fastened upon the fact that the law did not apply equally to all felons, since it made an exception for embezzlers. This opened the door to an equal protection analysis, and Douglas charged through. He identified the right to procreate as a fundamental right and said that any legislation restricting that right therefore would be subject to strict scrutiny by the courts. This law did not apply equally to all and failed the constitutional test.[58]

White shakes his head over the fact that Douglas could write an opinion like this at a time when the equal protection clause lay dormant, if not moribund; that the Court had never identified procreation as a fundamental right; that Douglas did not offer a single citation to justify this assertion; that he connected fundamental rights to a strict scrutiny standard without any support for that assertion; and that he pronounced the "invidious discrimination" in the law's enforcement as its chief evil—"all advanced without any textual or doctrinal support."[59]

Yet Douglas got it right, and in doing so breathed life back into the equal protection clause. As White notes almost in passing, in the twenty-three years between *Skinner* and *Griswold*, the Court began to make more and more substantive judgments on equal protection claims, and they adopted the same analytic model that Douglas had created in *Skinner*. Is there a fundamental right involved? If so, does it meet the standard of strict scrutiny? Is there any evidence of invidious discrimination?

One wonders why it was bad when Douglas engaged in that analysis in 1942. Was it because, as Professor White claims, Douglas had made this analysis without "any textual or doctrinal support"? Does it then become all right for another justice to apply that same model in 1956 or in 1963,[60] because now there was a precedent for it—namely Douglas's opinion in *Skinner*?

If there is one case that would stand for Douglas's willingness to be creative in reaching a particular result, it would have to be *Griswold*. A Connecticut statute prohibited the use of contraceptive devices. With a liberty argument under the due process clause still seemingly precluded by the legacy of the 1930s, Douglas had to engage in his highly creative and controversial analysis that found "emanations" and "penumbras"[61] in various parts of the Bill of Rights that created "zones of privacy." From this he concluded that a "right" to privacy existed, a right "older than the Bill of Rights," and in this context the association of marriage was "intimate to the degree of being sacred."[62] Thus Connecticut's invasion of this sacred and intimate area, one protected by a right to privacy, also impinged on the fundamental right to procreate, that right having been earlier established in *Skinner*.

According to Professor White, "the significance of Douglas' *Griswold* opinion was not that it chose the rubric of privacy on which to justify its result, but that it responded to what appeared to be a doctrinal impasse by simply creating constitutional doctrine on the spot, as Douglas had done in *Skinner*." White, it should be added, goes on to concede that the basic questions asked in both cases had obvious answers. "Would we allow the police to search the sacred precincts of marital bedrooms for tell-tale signs of contraceptives?" and "Should we allow the state to sterilize the chicken thief but not the embezzler?" should, of course, be answered in the negative. The only difficulties in reaching the obvious and easy answers, according to White, "were analytical, created by the presence of awkward doctrinal barriers. Douglas simply disregarded those barriers and created some new doctrine."[63]

Commentators have had trouble with *Griswold* ever since. Dinesh D'Souza could find no right to privacy in the Constitution. "Hold it up to the light, read it backwards in the mirror—still nothing." Robert Bork condemned Douglas's analysis, claiming that the penumbral

"right of privacy strikes without warning. It has no intellectual structure to it so you don't know in advance to what it applies." Thomas
Emerson worried about "the vagueness of the concept, and the general
lack of precise standards," while Paul Kauper condemned the
"accordion-like qualities of the emanations-and-penumbra theory." A
number of other scholars and jurists have found great difficulty with
the case, some with the holding and others with the analysis.[64]

And yet intuitively Americans do believe in a right to privacy, and
that it ought to be constitutionally protected. Years ago Louis D. Brandeis declared: "The makers of our Constitution . . . sought to protect
Americans in their beliefs, their thoughts, their emotions and their sen-
sations. They conferred, as against the Government, the right to be let
alone—the most comprehensive of rights and the right most valued
by civilized man."[65] Privacy is a value shared not just by liberals but
by conservatives as well,[66] and while both groups may have trouble
with the analysis that got Douglas there, most people agree with the
result. William O. Douglas never pretended that he was anything but
a results-oriented judge.

Only results can explain Douglas's rationale in a key illegitimacy
case, *Levy v. Louisiana,* in which the Court found a violation of equal
protection in a state law denying unacknowledged nonmarital children
the right to recover for the wrongful death of their mother. Douglas's
opinion hinted at both a simple rationality test and heightened scrutiny, but there is no doubt that he asked the right questions:

> We start from the premise that illegitimate children are not "non-
> persons." They are humans, live, and have their being. . . . The
> rights asserted here involve the intimate, familial relationship be-
> tween a child and his own mother. When the child's claim of dam-
> age for loss of his mother is in issue, why, in terms of "equal
> protection," should the tortfeasors go free merely because the
> child is illegitimate? Why should the illegitimate child be denied
> rights merely because of his birth out of wedlock? He certainly
> is subject to all the responsibilities of a citizen, including the pay-
> ment of taxes and conscription under the Selective Service Act.
> How under our constitutional regime can he be denied correla-
> tive rights which other citizens enjoy?[67]

Compare the common sense and humanity of this decision to that in
Labine v. Vincent three years later when a new majority upheld another

Louisiana law that subordinated the rights of acknowledged illegitimate children to those of other relatives in intestate succession. One
passage in Justice Black's opinion suggested that there might not even
be a minimal rationality review, since absent "a specific constitutional
guarantee, it is for [the] legislature, not [this] Court, to select among
possible laws."[68]

Results by themselves, of course, are not and should not be the sole
criterion by which we evaluate judicial performance. There is much to
be said in favor of the ability to reason from text and precedent and to
defer to the wisdom, or at least the judgment, of the elective branches
in policy determination. But judges who bind themselves to these as
the only standards rarely go down in the history books as great judges.

If any member of the Supreme Court in this century might be considered the paragon of "fidelity to constitutional text or doctrine and
institutional deference," it would certainly be Felix Frankfurter. For
the twenty-three years he occupied the "scholar's seat" on the Court,
Frankfurter wrote law review articles that masqueraded as judicial
opinions and carried judicial restraint to the point of judicial abdication. Yet Frankfurter's reputation for jurisprudence has never been
high with scholars, and his opinions have been ignored for the most
part by succeeding justices.

If one compares the records of the two men, there is no question
that Frankfurter's opinions are more scholarly, more in the mode of
analysis described by Professor White as the "norm," and more defer-
ential to the legislature. Indeed, from the early 1940s to the mid-1950s,
Frankfurter's jurisprudential views, and especially his beliefs in the
inherent institutional limits of the judiciary,[69] dominated the Court, although at all times he faced stiff challenges from Black and Douglas.
However, if we evaluate Frankfurter's opinions by their lasting impact
on American constitutional law, they appear insignificant.[70]

Douglas, by acting as a common-law judge, by asking the right
questions, by engaging in unorthodox analysis, got it right far more
often. Frankfurter's influence waned, and the Warren Court took a
distinctly more activist turn, when other members of the Court also
started asking the type of questions that Douglas had asked—is it
right, is it just, is the rule fair?

To take one example, in 1959 the Warren Court heard a case on
whether city health inspectors could enter premises without a search
warrant. Nearly everyone on the Court thought of it as a simple ques-

tion, since the Fourth Amendment previously had been held to apply only in criminal situations. Frankfurter, who considered the Fourth Amendment as his private preserve, got the assignment to write the majority opinion and buttressed it with copious references to prior rulings to show that the warrant clause could not apply to civil searches.[71]

Douglas disagreed, and set his clerk, Charles Miller, to work on a dissent. Miller got out two or three dozen books from the library, pored through numerous cases, but could not come up with anything to support a dissent. An angry and frustrated Douglas told Miller, "Bring in all the books you got, and let me see what I can do." For three days Douglas stayed in his office, working at the materials Miller had compiled, and at the end of that time "scratched" out ten pages that, according to Miller, "bowled me over. It was the most persuasive thing I had seen in my life."[72]

Douglas circulated the draft, and immediately Justices Warren, Black, and Brennan switched their votes. Justice Whittaker almost joined Douglas but, after intense lobbying by Frankfurter, stayed with the majority through a one-paragraph concurrence. Eight years later, the Court overruled the Frankfurter opinion and adopted the Douglas view that a search conducted by the government, whether by criminal or civil officials, is still a search subject to the limitations imposed by the Fourth Amendment.[73] There is little question that Frankfurter's formalistic analysis led to the wrong result, while Douglas's unconventional analysis asked the right question and got the right answer.

Douglas recognized that his reasoning and mode of argument often strayed from the ordinary. Rather than look at just the obviously related precedents, Douglas, like all good common-law judges, looked at "all the facts that surround."[74] Dorothy Glancy compares Douglas's examination in *Griswold* of "all sorts of legal rules and decisions in order to find the principle underlying them" as akin to what Louis Brandeis and Samuel Warren did in their pioneering 1890 article on the common-law right to privacy. The Douglas opinion in *Griswold* can best be described as "deliberately open-textured and suggestive, rather than closely argued and definitive," but the fact "that this type of impressionistic reasoning is unconventional does not necessarily mean that it is wrong."[75]

Vern Countryman reminds us that scholarship by itself is no guarantee that an opinion will be either sound or just, and in any case, scholarship is never a substitute for common sense.[76] Years ago Max Radin commented that judges decide on a result that seems correct. The necessity of writing an opinion to explain this result then gives them the "opportunity of working the judgment backward, from a desirable conclusion to one or another of a stock of logical premises." Douglas, a close friend of Radin, shared this view. In response to critics who charged that his opinions lacked scholarship, he said that "for those who liked the results, it was scholarship."[77]

V

Even if we accept the premise that Douglas can better be understood as a common law judge, that still leaves the question of whether that is an acceptable form of jurisprudence on the nation's highest court, and whether it is a legitimate means of constitutional interpretation. For someone like Edwin Meese who believes that there is only one correct interpretation of the Constitution, that intended by its framers, fidelity to constitutional text and institutional deference is the only jurisprudence acceptable. Yet one need not share Meese's extreme views to question whether a common-law approach is appropriate when dealing with the Constitution.[78]

In terms of historical perspective, however, the Supreme Court has been a common-law court as well as a statutory / constitutional court for much of its history. Until *Erie*,[79] a good portion of the Court's docket involved such traditional common-law cases as contract and negligence.[80] John Semonche, in his excellent study of the Court during the Progressive Era, concluded that it responded to the changes and challenges of the time in the finest common-law tradition.[81] Moreover, even if we accept the notion that constitutional interpretation must be closely tied to the text, there are many lacunae in that eighteenth-century text. As Justice Jackson once explained, the burden of judicial interpretation is to translate "the majestic generalities of the Bill of Rights, conceived as part of the pattern of liberal government in the eighteenth century, into concrete restraints on officials dealing with the problems of the twentieth century."[82] Translating "majestic generalities" sounds more like common-law practicality than fidelity to text and doctrine.

One wonders, especially in regard to the Warren Court, how many of the great changes it triggered would have occurred had the majority followed the Frankfurter school. We know that although Frankfurter did not sympathize with racial segregation, he doubted the power of the Court to apply the equal protection clause and reverse *Plessy v. Ferguson*.[83] Douglas, who had pioneered the resurrection of the equal protection clause, had no qualms over the results; moreover, the analysis he had suggested in *Skinner* over a decade earlier made perfectly good sense, and he pushed his colleagues in the direction of *Brown* from the time the cases first came to the Court.[84]

Would the Warren Court have been able to launch its great revolution in due process had it slavishly adhered to precedent in its interpretation of the Fourth, Fifth and Sixth Amendments? One can make a perfectly good argument, as Frankfurter did in *Wolf*, that the exclusionary rule—a judge-made common-law rule—did not apply to the states. But common sense tells us that restraints on misbehavior by the police ought to be at least roughly comparable whether they are agents of the federal or the state government.

Frankfurter lectured his brethren to avoid the "political thicket" of reapportionment and warned them that the courts had neither the power nor the wisdom to resolve the issue.[85] Black, Douglas, and Murphy dissented, and time proved them right. The Court, over Frankfurter's bitter protest, declared the question justiciable in 1962[86] and two years later required all the states to apportion their legislatures on an equitable basis.[87] Between *Baker* and *Reynolds*, however, Douglas came up with the answer to one of Frankfurter's major objections, that the courts could not fashion judicially discoverable and manageable standards. In a case involving the Georgia county unit system, Justice Douglas set forth the formula that not only provided judicial guidance but caught the popular imagination as well—"one man, one vote."[88] Despite Justice Harlan's complaint that the formula "flies in the face of history,"[89] again one senses the rightness of the decision, the common sense of this and the other apportionment decisions despite their alleged lack of analysis and fidelity to text.

Douglas has long been considered an activist in that he willingly reached out to decide issues and to expand the reach of constitutional protections. But Douglas always saw himself as a strict constructionist in the sense that he took the Constitution "to mean what it says." The most dramatic example of this is his and Justice Black's absolutist interpretation of the First Amendment speech clause: "Congress shall make *no* law . . . abridging the freedom of speech." While an absolutist position may be an excuse to avoid the problems of analysis in balancing individual freedom against the need for social order, it also provides a consistency that is often lacking in First Amendment analysis. Thomas Emerson, one of the nation's leading scholars on freedom of speech, lauded Douglas's use of the First Amendment "as a counter to all the pressures of modern life toward conformity. . . . In this respect, Justice Douglas has given a totally new dimension to the First Amendment."[90]

Douglas once said that "I'd rather create a precedent than find one. Because the creation of a precedent in terms of the modern setting means the adjustment of the Constitution to the needs of the time."[91] In his memoirs Douglas acknowledged the activist label, in terms that would have horrified Frankfurter: "My view has always been that anyone whose life, liberty or property was threatened or impaired by any branch of government—whether the President or one of his agencies, or Congress, or the courts (or any counterpart in a state regime)—had a justiciable controversy and could properly repair to a judicial tribunal for vindication of his rights."[92] This is certainly not the voice of judicial restraint; it is the voice of the common law.

There is a great deal to criticize about Douglas's opinions, above all that even when he got it right, he often failed to explain how he reached that result. A former law clerk and an admirer of Douglas, Lucas Powe, has written that Douglas did not take doctrine seriously and failed to appreciate that others, "including those not wedded to the judicial conservatism of Harvard, did take doctrine seriously. With his acknowledged abilities he could have played the doctrinal game superbly, but he saw doctrine as a waste of time and he had non-legal activities that were more pressing than authoring rationalizations for those silly enough to believe them."[93] Douglas, however, had nothing but contempt for those who failed to understand the meaning of his decisions unless they had a law review article attached as explanation. "I wrote for the common people," he declared, "hoping I could help them see the main contours, and seeing them, better understand the high vantage point we have reached with our form of government."[94] One might well recall the words of this nation's greatest common-law judge. "I think that to state the case shortly and the ground of decision as concisely and delicately as you can is the real way," Oliver Wendell Holmes told a friend. "It is the English fashion and I think it is civilized."[95]

One problem with complicated and unreadable opinions is that while they may appeal to the specialist, they are misunderstood by the general public.   In 1977 Irving R. Kaufman, then chief judge of the Court of Appeals for the Second Circuit, urged his fellow judges to write their opinions in a more intelligible form:

> Judges often play the role of teacher or leader in shaping the public's view. As the judicial opinion is the essential document of the third branch of government, the judge should explain his action in terms that enable the reader to understand precisely what he has done and why he has done it. The democratic character of the courts' active law-making role springs from judicial participation in the marketplace of ideas, and courts, like legislatures, must mobilize general understanding of their decisions.[96]

Douglas tried to do this, and one can hardly deny that an intelligent layperson would find Douglas's opinions far more accessible than those of Frankfurter.[97]

Another problem with involved analytical rationalizations is they might ignore common sense. While stare decisis might serve as a starting point in judicial decision making, Douglas remained aware of how uncertain a reed the past might be. Established law, he told Eric Sevareid, was not a sure guide because the past was not always relevant to the present. What did "the judges who sat there in 1875 know about electronic surveillance? They didn't know anything about it. . . . Why take their wisdom?" The law survived, Douglas said in 1949, because it adapted to new conditions. Precedents once correct might no longer be so, and he called it a "healthy practice (too infrequently followed) for a court to reexamine its own doctrine." Again, one hears the voice of the common-law judge.[98]

Douglas also has been criticized because he failed to build coalitions; he did not seem to care if he spoke for a majority or only for himself.[99] His colleague and fellow activist on the Court, William J. Brennan, disagrees, believing that Douglas cared passionately about the results in important cases.[100] Because he could not or would not play the game of coalition building, and because he would not take the time to explain some of his opinions in order to influence other judges in later cases, there is no question that Douglas exercised far less influence than his abilities and ideas deserved. A few years before he stepped down from the bench, he conceded that "I haven't been much of a proselytizer on the Court. I've had the theory that the only soul I had to save was my own."[101]

In interviews several Douglas clerks agreed that he cared passionately, but he would not act on his feelings. Typical is a comment from Jerome Falk, who clerked for Douglas in the October 1965 term: "I asked him about it, I said, 'Why don't you talk to these guys?' And he said several times that was not his view of what was appropriate. He would put his views out, and see what happened. He was perfectly willing to talk to people about changes, but he would never call one of them up and say, 'What do I have to do to get you on board here?' Never!"[102]

Many of the criticisms leveled at Douglas are true, and no doubt future historians will wonder why a man who exercised such influence on the development of American constitutional law enjoyed such a poor reputation. For, in the end, Douglas did exercise influence. According to Kenneth Karst, a self-described "second-generation disciple of Felix Frankfurter," Douglas "went his own way; he did not make concessions—and no Justice of his era did more to remake the landscape of constitutional doctrine. Justice Douglas was the unrivaled leader of the most important constitutional development of his time: the growth of the equal protection clause. He was also a major figure in the revival of substantive due process as a protection of personal liberties. His leadership, in other words, was precisely doctrinal leadership. What was missing from his opinions was the logic of the syllogism."[103] This is a generous and a fair assessment. Douglas would have been among the first to admit that the logic of the syllogism was indeed missing. In terms of the common law, however, Holmes reminded us a century ago that the life of the law has not been logic but experience, and all sorts of things in the real world, including the prejudices of the judges, had a great deal more to do with the law than the syllogism.[104]

William O. Douglas should not be characterized as an anti-judge simply because he refused to play by certain formalistic rules. Nor, as a third-generation Harvard disciple of Frankfurter claimed, was Douglas the "loose gun on the deck of the sinking ship of American liberal jurisprudence."[105] White is right in characterizing him as an individualist, and as such he brought certain values to the Court that others did not have and often did not appreciate. Further, his common-law proclivities also contributed to the work of the Court in his lengthy tenure.

This is not to say that we would want a Court of William O. Douglas clones, anymore than we would want nine Felix Frankfurters. But for the Court to be responsive to the needs of a changing society, as the Warren Court most certainly was, it needs the occasional nonconformist, the result-oriented judge who asks the right questions even if he or she cannot rationalize the right results. Louis Jaffe, in an article about Justice Brandeis, wrote that "we should perhaps rid ourselves of the implicit assumptions that there is any single model of judicial greatness. Once we recognize that the Supreme Court is a supreme policy-maker we should welcome on the Court a variety of talents and attributes—the 'activist,' the exponent of 'judicial restraint,' the liberal, the conservative, the moralist, the skeptic. Each can be great in his own way; each can contribute to the institutional product of the Court."[106] For all his faults, and there were many, Douglas played a critical role on the Supreme Court for thirty-five years. He asked the right questions, and more often than not, he got the right answers. In doing so, he helped his colleagues on the bench keep the law, constitutional and otherwise, sensitive to the needs of a rapidly changing society. "The flexibility and capacity for growth and adaptation," the Supreme Court noted in the nineteenth century, "is the peculiar boast and excellence of the common law."[107] In this century William O. Douglas helped keep that common-law tradition alive.

5 *TONY FREYER*

Hugo L. Black and the
Warren Court in Retrospect

After twenty years the image of the Warren Court has become blurred. Conservative and liberal commentators agreed that Earl Warren's tenure as chief justice coincided with the Court's most extensive reinterpretation of the status of individual rights under the Constitution since the time of John Marshall. A point of contention, however, was the extent to which this constitutional transformation could survive continuous reconsideration and limitation by a Supreme Court possessing a different dominant ideology. Occupying a central if incongruous place in this debate was Hugo L. Black. During most of the Warren Court era, critics such as Phoenix lawyer William H. Rehnquist often denounced Black and his colleagues as "left-wing" and condemned them for making the "Constitution say what they wanted it to say." Yet as the Warren Court ended, friend and foe alike perceived a "new" Black advocating greater judicial self-restraint. Twenty years later Chief Justice Rehnquist and those sharing his beliefs found in the thinking of this "new" Black grounds for eroding the Warren Court's constitutional principles.[1] Given the curious evolution of Black's image, a reassessment of his role within the Warren Court seems timely.

Still, the essence of the man himself and his impact on the Warren

Court have remained elusive. Detractors attributed his influence to a bullying propensity and claimed that his constitutional thought was simpleminded and inconsistent. Generally, however, such views rested upon a partial understanding of Black's relation to fellow justices and an incomplete reading of his numerous decisions. The critics who took the trouble to read a broad range of these decisions conceded, more-over, that generally they embodied a jurisprudence which was neither inconsistent nor superficial. At the same time the justice did not want for defenders, including, most recently, political scientist Tinsley E. Yarbrough. Yarbrough's incisive examination of Justice Black and his critics concluded that an underlying positivism gave Black's constitu-tional thought a cohesion and sophistication which the critics either misunderstood or misconstrued. In addition, like other older and more recent authors, Yarbrough supported the conclusion that Black's influ-ence on the Warren Court owed more to the strength of his ideas than to the force of his personality.[2]

This chapter argues that throughout the Warren era Black's constitu-tional principles did not change. Instead, Black applied his distinctive constitutional faith to new issues to achieve results that departed from those he had fought for in earlier cases. His faith, rooted in core values possessed since youth, assumed that freedom depended on main-taining a balance between individual rights and community welfare. Individual rights were thus a means rather than an end in themselves. Between Frankfurter, who favored giving primacy to the conformism inherent in majoritarian democracy, and Douglas, for whom individu-alism was of first importance, Black occupied the middle ground.[3]

I

No clerk was long in the justice's service before Black urged him to read some volume of the classics or history. He always asked, "Have you read these books?" Usually the clerk answered in the negative, whereupon Black replied: "Well, they're your first assignment. What they have to say about human nature and history is more relevant than anything I can think of to the issues now before the Court." Gradually, the young lawyers perceived that the justice believed that human na-ture was changeless. "Well, of course this has been the problem since the time of Tacitus," he would observe, regarding some current issue.

If the clerk said he had not read Tacitus, Black would retort, "Well, you can't be a lawyer if you haven't."[4]

The contrasting styles of Black and Frankfurter within the Warren Court suggest the influence of Black's roots and his self-education. Because the Alabamian purportedly sought "JUSTICE" and placed achieving it above the canons of judicial self restraint, Frankfurter labeled him a "politician."[5] Yet, according to Brennan, Black "was not a court politician, lobbying in the invidious sense of that term." He "listened well, although one had to be wary that his patient attention might be only a delaying tactic to gain time to marshall arguments to demolish you."[6] Perhaps no one provided a more balanced assessment than Stewart. When he first arrived on the Court, he recalled, the two senior antagonists "courted" him: "Felix was so unsubtle and obvious that it was counterproductive. Hugo didn't impress me that way. He was largely self-taught and an old-fashioned populist who acted like a young fellow just appointed to the Court — until the end of his life."[7]

Yet the image of Black as the self-taught populist was imprecise. He grew up during the late nineteenth century in the small, isolated northeast Alabama town of Ashland located in the Appalachian foothills. The population of Ashland at the time was 350. His mother and storekeeper father were prominent and respectable members of the local middle class, his older brothers and sisters all acquired success as teachers, doctors, or lawyers.[8] The influence of his father's identification with the Democratic party establishment of Grover Cleveland was strong enough that the eighty-two-year-old Black claimed that for him, the "sweetness and satisfaction" of Cleveland's victory of 1892 had "never been surpassed."[9]

Even so, the influence of place, time, and family was complex. The success of brothers and sisters and the firm direction of a loving and caring mother, combined with intellectual skills sufficient to win a Phi Beta Kappa key and top honors in law school, fed Black's ambition and drive. Legislative malapportionment, however, subjected the state's more populated northern section to the control of the south. A still more fundamental source of conflict was race. Many north Alabamians, like Black's parents, condoned racial separation maintained in private relations as a matter of custom but adamantly opposed segregation imposed by law, which south Alabama won in the Constitution of 1901.[10]

From the Populists, Black learned how to challenge the conservative bosses' primacy within the Alabama Democratic party. The Populists taught Black the value of a constituency-oriented, face-to-face political style emphasizing an instinctive preference for the underdog; their defeat revealed that in the future only Democratic candidates were likely to get elected by using it.

Religion and personal tragedy also influenced Black's formative years. As far as young Hugo knew, the only churches in Clay County were Protestant, with the evangelical Baptist church by far the largest denomination. Black's mother saw to it that her children attended all Baptist church services. Probably the most significant factor influencing Black's religious beliefs, however, was that his own father and two uncles were publicly expelled from a Baptist congregation because they drank alcoholic beverages. In addition, an older brother to whom Black was quite close drowned, apparently because he was drunk. Incidents such as these led many evangelical Protestant sects to urge injecting the state into the community's private life to enforce prohibition.

The tensions engulfing Black's family members heightened his sensitivity to respectability. Intimately familiar with slavery and racial segregation, southern communities like Ashland prized independence and moral accountability. Respectability was integral to preserving the balance between community unity and individuality because those possessing it were considered liberated from material or social dependency. The success of Black's storekeeper father and lawyer brother entitled them to respect as pillars of ordered community life. But in a society dominated by evangelical Protestant proscriptions, their behavior jeopardized the respectable individual conduct on which the well-being of individuals, family, and the community depended. These values were central to Black's formal education, which stressed the classics, Greek and Roman history and literature, and the cultural and political heritage of the Anglo-Saxon peoples. Anxieties arising from the ambiguous social standing of his family intensified his sensitivity to the individual's status *within* the community.

Black proved remarkably capable of finding the right balance, as he fulfilled his legal and political ambitions in Birmingham. His law career and attainment of public office depended on the ability to represent and touch the emotions of all ethnic, racial, religious, and economic groups, whose personal relations with one another were dominated by conflict.

Black's sensitivity to the dynamics of persuasion blended opportunism and fundamental convictions about human behavior. A lawyer "whose career depends to a very large extent on his capacity to persuade" should, he wrote his son, Hugo, Jr., "possess internal wisdom and goodness" if he seeks to "appeal to exalted ideals" of his "hearers."[11] Like most lawyers, Black would subordinate abstract issues of justice to the necessities of winning a case. In so doing, he might snatch points from history and the classics — often out of context — in order to support whatever case he needed to make. Expediency alone, however, did not explain Black's frequent use of classical and historical references. His success before juries convinced him that human nature was changeless. This presumption led in turn to the conviction that an understanding of human action recorded by historians such as the Roman scholar Tacitus provided guidance for those seeking to convince people in modern times.[12]

Lawyer and politician, Black often won cases and campaigns by convincing jurors and voters that community unity and individual rights were interdependent. As a police judge, county prosecutor, and then special federal prosecutor, he enforced the prohibition laws supported by evangelical Protestants. Repeatedly also, however, he effectively defended the rights of blacks or ethnic minorities in court and as a public official.[13]

Even so, lacking the support of the elite and the bosses during the 1920s, his election to the United States Senate was unlikely without Ku Klux Klan affiliations. As a result, although he condemned the Klan's violence, like tens of thousands of fellow Alabamians and other Americans throughout the nation he took the oath of eternal loyalty to the Invisible Empire. Moreover, although Black felt no prejudice toward individual Catholics, he profoundly distrusted the Roman Catholic church. He resented the fact that rental property owned by the church was not taxed; most of its revenue came from the poor, and not enough was being returned. Black's success as a trial lawyer also hinged on the Klan. Years later in a confidential interview, Black explained: "I was trying a lot of cases against corporations, jury cases, and I found out that all the corporation lawyers were in the Klan. . . A lot of the jurors were too, so I figured I'd better be even-up."[14] Thus, the community's fears and prejudices converged with his own antipathies, political ambitions, and livelihood as a lawyer, encouraging his short membership in the organization that threatened the very social order that he otherwise defended.

However, there was a firmer foundation to Black's convictions. "So long as you do your duty" and "live so as to keep your own self-respect, and keep your head in the midst of temporary disappointments," he wrote Hugo, Jr., "I shall be . . proud of you." Nothing was "really disgraceful except that which is dishonorable, and it is never dishonorable to fail to achieve something if the person does the best he can." At another point he wrote his other son, Sterling, that there was "much evidence that while human progress is slow, it is nevertheless sure. While we may have a relapse at any time, I think that this country has, during my lifetime, moved in the direction of a better distribution of justice." He observed, "I think we have a much better government [now] than we had in 1789, and will have a still better one in 1989."[15] The interplay between Black's past and self-education shaped the constitutional principles he defended on the Warren Court.

II

As Derrick Bell has argued, the *Brown* desegregation decision resulted from a convergence of the interests of whites and African-Americans. Within the Supreme Court this convergence was reflected in the way Chief Justice Warren worked with both Black and Frankfurter to achieve unanimity. Yet the tensions and ambiguities shaping *Brown II* and culminating in the clash between Black and Frankfurter over the latter's concurrence in *Cooper v. Aaron* revealed how limited were the shared interests. To a considerable extent, these conflicts rather than the pressures facilitating unanimity in *Brown* determined the course of the Warren Court's civil rights decisions.[16]

Black's understanding of human nature shaped his views of the civil rights revolution. "If you live long enough, you will see [among all races] many more evidences of cruel propensities in individuals," Black assured his son. "Racial intolerance as a rule rests upon egotism, or a concealed inferiority complex." In addition, the Nazis' persecution of ethnic and racial minorities and political dissenters were "simply a repetition of the course of history when people get too much power." During the Cold War these considerations also led Black to note with concern how Soviet propaganda effectively exploited the contradiction between America's espousal of freedom and the South's system of racial segregation.[17]

Moreover, as the Court's undermining of racial segregation accelerated from the 1930s on, the influence of Black's north Alabama past remained strong. White southerners needed to understand, he wrote a Georgia cousin in 1962, that devising "ways to defy and defeat the will of the Nation" would, as it had in the Civil War, "again bring on unnecessary pain and suffering." States could not prevent the "overwhelming majority" from living "true to their constitutional ideas of equal freedom for all." The foundation of the Constitution was a "belief that all people, whatever their color and whatever their history," were "human beings created by the same creator, all entitled to have equal opportunities to do their part in helping to carry out the great national plan under which all our people must live." Black traced these convictions back to his boyhood: "I do not recall ever having heard anything contrary to them in my home," he said, "and I am sure that any Sunday school teachers in the little churches in Ashland, Alabama, came very near to expressing this same philosophy when they talked to me about the Sermon on the Mount and repeated the story of the Good Samaritan." America was "great" because the Constitution did not foster "slavery, hatred, and a caste system" but instead was dedicated to the "principle of Equal Justice Under Law."[18]

Other justices shared these values and concerns to a degree. In Black's case, however, they engendered a leading role in the Warren Court's pathbreaking *Brown* decision. Since 1938 Black had supported the gradual erosion of *Plessy*'s separate-but-equal doctrine, but by 1950 he became one of the only three or four justices who supported reversing outright the entrenched precedent governing the application of the Fourteenth Amendment's equal protection clause.[19]

Black was sure that overruling *Plessy* would mean the "end of political liberalism in the South" and would bring extremists "out of the woodwork." The Klan would ride again. However, his own long-held values and the awareness of the propaganda gains the Soviet Union made because of segregation led him to support Warren's efforts to achieve unanimous support for overruling the *Plessy* doctrine. In addition, Black and Frankfurter agreed on the importance of unanimous decisions in segregation cases in order to establish public support for the Court. Meanwhile, the NAACP influenced the Court's opinion by presenting social science data that suggested racial discrimination in public education hurt black children's self-respect. The evidence was of particular interest to Black, whose success as a lawyer and public official had been due in large part to his keen appreciation of the importance of respectability to individual and community welfare.[20]

Above all, however, Chief Justice Warren stressed that the Court should postpone determination of the standard governing implementation of desegregation. With Frankfurter's help, he convinced the justices that a unanimous decision overruling *Plessy* would facilitate the formulation of an enforcement decree later on. By May 17, 1954, Warren achieved the unanimity that Black and Frankfurter had considered essential in *Brown I*.[21] On the same day, in *Bolling v. Sharpe*, Warren declared that racial segregation in Washington's public schools was unconstitutional. He followed Black's and Frankfurter's idea of reading into the due process clause of the Fifth Amendment the constitutional principle of equal protection. Such judicial activism, according to Black, was justified by "the understanding shared by many of the draftsmen of the Fourteenth Amendment, that the whole Bill of Rights, including the Due Process Clause of the Fifth Amendment, was a guarantee that all persons would receive equal treatment under the law."[22]

Though Eisenhower followed *Bolling v. Sharpe* and desegregated the Washington, D.C., schools, he explicitly refused to support *Brown*. Meanwhile, Frankfurter surreptitiously contacted one of his former law clerks involved in the presentation of the government's brief, which resulted in the inclusion of the phrase which subsequently epitomized the Court's *Brown II* decision. On May 31, 1955, Warren announced a unanimous opinion outlining the terms governing the enforcement of *Brown* which concluded with the phrase secretly contrived by Frankfurter: desegregation should proceed "on a nondiscriminatory basis with all deliberate speed."[23]

The ambiguity inherent in the concept of "deliberate speed" encouraged the South's campaign of massive resistance, which reached a peak in Little Rock with Arkansas governor Orval E. Faubus's defiance of a federal desegregation decree during September 1957. The following summer in *Cooper v. Aaron* (1958), in a virtually unprecedented action, all nine justices signed an opinion holding the conduct of Faubus and the state unconstitutional. Yet Black and Frankfurter reached an impasse over the Little Rock case. Frankfurter urged the Court to make an appeal to the South's white moderate lawyers. Black opposed the idea. He understood that southern moderates were isolated and relatively weak. Moreover, moderates succeeded only after protracted disorder and with the assistance of the African-American community. When Frankfurter got his way, Black was so angry that he threatened to write a dissent, though because of Warren's persuasion he remained quiet.[24]

The clash with Frankfurter also suggested how Black's personal values shaped his perception of the sit-in cases. Warren's attainment of unanimity in *Brown I* indicated that the justices had accepted the convergence of white and African-American interests to the point that they believed American public opinion and therefore the Eisenhower administration were ready to accept a revolutionary interpretation of the equal protection clause. Little Rock revealed, however, that the Eisenhower administration would enforce the new principle in only the most extreme cases, which encouraged defiance.[25]

To the South's massive resistance, Martin Luther King, Jr., led a campaign of nonviolent, passive resistance. The growing emphasis on public demonstrations and the corresponding and often brutal repression by officials in Oxford, Mississippi, and Birmingham and Selma, Alabama, resulted in still more disorder. Black, however, told his wife Elizabeth shortly before Congress passed the pioneering civil rights legislation of 1964 and 1965 that the courts, though "not as glamorous as the streets," were the "route by which the only lasting civil rights will come."[26]

Black was convinced that the sit-ins were a form of public demonstration which undermined the common ground of whites and African-Americans. Initially at least, most African-American leaders, the major African-American newspapers, and the leading civil rights organizations shared this view. At first, King was perhaps the only prominent African-American leader supporting the new demonstrations, and the NAACP Legal Defense Fund did not defend the first students arrested. But the NAACP and the Legal Defense Fund soon came around. The sit-ins began February 1, 1960, in Greensboro, North Carolina. Three months later the Fund's leading lawyer, Thurgood Marshall, stated publicly that legal assistance was available to those involved in the sit-ins. Justice Black, however, never changed his mind concerning the issue.[27]

For the Warren Court the constitutional question involved the distinction between state and private action. Douglas argued that the sit-ins raised the question of whether public officials could constitutionally enforce private discrimination. Black's view was more restricted. He readily acknowledged that Congress or a state could enact a law forbidding racial discrimination even in private businesses. Recalling his "Pappy's" store in Ashland, however, Black declared further that "I don't think the Constitution forbids the owner of a store to keep people out," so long as the business was "really wholly your own and neither in its origin nor in its maintenance" was involved "directly or indirectly" in issues of state or federal authority.[28]

The conflict within the Court became increasingly irreconcilable. In several early cases the Court, including Black, overturned convictions of protestors where discrimination by private businesses involved state action. Black, however, was one of several justices arguing that the Fourteenth Amendment did "not of itself, standing alone, in the absence of some cooperative state action or compulsion, forbid property holders, including restaurant owners, to ban people from entering or remaining upon their premises, even if the owner acts out of racial prejudice."[29]

Ultimately, however, Black's opposition became moot. He supported the Civil Rights Act of 1964, including Title II prohibiting racial discrimination in restaurants and other public accommodations. Title II relied on the commerce clause to enforce federal power; now that authority was aligned against racial injustice and the end of the "deliberate speed" standard.[30]

Black's role was also significant in the voting rights and apportionment cases. Since World War II the Court had steadily eroded the southern states' control of African-American voting rights by broadening the scope of state action proscribed by the Fifteenth Amendment. The process reached a turning point in *Gomillion v. Lightfoot* (1960) where, through Frankfurter's opinion, the Court struck down Alabama state and municipal rules which enabled white city officials to establish boundaries excluding nearly all eligible African-American voters from Tuskegee municipal elections.[31]

The underlying convergence of African-American and white interests became conspicuous when a majority of the Warren Court extended the judiciary's jurisdiction beyond the race cases established in *Gomillion v. Lightfoot* to include the malapportionment of primarily white voting districts, a shift which reversed Frankfurter's "political question doctrine" in favor of Black's theory. His Clay County childhood, public career in Birmingham, and tenure in the Senate had taught Black that the disenfranchisement of African-Americans and the underrepresentation of white voters in places such as Birmingham were linked. Despite considerable criticism the Warren Court adopted Black's "one man–one vote" principle for United States congressional and state voting districts.[32]

Black's support for the Voting Rights Act of 1965 was equivocal, however. In *South Carolina v. Katzenbach* (1966), he concurred with Warren's opinion upholding the law's imposition of federal supervision of southern state franchise requirements except regarding the requirement of "preclearance." In lone dissent he argued that preclearance discouraged state attempts to remedy racial disenfranchisement on their own, which in turn undercut white southerners' self-respect, breeding resentment and resistance.[33]

Similarly, Black dissented when the Court struck down the poll tax in *Harper v. Virginia* (1966). Noting that he had concurred in the unanimous 1937 opinion upholding the tax, he held to the position that legislation was better than a Court ruling to resolve any "invidious discrimination" arising from the poll tax. In his view a fairly administered tax would encourage a far greater interest in democratic government.[34]

Although the Warren Court generally remained united on the enforcement of *Brown,* it often divided in related cases. The conflict within the Court reflected how shaky was the convergence of white and African-American interests supporting racial justice throughout American society. After King's assassination on April 4, 1968, the unrest climaxed in nationwide riots. Elizabeth Black remarked in her diary that "Hugo has been saying that the demonstrations would lead to riots and anarchy, and he is borne out." The domestic disorder concerned Black for deeper reasons. The scale of unrest and the often vicious response of officials left Black wondering whether a majority might not ultimately endorse a more repressive government. He told Elizabeth that the "people in this country subconsciously want a change in government, since all seem to want a government by demonstrations and marching." Moreover, Black warned, "Hitler took to the streets before he took over." Yet he was sure that the constancy of the human character also demonstrated the truth of Tacitus's observation that authorities should "appeal to exalted ideals" of the people.[35] The Court's chief responsibility was to encourage higher rather than lower sentiments in the people.

III

Black's unique contribution to American constitutionalism was the consistent application of a contractarian theory to the Bill of Rights. According to Alexander Bickel, the contractarian tradition of John Locke assumed "a vision of individual rights" possessing a "clearly defined, independent existence predating society . . .derived from nature and from a natural, if imagined, contract. Society must bend to these rights." Bickel, however, preferred the alternative "conservative whig" tradition in which rights depended entirely on "culture" and "time-and-place-bound conditions," ultimately leaving lawmakers "no choice but relativism." As early as 1929, in a Senate speech, Black blended the teachings of Locke and Jefferson to resist government interference with free expression on the basis of the contractarian principle. Thirty years later on the Warren Court, he applied the same theory in many opinions pitting individual rights against national security.[36]

Black accepted Locke's theory in part because he believed that Jefferson had incorporated it into the Declaration of Independence. Applying the ideas of a close friend, the philosopher Alexander Meiklejohn, Black attempted to prescribe the limits of both individual rights and majoritarian democracy, particularly as they related to the distinction between speech and conduct. During the 1950s and 1960s, Black accepted Meiklejohn's reading of the Declaration of Independence as an expression of the tension between liberty and authority stated by Socrates in the *Apology* and the *Crito* dialogues. Meiklejohn interpreted Jefferson's pledge of "lives," "Fortunes," and "sacred Honor" ending the Declaration as "a voluntary compact among equals." From this view it flowed that free expression was so vital to preserving the contract creating a free society that it should receive absolute protection. Yet Black and Meiklejohn agreed, too, that protection of the content of expression did not extend to the "time, place, or manner of the utterance," and the judge's duty was to establish the boundary separating each.[37]

The judge was bound by what Black believed was the fundamental intent of the framers of the Bill of Rights. The First Amendment, Madison declared, placed freedom of expression "beyond the reach" of Congress. Frankfurter, and even Douglas in brilliantly refined form, applied Justice Oliver Wendell Holmes's clear-and-present danger test to achieve this purpose. Justice Robert Jackson, by contrast, said that doctrine made the government captive in a "judge-made verbal trap," which he preferred replacing with a rule of reason.[38] Black, however, believed neither test protected free expression from government authority (including that of judges themselves) to a degree consistent with the contractarian theory implicit in the intent of Madison's Bill of Rights and Jefferson's Declaration of Independence. Black said in his *Barenblatt v. U.S.* (1959) dissent that "the First Amendment sought to leave Congress devoid of any kind or quality of power to direct any type of national laws against the freedom of individuals to think what they please, advocate whatever policy they choose, and join with others to bring about the social, religious, political, and government changes which seem best to them." A decade later, in *Brandenberg v. Ohio* (1969), as the Warren Court came to an end, it accepted Black's reasoning rather than that of either the clear-and-present danger or reasonableness test.[39]

Black extended full protection to a relatively broad expression of ideas which were, to use Douglas's phrase, not "brigaded with action." Accordingly, the national security cases were relatively easy for Black from the perspective of contractarian theory, because Communists, though advocating radicalism, generally only talked. Similarly, it was not difficult to extend the absolutist principle to libel laws and, more problematically, to obscenity.[40]

Near the end of 1968, in a one-hour CBS news special, he explained why he advocated extending this absolute guarantee to pornography. The community could not agree on what was obscene or pornographic. The best safeguard against unacceptable contact with offensive material was, Black observed, the family's teaching of appropriate values to children. Parents "ought" to take care of their "children and warn them against things themselves rather than try to pass a law." If parents did their duty, children would have the strength of character to reject the obscene, as Black himself said he had done because of his upbringing.[41]

Still, the line separating that which was and was not absolutely protected was often difficult to establish. In *Cox v. Louisiana* (1965), Black agreed to overturn the conviction of civil rights activists demonstrating near a local courthouse where state measures and actions violated the equal protection clause. At the same time, he dissented to support related convictions where equal protection was not at issue, expressing "no doubt" that the state had the "power to protect judges, jurors, witnesses, and court officers from intimidation by crowds" seeking to "influence them by picketing, patrolling, or parading in or near the court houses in which they do their business or the homes in which they live."[42] A majority of the Warren Court accepted this principle in Black's opinion *Adderly v. Florida* (1966).[43]

There was no more conspicuous attempt to establish the boundary than the *Tinker* case. Early in 1969 the Supreme Court reversed a federal district court's sustaining of a local Iowa school policy prohibiting the wearing of black armbands protesting the government's Vietnam policy. Black dissented, contending that Justice Abe Fortas's majority opinion pushed free expression beyond proper limits, undercutting traditional sources of order. "School discipline, like parental discipline, is an integral and important part of training our children to be good citizens—to be better citizens."[44]

Black reiterated his and Meiklejohn's distinction between speech and conduct. The First Amendment guaranteed the "right to think, speak, and write freely without governmental censorship or interference."[45] Where there was more action than speech, however, the democratic system of government that free debate made possible was subverted. Social order, no less than vigorous written and spoken expression, was essential to democracy. Unrestrained conduct too easily disintegrated into disorder, he wrote, and "the crowds that press in the streets for noble goals today can be supplanted tomorrow by street mobs pressuring" for "precisely opposite ends."[46]

He thus acknowledged the limits of the absolute defense of free expression that he had proclaimed during the McCarthy era, when anticommunist prosecutions excluded controversial ideas from the intellectual marketplace. The resulting fear, ignorance, and guilt by association undermined democracy and faith in constitutional rights. Americans would have rejected the Communists' ideas if given the opportunity to consider them objectively. Such evaluation, in turn, would have strengthened both the public's faith in democracy and respect for individual rights.

The symbolic protest in *Tinker* expressed a similar attitude from an opposite direction. For Black, despite evidence to the contrary, the protestors' armbands disrupted the educational process. In light of the period's massive unrest, Black believed that the armband protest undermined the orderly discourse in the classroom essential to both community stability and individual rights.

Black remained consistent on the establishment clause. *Engel v. Vitale* (1962) involved a New York law establishing in public school classrooms daily observance of a brief nondenominational prayer, with voluntary individual participation. Black's majority opinion declared the law invalid because it mandated a clear religious preference. The framers based the establishment clause, he said, "upon an awareness of historical fact that governmentally established religions and religious persecutions go hand in hand." Religion was "too personal, too sacred, too holy, to permit its 'unhallowed perversion' by a civil magistrate."[47]

To be sure, Black admitted a narrowly circumscribed place for government action touching the establishment issue. In the *Everson* decision of 1947, his majority opinion sustained a New Jersey law authorizing local school boards to reimburse parents for bus fares their children paid to attend either public or Catholic schools. Black reviewed the history of the nation's experience with the religious establishment, concluding that the First Amendment required the "state to be a neutral in its relations with groups of religious believers and unbelievers." In this case, the state neither contributed money nor otherwise supported the parochial schools. It merely provided a "general program to help parents get their children, regardless of their religion, safely and expeditiously to and from accredited schools."[48]

Black's *Everson* and *Vitale* opinions sparked enormous criticism within and outside of the Court. The critics underestimated Black's attempt to apply the contractarian theory to the establishment and free exercise clause of the First Amendment. Black was no more willing than his critics to breach the wall separating church and state. At the same time, he was certain that establishing the principle of government neutrality where safety was at stake successfully preserved the inviolability of the establishment clause. After all, New Jersey's legislature had conferred the reimbursement authority upon local school officials to assist without preference both the public school majority and the Catholic school minority. As for *Vitale,* Black responded that he had preserved the welfare of the community by protecting the rights of religious minorities. He had remained consistent in this view by dissenting when the Warren Court in 1968 upheld a New York law providing free textbooks to children in both public and private schools.[49]

As disagreements with Douglas, Warren, and Fortas appeared during the late 1960s, some observers argued that Black was retreating from activism.[50] The apparent shift, however, was a renewed emphasis upon community welfare. In the sixties he continued to seek a balance between majoritarian democracy and individual liberty, and in the search for balance he relied upon clear prescriptions. He hedged his famous assertion that the First Amendment's guarantee of speech was absolute by distinguishing pure speech from conduct which was not protected absolutely. The distinction was like that between advocacy of action and overt action itself. The First Amendment permitted advocacy of controversial ideas until evidence proved that some unlawful act resulted. Similarly, Black held that the strict separation between church and state under the establishment clause did not preclude the state from providing safe transportation for both public and parochial schoolchildren. Since only economic and safety considerations determined eligibility for financial assistance, he said, on the issue of religion, the state was neutral. Yet the state was forbidden from imposing religious beliefs upon the individual's conscience by instituting a school prayer. Black thus balanced activism and restraint by limiting the state's power up to the point he believed was consistent with Meiklejohn's contractarian theory of the Declaration of Independence and the intent of the framers of the Bill of Rights.

IV

Black pronounced his theory of total incorporation in a dissenting opinion in *Adamson v. California* (1947). The Court held that the Fifth Amendment did not apply to the states under the due process clause. Black argued to the contrary that the entire Bill of Rights restricted the states. But he also sought to establish specific guidelines limiting judicial discretion. "I would follow what I believe was the original purpose of the Fourteenth Amendment to extend to all the people of the nation the complete protection of the Bill of Rights," he said. "To hold that this Court can determine what, if any, provisions of the Bill of Rights, will be enforced, and, if so, to what degree, is to frustrate the great design of a written Constitution."[51]

Black's critics argued that the intent of the framers of the Fourteenth Amendment's due process clause was not clear. Black's historical inquiry, however, was not as misguided as the critics implied. Indeed, the most comprehensive research by recent scholars is not inconsistent with Black's conclusion.[52] As Black said, "I served in the United States Senate for ten years and I believe I have some knowledge of .. the use of committee reports. Applying this knowledge and experience to the legislative history surrounding the adoption of the Fourteenth Amendment, I come to my conclusion that the purpose of the Amendment was to make the Bill of Rights applicable to the states."[53]

Black opposed Harlan F. Stone's well-known "Footnote Four" because it failed to establish adequate guidelines circumscribing the judges' discretion. In cases involving racial discrimination imposed by state action, he wanted the Court to rely on the intent of the framers of the Fourteenth Amendment's equal protection clause. When the Court overturned state restrictions on individual liberty as contrary to the Fourteenth Amendment's due process clause, Black accepted the theory that Justice Cardozo pronounced in *Palko v. Connecticut,* holding that certain rights guaranteed in the Constitution's Bill of Rights had— through "a process of absorption"—become part of the due process clause of the Fourteenth Amendment.[54]

Yet Black's search for rules to govern the application of the Bill of Rights to the states was part of a larger conflict. The brand of judicial restraint advocated by Frankfurter supported a position that the liberties applicable to the states through the due process clause were merely *similar* to those in the Bill of Rights. As a result, the judge was free to prefer the majority's interest to the individual's. Black countered, however, that the rights found in the due process clause and the first eight amendments were *identical.* Accordingly, judges were bound to protect individual liberty to a degree neither more nor less than that specifically required by the Bill of Rights. He believed that total incorporation limited judicial discretion and increased individual freedom. The theory of incorporation frightened Frankfurter and others because, in effect, due process under the Fourteenth Amendment could stretch almost indefinitely. But Black countered that a strict regard for the intent of the framers of the Bill of Rights, read literally, restricted the judge.[55]

Black faced this challenge in cases involving the rights of the accused. In *Griffin v. Illinois* (1956), Black for a five-to-four majority held that making the appeal of a noncapital offense contingent upon the ability to pay the costs of reproducing a trial transcript violated the due process and equal protection clauses of the Fourteenth Amendment.[56] The next year, in *Breithaupt v. Abram*, however, the Court blunted Black's attempt to broaden the amendment's due process guarantees. With Black in dissent, the Court held that a New Mexico conviction of an individual based on the authorities' use of a blood test taken when he was unconscious did not violate the due process clause.[57] Still, on a selective basis the Warren Court did significantly expand the Bill of Rights guarantees applicable to the states under the due process clause. In the pathbreaking decisions of *Mapp v. Ohio* (1961), *Escobedo v. Illinois* (1964), and *Miranda v. Arizona* (1966), it declared that the Fourth Amendment's proscription of unwarranted search and seizures, the Sixth Amendment's right to counsel, and the Fifth Amendment's provision against self-incrimination all controlled state trials and police conduct. Black supported each of these opinions and contributed one himself in *Gideon v. Wainwright* (1963).[58]

Particularly on the issue of self-incrimination, Black always preferred to rely on the Fifth Amendment, rather than on what he believed was the vaguer standard of "reasonableness" in the Fourth Amendment. In *Benton v. Maryland* (1969), the Warren Court held that the double jeopardy clause of the Fifth Amendment applied to the states through the Fourteenth Amendment's due process clause. Yet Black dissented when the Court limited the state's authority in criminal cases as contrary to the Fourth Amendment's proscription of unreasonable searches and seizures. Even so, selective rather than full incorporation triumphed, a result consistent with the spirit if not the letter of Black's theory.[59]

Griswold v. Connecticut (1965), establishing the right of privacy, revealed the limits of Black's constitutional principle. Douglas wrote the Court's decision, holding that the law violated a "marital right of privacy" implicit in the First, Fourth, and Fifth Amendments and the due process clause. Black vigorously dissented. The Court had transcended his presumption that it should apply the Bill of Rights as fully as, but no further than, a literal reading established.[60]

The turmoil of the sixties reflected the public's growing acceptance of extralegal action. Acquiescence in violence eventually produced a backlash aimed at the Court. Black knew that this attack on the Court reflected profound emotions. "Sir, I am just a common laborer, without any influence, except to vote, and I use this to the best of my knowledge," said an anonymous letter writer. "I was very much afraid the communists would take over this country, because I have five small sons and I want to live in freedom."[61] Such sentiments made the wide-spread disorder of the sixties particularly dangerous. However good the motives of demonstrators, the unrest aroused America's deepest anxieties and could lead to the election of those who would use fear to justify restricting freedom. Black perceived the initial steps in this direction during the state gubernatorial elections of 1966; he told Elizabeth that Ronald Reagan's victory in California over liberal Pat Brown was "bad." He thought the same of George Wallace's triumph through the election of his wife, Lurleen.[62] The victories of Reagan and Wallace resulted, he told his clerks, from human anxieties that "had been the problem since the time of Tacitus."[63]

The Court's due process revolution, which imposed national standards on local law enforcement authorities, was also central to Richard Nixon's 1968 presidential campaign. Nixon exclaimed repeatedly that the Court's decisions had "gone too far in weakening the peace forces as against the criminal forces of this country."[64] Black, however, struggled to establish the total incorporation principle primarily because he believed that uniform constitutional rules controlling state police and courts would improve law enforcement. "Having served as a prosecutor myself for so long a time," he replied to a letter from a prosecuting attorney in Indiana, "I have great sympathy with efforts of prosecuting officers to enforce the law of the States and Nation."[65]

Black publicly addressed the tensions in a one-hour CBS news special in which journalists Eric Sevareid and Martin Agronsky interviewed the justice. When the interviewers raised the "public clamor" involving the Court and the "notion" that its decisions had somehow restricted police and aided criminals, Black responded without hesitation. "Well, the Court didn't do it," he said. "No, the Constitution-makers did it. They were the ones that put in 'no man should be compelled to convict himself.'" And Black made clear his conviction that the Court's enforcement of the framers' intent was correct. "Certainly, why shouldn't they?" he said. "Why did they write the Bill of Rights? They practically all relate to the ways cases shall be tried. And practically all of them make it more difficult to convict people of crime."[66] He wrote in *A Constitutional Faith*, moreover, that his duty was to follow as nearly as possible the literal meaning of the Constitution's words. In so doing, he looked to the framers for guidance, to the historical context in which they worked, and only then did he exercise his own judgment. The framers knew intimately history's long record of oppressions and wrote the Constitution to limit government, thereby limiting the perpetuation of oppression in the future.

V

From the time Warren joined the Court, he and Black shared a similar vision of American liberalism. When critics charged that Black's influence had changed Warren's views, Black emphasized the unity of their convictions. "He came into the Court with the same ideas I had," Black insisted. "He got them in California, I in Alabama."[67] Nevertheless, Black found himself disagreeing with Warren and others on leading cases involving the expansion of individual rights.

After years of rigorous self-education, Black believed that human nature did not change. Thus, people living today could learn useful lessons from history, classical literature, and philosophy. This logic meant that the Constitution, even though written two centuries ago, could be an appropriate guide for the conduct of contemporary Americans. In fact, for Black, the Constitution was the primary standard controlling conduct throughout the nation's history. Through provisions of the Fourteenth Amendment and the Bill of Rights, it placed limitations upon the power of state and federal government. Judges were bound to adhere to these limitations without altering them, and as faithful servants of the document, they exercised an authority which extended beyond all other lawmaking branches.

No one believed in or fought for the liberties guaranteed by the Fourteenth Amendment and the Bill of Rights more than Black. Yet he was convinced, too, that unless citizens accepted the responsibilities these liberties imposed, freedom could neither thrive nor endure. He devoted his role on the Warren Court to restricting government's power over individual rights without minimizing the equally compelling need for individuals to embrace the obligations this freedom demanded. Few judges have been as effective as Black in developing a constitutional theory which maintained this vital balance.

PART II

THE CENTRAL

FIGURES OF

THE SECOND

GENERATION

John Marshall Harlan
and the Warren Court

Justice John Marshall Harlan was an indispensable component of the Warren Court. This is true not only, as a wiseacre might say, because losers are needed if there are to be winners, but because he provided a form of resistance to the Court's dominant motifs that was intelligent, determined, professionally skillful, and above all principled. In a sense he defined that Court by his dissents. For this performance over sixteen years Harlan received extraordinary praise. Earl Warren himself said, "Justice Harlan will always be remembered as a true scholar, a talented lawyer, a generous human being, and a beloved colleague by all who were privileged to sit with him." Judge Henry Friendly, who first worked with Harlan as a young lawyer in the early 1930s, boldly asserted, "There has never been a Justice of the Supreme Court who has so consistently maintained a high quality of performance or, despite differences in views, has enjoyed such nearly uniform respect from his colleagues, the inferior bench, the bar, and the academy." There have been many similar accolades.[1]

This chapter indicates the nature and extent of Harlan's views as a counterpoint to the Warren Court majority and suggests that it would be a mistake to conceive of Harlan solely in this light, as an inveterate reactionary seeking to forestall the brave new work that his brethren sought to welcome or even to create. To a surprising degree Harlan concurred in the liberal activism of the Warren Court, picking his spots carefully and above all seeking (though not always successfully) to be true to his core values of federalism and a limited judicial function. What emerges, in sum, is not a right-wing justice as he is sometimes conceived but rather someone much closer to the center, a moderate figure avoiding the extremes.

I

Harlan dissented from the principal themes of the Warren Court. Perhaps the most central of these is equality, an idea that "[o]nce loosed .. is not easily cabined," as Archibald Cox said in his valuable book on the Warren Court.[2] Harlan vigorously opposed egalitarian rulings of many kinds. He was most vehement in condemning the reapportionment decisions, first *Baker v. Carr*[3] in which the Court acknowledged federal jurisdiction to decide the issue whether state legislative districts were malapportioned, then *Reynolds v. Sims*[4] in which the Court established the one person–one vote rule, and then the many sequels to these rulings.[5] Harlan never became reconciled to what he regarded as a wholly unjustified encroachment into the political realm, saying in *Reynolds* that "it is difficult to imagine a more intolerable and inappropriate interference by the judiciary with the independent legislatures of the States."[6]

Closely related to the apportionment cases are those dealing with the right to vote. Here, too, he dissented, from the ruling invalidating Virginia's poll tax, from a decision opening school board elections to a person who was neither a parent nor a property holder in the district, and from the decision upholding Congress's power to extend the franchise to eighteen-year-olds.[7]

The poll tax case illustrates an aspect of the Court's egalitarianism to which Harlan especially objected, its acceptance of the idea that government has an obligation to eliminate economic inequalities as a way to permit everyone to exercise human rights. The leading case was *Griffin v. Illinois,* in which a sharply divided Court held that where a stenographic trial transcript is needed for appellate review, a state violates the Fourteenth Amendment by refusing to provide the transcript to an impoverished defendant who alleges that reversible errors occurred at his trial. Harlan's dissent maintained that "all that Illinois has done is to fail to alleviate the consequences of differences in economic circumstances that exist wholly apart from any state action."[8] He later dissented from *Douglas v. California,* which held that a state could not deny counsel to a convicted indigent who seeks his only appeal by right to a higher court.[9] Another example of the genre is Harlan's protest at efforts to transform welfare payments into entitlements. Thus, in a major effort, he maintained that states could deny such payments to otherwise eligible welfare applicants who had not resided in the state for a year or more.[10]

Harlan also found himself out of step with the prevailing view of criminal procedure, where the Warren Court rewrote the book, transforming the law relating to confessions and lineups, the privilege against self-incrimination, the use of wiretapping and eavesdropping, and the admissibility of illegally obtained evidence, among other aspects of criminal cases. The linchpin of most of the rulings was the doctrine of selective incorporation, under which the Court applied to state criminal trials under the Fourteenth Amendment's due process clause the protections of the first eight amendments to the Constitution that were deemed "fundamental." Rejecting Harlan's view that the due process clause established a general test of "fundamental fairness" not tied to the particular provisions of the Bill of Rights, the Court completed a massive reform of criminal procedure in an astonishingly brief period.[11] Harlan vigorously dissented from most of the seminal decisions, including those applying the exclusionary rule to illegally seized evidence, incorporating the privilege against self-incrimination, establishing the Miranda rules for warning individuals being taken into police custody, and requiring a jury trial in criminal cases. He equally opposed the Court's conclusion that the guarantees of the Bill of Rights that were "selectively" incorporated should apply to the states in exactly the way in which they applied to the federal government.[12] In these cases he asserted that a "healthy federalism" was inconsistent with the assertion of national judicial authority.[13]

Harlan also objected in the interests of federalism to extensions of congressional power. The two most significant cases of this sort were *Katzenbach v. Morgan*[14] and *United States v. Guest,*[15] which adopted broad theories in sustaining, respectively, the authority of Congress to invalidate state English language literacy tests for voting as applied to individuals who completed sixth grade in Puerto Rican schools and to punish private (not state) action that interferes with constitutional rights.

At the same time Harlan, often contrary to the majority, deferred to congressional judgments that impaired civil liberties. For example, he conceded broad authority to Congress over citizenship, rejecting any constitutional right to prevent involuntary denationalization;[16] he protested a softening of the immigration law that provided for deportation of an alien who had ever been a member of the Communist party, however nominally;[17] and he did not recognize a constitutional right to travel abroad, first recognized in *Kent v. Dulles*[18] and solidified in *Aptheker v. Secretary of State.*[19] In all these cases he refused to overturn actions of the elected branches of government that resulted in severe and arguably unjustified harm to individuals.

There is no doubt, in light of these cases and others, that Justice Harlan was a regular and frequent dissenter from many of the Warren Court's key liberal decisions. In addition, especially in his early terms, there were many important cases in which Harlan was part of a majority that rejected constitutional theories supported by the liberal justices. For example, he wrote the prevailing opinions in cases rejecting First Amendment claims by individuals who were held in contempt by the House Un-American Activities Committee and denied admission to the practice of law for refusing to respond to questions concerning Communist activities and by a man sentenced to prison because of membership in the Communist party.[20] These cases have not been overruled, but later actions overturned majority decisions of which Harlan was a part that, for example, permitted states to question criminal suspects without concern for the privilege against self-incrimination and to deny women the right to serve on juries equally with men. Here, too, Harlan was out of step with the liberal activism that distinguished the Warren Court.[21]

II

But this is far from the whole story. Justice Potter Stewart, one of Harlan's closest colleagues, recognized this when he said, "I can assure you that a very interesting law review article could someday be written on 'The Liberal Opinions of Mr. Justice Harlan.'"[22] In virtually every area of the Court's work, there are cases in which he was part of the consensus and, indeed, in which he spoke for the Court.

Harlan joined *Brown II*[23] and *Cooper v. Aaron,*[24] decisions instrumental in protecting the principle of the initial school segregation case, *Brown I.*[25] He also joined every opinion decided while he was on the Court that applied the principle of *Brown* to other sorts of state-enforced segregation.[26]

He concurred in *Gideon v. Wainwright,*[27] the right-to-counsel case, and wrote the opinion in *Boddie v. Connecticut,*[28] which held that a state could not deny a divorce to a couple because they lacked the means to pay the judicial filing fee. Although both of these cases were decided under the due process clause, they were, at bottom, judicially mandated equalization of economic circumstance in situations where Harlan concluded that it would be fundamentally unfair to deny poor people what others could afford.

In the criminal procedure area, while opposing the exclusionary rule in state prosecutions, he consistently supported a strong version of the Fourth Amendment protection against unreasonable searches and seizures by federal authorities, including application of the principle to wiretapping and eavesdropping.[29] He also wrote a separate opinion to underscore his agreement with the ruling that extended criminal due process protections to juveniles accused of delinquency.[30] And he joined the decision overruling earlier cases upholding federal registration requirements for gamblers, concluding that they could avoid prosecution for violation of the statutes by pleading the privilege against self-incrimination.[31]

Turning to free expression, one finds a host of important cases in which Harlan supported the constitutional right. For example, he wrote the important opinion in *NAACP v. Alabama,*[32] which held that the right of individuals to join civil rights groups anonymously when exposure would have entailed great personal risk was a form of freedom of association protected by the First Amendment. He joined *New York Times Co. v. Sullivan,*[33] which first imposed limits on libel judgments against the media, and some (though not all) of the sequels to that case.[34] He joined majority opinions that barred states from seating an elected legislator who had been denied his seat because of his sharply critical views on the Vietnam War and from convicting a leader of the Ku Klux Klan for "seditious" speech.[35] And he wrote for the Court to protect the right of a black man, unnerved by the fact that a civil rights leader had been shot, to express himself strongly about the country while burning the flag.[36]

Harlan also wrote a number of opinions, all curbing variants of Mc-Carthyism, that nominally were decided on nonconstitutional grounds but rested on First Amendment principles. In the first of these, *Cole v. Young,* which invalidated the discharge of a federal food and drug inspector, Harlan interpreted a statute authorizing dismissals of government employees "in the interests of national security" to apply only to jobs directly concerned with internal subversion and foreign aggression.[37] The next year, in what Anthony Lewis has described as a "masterfully subtle opinion," Harlan construed the Smith Act to permit prosecution of Communist party leaders only for speech amounting to incitement to action rather than for "abstract doctrine" advocating overthrow.[38] A third instance involved companion cases in which the government had revoked the naturalization of two persons were alleged to have obtained their citizenship improperly.[39] The government contended that they were Communists and therefore not "attached to the principles of the Constitution of the United States" as required by the applicable statute. Harlan's opinion found that "clear, unequivocal and convincing evidence" was lacking that the individuals were aware, during the relevant period prior to their becoming citizens, that the Communist party was engaged in illegal advocacy. During the 1950s these decisions were milestones in lifting the yoke of political repression.

Freedom of religion also showed Harlan as frequently, but not invariably, protective of constitutional guarantees. He joined decisions that prohibited organized prayer in the public schools and invalidated a requirement that state officials declare a belief in God.[40] And while approving state loans of textbooks to church schools, he balked when tax-raised funds were used to reimburse parochial schools for teachers' salaries, textbooks, and instructional materials.[41] Similarly, while unwilling to protect adherents to Sabbatarian faiths who objected to Sunday closing laws and to unemployment compensation laws that required a willingness of the applicant to work on Saturdays,[42] Harlan wrote a powerful opinion during the Vietnam War declaring that a statute that limited conscientious objection to those who believed in a theistic religion "offended the Establishment Clause" because it "accords a preference to the 'religious' [and] disadvantages adherents of religions that do not worship a Supreme Being."[43] In all these cases Harlan emphasized that "the attitude of government towards religion must . . . be one of neutrality."[44] Harlan was sophisticated enough to appreciate that neutrality is "a coat of many colors."[45] Nevertheless, as Professor Kent Greenawalt has observed, "no modern Justice ha[s] striven harder or more successfully than Justice Harlan to perform his responsibilities in [a neutral] manner."[46]

A final area of civil liberty, sexual privacy, is of particular importance because Harlan produced the most influential opinions on this subject written by anyone during his tenure. In the first case a thin majority, led by Justice Frankfurter, refused to decide whether a Connecticut law that criminalized the sale of contraceptives to married and unmarried people alike violated the Constitution, finding that there was no threat of prosecution. Harlan's emotional opinion — a rarity for him — not only differed with this conclusion but extensively defended the proposition that Connecticut's law violated the due process clause of the Fourteenth Amendment,[47] a position that prevailed four years later in *Griswold v. Connecticut.*[48] It is impossible to know whether Harlan would have extended this reasoning to support the result in *Eisenstadt v. Baird,*[49] which held that a state could not punish the distribution of contraceptives to unmarried persons, or to *Roe v. Wade's*[50] recognition of abortion as a personal right, both decided soon after he retired. At a minimum, he surely would have protected the right of a married woman to proceed with an abortion that was dictated by family financial considerations.

Harlan's participation in the major thrusts of the Warren Court was not confined to civil liberties and civil rights. In economic cases, too, he often went along with the majority's support of government regulation of business, despite the fact that his private practice of law often involved the defense of antitrust and other actions against the government and that he was acutely aware of the effect of regulation on business. To be sure, he frequently voted to limit the impact of regulatory statutes, but there are also many important antitrust cases in which he sided with the government or private plaintiff.[51]

III

What should one conclude from the many decisions in which Justice Harlan, a conservative, supported constitutional rights, often in highly controversial cases in which the Court was split? That he was in step with the majority of the Warren Court? Plainly not; there are too many instances where he marched separately. That he was essentially a civil libertarian? No, again; not only are there too many cases to the contrary, but at a basic level that is not the way Harlan reacted to injustice. This is not to say that he was insensitive to human suffering or unmoved by evidence of arbitrariness. It is rather that something else was at the core.

That something was Harlan's deep, almost visceral, desire to keep things in balance, to resist excess in any direction. Many times during my year with him he said how important it was "to keep things on an even keel." That is the master key to Harlan and his jurisprudence. One recalls Castle, the hero of Graham Greene's novel *The Human Factor,* as he muses on those who are "unable to love success or power or great beauty." Castle concludes that it is not because such people feel unworthy or are "more at home with a failure." It is rather that "one wanted the right balance." In reflecting on some of his own perplexing and self-destructive actions, Castle decides that "he was there to right the balance. That was all." [52] Harlan was not a man who avoided success or power or, if one knew Mrs. Harlan, great beauty, but nevertheless in his own eyes he was there to right the balance. It is significant that he entitled a major speech at the American Bar Association "Thoughts at a Dedication: Keeping the Judicial Function in Balance." [53]

There is evidence of balance not only in the decisions discussed above but in his elaborate views on doctrines of justiciability as well. These are closely related to his frequent preoccupation with judicial modesty or, put negatively, his opposition to excessive judicial activism, which in turn is related to the central theme of his judicial universe—federalism. As I suggested in 1969, "His pervasive concern has been over a judiciary that will arrogate power not rightfully belonging to it and impose its views of government from a remote tower, thereby enervating the initiative and independence at the grass roots that are essential to a thriving democracy." [54]

Harlan's thinking on jurisdictional issues was also related to his long years as a practicing lawyer, where he customarily represented defendants in litigation. In that role he had to be "constantly aware that it is easier and quicker to achieve victory on grounds such as want of federal jurisdiction, lack of standing or ripeness, of failure to join an indispensable party, than to prevail on the merits of a lawsuit." [55]

That this earlier sensitivity to issues of justiciability carried over to his judicial years is seen in the many instances where Harlan urged jurisdictional rules to avoid deciding controversial cases. Among the most notable are his dissenting opinions in *Baker v. Carr*[56] and *Reynolds v. Sims*[57] where he concluded that the issue of legislative reapportionment was a political question; in *Dombrowski v. Pfister*,[58] where he objected to the adjudication of the constitutionality of Louisiana's Subversive Activities and Communist Control Act in a federal suit to enjoin a state criminal prosecution under the statute; in *Fay v. Noia*[59] and *Henry v. Mississippi*,[60] where he criticized expansion of federal judicial authority to review state criminal convictions which previously were unreviewable because the convicted person had not complied with state procedural requirements; and in *Flast v. Cohen*,[61] where he dissented from the Court's holding that taxpayers had standing to challenge federal financial aid to religious schools.

On the other hand, reflecting his balanced approach, Harlan wrote or joined many opinions that expanded the Court's jurisdiction. Perhaps the most celebrated was *Poe v. Ullman*, where he vigorously rejected, in a dissent, the reasoning of Justice Frankfurter in dismissing an early challenge to Connecticut's birth control law on the ground that the statute was not being enforced.[62] Again, in *NAACP v. Alabama*, the first case explicitly recognizing a freedom of association, his opinion for the Court proceeded to its First Amendment conclusion only after overcoming difficult procedural obstacles involving the doctrines of standing and independent state grounds.[63] In the first school prayer case,[64] and again in the ruling that ordered the House of Representatives to seat Adam Clayton Powell,[65] both decisions of unusual sensitivity, Harlan joined majority opinions that rejected substantial justiciability defenses.[66]

Harlan's often unappreciated willingness to expand judicial authority can be seen in several cases involving the broadening of remedies in civil rights and economic cases alike. In one case, again differing with Frankfurter, he wrote a concurring opinion sanctioning the expansion of federal remedies against municipal officials who violated an individual's civil rights.[67] In a second ruling, involving a provision of the Securities and Exchange Act that prohibited false and misleading proxy statements in respect to mergers, Harlan agreed that a stockholder could sue for rescission and damages even though the statute was silent on private lawsuits to enforce the statute.[68]

Stare decisis is another important area relating to legal process and the judge's role in which Harlan's actions betrayed a more activist spirit than is commonly recognized. His general insistence on adhering to precedent was "the product of a conservative mind, one that is distrustful of abrupt change, comfortable with accustomed rules and practices, and therefore reluctant to revise the judgments of predecessors. It can also be partially traced to his long career at the bar, where, in advising clients and preparing for litigation, Harlan worked with precedent, relied on it, and was imbued with its significance in ordering day-to-day affairs."[69]

There are many examples of his unwillingness to reach beyond accustomed boundaries.[70] But there are also many contrary instances. He voted to overrule *Betts v. Brady* and grant an absolute right of counsel to defendants in felony prosecutions.[71] In *Marchetti v. United States* he spoke for the Court in overruling a decision that denied the privilege against self-incrimination to gamblers prosecuted for failing to register and pay taxes.[72] And in *Swift & Co. v. Wickham,* he wrote in the course of overruling an earlier decision that "unless inexorably commanded by statute, a procedural principle of this importance should not be kept on the books in the name of stare decisis once it is proved to be unworkable in practice."[73]

A striking aspect of Harlan's approach to *stare decisis* is that he would often follow precedent from which he had dissented when it was initially established.[74] Equally striking is that Harlan followed this principle even as it carried him to dissent from the Court's failure to follow precedent with which Harlan disagreed. Thus, in *Green v. United States* the Court held that where a defendant is convicted of a lesser included offense and then secures reversal of the conviction, the defendant may be retried only for the lesser included offense.[75] Although Harlan dissented in *Green,* he dissented again in *North Carolina v. Pearce* where he found, contrary to the Court, that *Green* mandated the conclusion that a defendant once "convicted and sentenced to a particular punishment may not on retrial be placed again in jeopardy of receiving a greater punishment than was first imposed."[76]

Finally, one may point to cases in which Harlan exhibited a trait familiar to all of his law clerks — his exceptional open-mindedness and willingness to listen to new arguments. In these cases he dissented from the Court's refusal to hear oral argument on constitutional claims, although in each of them he was not predisposed to agree that the appeal had merit. Thus, he joined Justice Douglas's dissent from the refusal to hear a plea of the Veterans of the American Lincoln Brigade that the organization was improperly ordered to register as a Communist front organization under the Subversive Activities Control Act.[77] Similarly, despite his earlier *Barenblatt*[78] ruling, he would have heard a challenge to contempt citations by the House Un-American Activities Committee against an uncooperative witness.[79] And in perhaps the most far-reaching action, he would have set down for oral argument a complaint by the state of Massachusetts that raised the issue of the legality of the Vietnam War, although he ordinarily accorded great deference to decisions of the elected branches of government on matters of war and peace.[80]

In one area Harlan was inflexible; he consistently refused to widen the scope of "state action" under the Fourteenth Amendment to encompass discrimination engaged in by what he regarded as private actors.[81]

IV

The Warren Court ended in mid-1969, but Harlan remained for two more terms, a brief period in which he was the leader of the Court. Possessing seniority and an unmatched professional reputation, he took advantage of the replacement of Earl Warren and Abe Fortas by Warren Burger and Harry Blackmun to regain the position of dominance that Justice Frankfurter and he shared until Frankfurter retired in August 1962. Thus, as Judge Friendly has noted, against an average of 62.6 dissenting votes by Harlan per term in the period between 1963 and 1967, he cast only 24 such votes in the 1969 term and 18 in the 1970 term.[82]

This new situation meant that Harlan could reassert conservative themes in his own opinions for the Court or join such expressions in the opinions of others. For example, during this period he adhered to his long-standing opposition to expansion of the constitutional rights of poor people to public assistance by voting with the majority in the leading case rejecting welfare as an entitlement.[83]

He prevailed in a series of criminal justice decisions, including those that confined the reach of the confrontation clause, denied a jury trial in juvenile delinquency proceedings and permitted the closing of such hearings to the public, and authorized capital sentencing without guidelines.[84] And in an important case that involved both the rights of poor people and procedural due process, he joined Justice Blackmun's opinion that rejected Fourth Amendment claims in sustaining the power of caseworkers to make unannounced visits to the homes of welfare recipients to check their eligibility and to provide rehabilitative assistance.[85]

In the First Amendment area Harlan also maintained long-standing positions, but here he was more often in dissent. The most notable occasion was the *Pentagon Papers* case, where he would have permitted a prior restraint of newspaper publication of an extensive and often embarrassing history of the Vietnam War.[86] He also dissented in an important libel case and in two decisions confining the authority of bar examiners to probe into the associations of applicants.[87] But he prevailed in another bar admission case, recalling issues from earlier days, that sustained questions about Communist associations, and he again joined the majority in an obscenity prosecution that rejected privacy as well as free speech claims.[88]

With regard to the breadth of the judicial role, he maintained his strong opposition to expansion of the state action doctrine, even when the consequence was to limit racial equality, and he took a similar position in rejecting a Fourteenth Amendment claim against an amendment to a state constitution that provided for a community referendum before a low-rent housing project could be constructed or acquired.[89]

At the same time that Harlan was, under Chief Justice Burger, renewing his formidable conservative record, he nevertheless adhered to a balanced judicial profile. Although liberal activist rulings did not dominate his last biennium on the Court, there surely are many examples of the genre. Thus, in the equality area, he maintained his support for desegregation,[90] and he joined the new chief justice's important opinion that expanded remedies against discriminatory employment tests.[91] And his opinion in *Boddie*, which invalidated a state statute that denied poor couples the right to divorce because they could not afford court filing fees, came during this period.[92] Harlan's reliance on the due process clause to reach this result was widely criticized, and the doctrine has not survived, but the case stands as a rare example of Harlan's reaching out to right an economic imbalance that prejudiced poor people in American society.[93] In another such case involving criminal justice, Harlan joined the Court's opinion prohibiting the incarceration of indigents who were unable to pay criminal fines.[94] He continued his deep concern for Fourth Amendment rights,[95] and wrote an extensive concurring opinion in support of "beyond reasonable doubt" as the proper standard of proof in juvenile delinquency hearings.[96]

And in the First Amendment field he wrote a widely cited opinion that protected display in a state courthouse of a "scurrilous epithet" ("Fuck the draft") in protest against conscription.[97] From 1969 to 1971, Harlan also manifested his flexibility by joining majorities that considerably expanded federal remedies for civil rights violations and overcame rigid theories of *stare decisis* in a variety of cases.[98]

V

The pattern of decisions provides ample proof that Harlan was not a one-dimensional justice. What is less clear is the source of his drive to keep things in balance, to eschew an extreme ideology.

Two possibilities may be suggested. The first is the familiar notion that in any society patricians (like Harlan) are concerned less with results in particular controversies, and certainly less about pressing any group against the wall, than in assuring the smooth functioning of institutions without the precipitation of volatility or deep-seated enmities. This means that dissent should be allowed an outlet, that racial minorities should be able to hope, that political power should not become centralized and therefore dangerous. Thus, his decisions supporting desegregation, a strong federal presence, and law and order. Thus also his fears about court-dominated reapportionment and about an "incorporation" of the Bill of Rights through the Fourteenth Amendment that represented too dramatic a break with established doctrine. But thus also Harlan's willingness to take reformist steps, to overrule outdated precedent selectively and before a problem worsened, and above all to listen closely to many voices.

A second source of Harlan's overall philosophy is legal process theory, which had its heyday for almost exactly the period that he served on the Supreme Court. In the early 1950s Henry Hart produced an early draft of the work that he and Albert Sacks published at Harvard Law School in a "tentative edition" in 1958 (it was also the final edition). The moderate philosophy embodied in these materials was tailor-made to Harlan's personality. It emphasized the central role that procedure plays in assuring judicial and legislative objectivity and argued that "just" policies will result when each government branch works within its assigned role. In this way courts through "reasoned elaboration" of decisions, and legislatures through public-seeking interpretations of statutes, will assure maximum fulfillment of society's expectations. Not surprisingly, Harlan was attracted to this theory, which enabled him to take constitutional steps as long as they were not too long or jarring, while simultaneously offering him ample institutional reasons for resisting excessive judicial authority.[99]

By 1971, when Harlan left the Supreme Court, legal process theory, buffeted by events in society at large, was beginning to lose its hold, even at Harvard, and the more extreme philosophies of law and economics and critical legal studies moved to the forefront. The struggle within the Court became ever more polarized as strong civil libertarians, which Harlan was not, waged battle with doctrinaire conservatives, which Harlan also was not.

VI

It fell to John Marshall Harlan, by nature a patrician traditionalist, to serve on a Supreme Court which, for most of his years, was rapidly revising and liberalizing constitutional law. In these circumstances it is not surprising that Harlan would protest the direction of the Court and the speed with which it was traveling. He did this in a remarkably forceful and principled manner, thereby providing balance to the institution and the law it generated. Despite this role, Harlan joined reformist rulings on the Court during his tenure to a degree that his overall jurisprudence can fairly be characterized as conservative primarily in the sense that it evinced caution, a fear of centralized authority, and a respect for process. In short, the nature and results of Harlan's jurisprudence were far more mixed than his conservative reputation would allow.

7 *ROBERT C. POST*

William J. Brennan

and the Warren Court

Justice William J. Brennan's eminent, if not preeminent, position in the annals of the Warren Court is now well established. The depth and clarity of his vision, the lucidity of its doctrinal expression, his uncanny knack for creating crucial court majorities from the splinters of disparate perspectives have all been amply documented. In the words of one commentator, "To the extent that the Court over which Warren presided has any intellectual legacy that is accessible to those trained in doctrine and not in ethics, it is Brennan who is responsible."[1] This chapter isolates and assesses Brennan's distinct contribution to that legacy.

The immense influence of the Warren Court on American constitutional law can ultimately be traced to three discrete achievements: the reconstruction of constitutional law on individualistic principles; the redesign of doctrine based upon a pragmatic conception of legal rules; and the vigorous articulation and revivification of egalitarian values. Although Justice William J. Brennan importantly participated in all three of these achievements, his work as a justice was particularly decisive to the first two.

I

When Brennan was appointed in October 1956, *Brown v. Board of Education,*[2] perhaps the most important decision of the Warren Court, had already been decided. The principle of equality, whose awesome power in our democracy had long ago been theorized by Alexis de Tocqueville, had been unleashed. Indeed, Brennan later remarked that "the equality principle . . . is the rock upon which our Constitution rests. . . . The judicial pursuit of equality is, in my view, properly regarded to be the noblest mission of judges; it has been the primary task of judges since the repudiation of economic substantive due process as our central constitutional concern."[3] During the Warren Court era, Brennan strongly supported and developed the equality principle in major opinions like *Cooper v. Aaron*[4] and *Green v. County School Board.*[5] In these efforts, as he recognized, he was ultimately carrying forward—albeit enthusiastically, creatively, and forcefully—a task assumed before his appointment.

The importance of this task had been foreseen by Tocqueville, who presciently argued that the people of the United States would evince "a more ardent and enduring love of equality than of liberty."[6] This point was astonishingly unappreciated by Herbert Wechsler when in 1959 he criticized *Brown* as not involving a question "of discrimination at all" but rather one of "freedom of association."[7] Precisely because in the end the Warren Court subordinated the latter to the former, it cannot strictly be called libertarian in sentiment.

It is more accurate to characterize the perspective of the Warren Court as individualist. And individualism, as Tocqueville also explained, is not only compatible with but directly implied by the principle of equality. In fact, Tocqueville argued that "individualism is of democratic origin, and it threatens to spread in the same ratio as the equality of conditions."[8] Individualism and equality are linked because the institution of democracy created pressure to measure equality in terms of persons.

By the end of the Warren Court, it is true, glimpses could be caught of a form of equality measured in terms of groups rather than individuals.[9] Brennan's opinion in *Green* rejecting a freedom-of-choice school desegregation plan is a prime example. In the years after the Warren Court the difference between these two forms of equality would lead to heated debates over affirmative action,[10] debates in which Brennan chiefly supported a concept of equality rooted in groups.[11] But in time of the Warren Court this tension between equality and individualism remained largely latent, and one of Brennan's most important contributions was the development and amplification of the logic of individualism.

The nature of that logic and its connections to equality can perhaps best be seen in Brennan's opinion in *Baker v. Carr*,[12] which Earl Warren viewed as "the most important of my tenure on the Court."[13] *Baker* was a lawsuit alleging that the gross malapportionment of the Tennessee legislature violated the equal protection clause; the issue before the Court was whether such a lawsuit was justiciable, or whether it was, as prior precedents like *Colegrove v. Green*[14] construing the guaranty clause of the Constitution[15] had concluded, a "political question." Brennan's long and exegetical opinion in *Baker* conceded that suits based upon the guaranty clause were nonjusticiable because the clause did not offer "a repository of judicially manageable standards which a court could utilize." But it insisted that, by contrast, "judicial standards under the Equal Protection Clause are well developed and familiar," and hence "that the complaint's allegations of a denial of equal protection present a justiciable constitutional clause of action upon which [plaintiffs] are entitled to a trial and decision."[16]

Why would the equal protection clause supply the judicial standards absent from the guaranty clause? The plaintiffs in *Baker* had alleged in their complaint that Tennessee malapportionment violated the equal protection clause because it constituted a "debasement of their votes." But, as Justice Frankfurter trenchantly noted in dissent, "talk of 'debasement' or 'dilution' is circular talk. One cannot speak of 'debasement' or 'dilution' of the value of a vote until there is first defined a standard of reference as to what a vote should be worth." Necessarily implicit in Brennan's conclusion, therefore, was the notion that the equal protection clause required "if not the assurance of equal weight to every voter's vote, at least the basic conception that representation ought to be proportionate to population, a standard by reference to which the reasonableness of apportionment plans may be judged."[17]

That legislative apportionment ought constitutionally to be based upon population, rather than upon geography, is not an obvious proposition in a country whose national Senate has since the eighteenth century represented states instead of people. It is the proposition, however, that underlies Brennan's opinion in *Baker v. Carr*. It is the proposition that would subsequently form "the foundation," in Earl Warren's words, "upon which rest all subsequent decisions guaranteeing equal weight to the vote of every American citizen for representation in state and federal government."[18]

What lends the proposition its power and makes it exemplary of the Warren Court's jurisprudence, is its democratic, as distinct from republican, logic. If democracy is that form of regime in which the people ultimately choose their government, then equality must ultimately be measured in terms of persons. In this manner the Warren Court used the solvent of democracy to fuse equality with individualism. As Brennan would later remark, the Constitution "is a sparkling vision of the supreme dignity of every individual. This vision is reflected in the very choice of democratic self-governance: the supreme value of a democracy is the presumed worth of each individual."[19]

The most salient characteristic of individualism is its focus on the individual as the privileged unit of social action. This focus has the powerful effect of delegitimating forms of social organization that do not flow from processes of individual choice. Thus the individualism of *Baker v. Carr*, which would later find explicit expression in Warren's opinion in *Reynolds v. Sims*,[20] undermines forms of representation that depend upon geography or upon maintaining an urban / rural balance. These forms of representation are entailed by visions of social identity that cannot be reduced to individual choice. By disallowing them, the Warren Court essentially turned its back, as Justice Harlan pointed out in his dissent, "on the regard which this Court has always shown for the judgment of State legislatures and courts on matters of basically local concern."[21] Individualism, in other words, meant the death knell of federalism as a source of limitations on the construction of civil rights and liberties.

Federalism is a form of cultural pluralism that valorizes the diversity of local cultures.[22] Individualism, on the other hand, valorizes the diversity of persons, who are understood to choose or to create their cultures. From the perspective of individualism, it makes no sense to curtail individual freedom for the purpose of promoting local culture. Similarly, for Brennan and the dominant members of the Warren Court, it was incomprehensible to appeal to federalism as a reason not to protect individual rights. In their eyes the very purpose of federalism, as Brennan told the Conference of Chief Justices in 1964, was to secure "individual freedom,"[23] a formulation that justices Frankfurter and Harlan would no doubt have found most distasteful.

Brennan's disaffection with federalism was reinforced by his perception that "the rise of mass education and mass media of communication" in the "two decades since the end of World War II" had materially contributed to the creation of a cultural uniformity inconsistent with the premises of federalism. He also perceived the most important social development of the time to be the growth of the state, creating the potential for "more and more collisions of the individual with his government."[24] And he conceived government not as a reflection of indigenous culture but rather as an impersonal "bureaucracy," as a rational deployment of state power.[25] His primary concern, then, was the protection of persons in their conflict with government, and from this perspective it made no difference whether the government at issue was federal or state.

It is for this reason that Brennan viewed the incorporation decisions "the most important of the Warren era."[26] These decisions, which applied the Bill of Rights against the states,[27] crushed federalism as an effective counter to the logic of individual liberty. Brennan believed that the logic of both individualism and equality entailed incorporation. The decisions were made possible by the Fourteenth Amendment, which thus "'served as the legal instrument of the equalitarian revolution which has so transformed the contemporary American society,' protecting each of us from the employment of governmental authority in a manner contravening our national conceptions of human dignity and liberty."[28] By focusing on the individual as the privileged unit of legal and social analysis, the incorporation decisions eliminated local cultural variations. They were egalitarian because they insisted that all individuals throughout the nation be treated equally. The nationalism which was so characteristic of Warren Court jurisprudence can thus be seen as implied by its evacuation of the space between individuals and the federal government.

The lengths to which Brennan was willing to take this nationalism is revealed in his important opinion in *Shapiro v. Thompson*,[29] from which even Earl Warren dissented. In *Shapiro*, the Court invalidated regulations imposing one-year residency requirements on welfare applicants. In Warren's view the requirements had been approved by Congress, and consistent with traditional New Deal nationalism, he

was therefore prepared to hold that Congress need only "have a rational basis for finding that a chosen regulatory scheme is necessary to
the furtherance of interstate commerce."[30] Brennan, on the other hand,
revealing the distance that he had traveled from the New Deal Court,
concluded that the regulations impinged upon the "fundamental"
right to interstate travel and were therefore a violation of the equal
protection clause unless justified by "a *compelling* government interest."[31] State attempts to use residency requirements to partition off local cultures were therefore precluded, as were most variations among
states. In this manner the Warren Court, under Brennan's lead, moved
decisively to articulate a nationalism that went beyond notions of plenary congressional power and derived instead from a vision of individuals uniformly equal before the Constitution.

The facts of *Shapiro* confirmed for Brennan his general analysis of
contemporary society. The case concerned a contest between government, in its capacity as a large and unfeeling bureaucracy, and desti-
tute welfare recipients, whose very necessities of life were being manipulated. The issue thus reduced to a conflict between individual
freedom and the impersonal and administrative prerogatives of state
power. For Brennan, the judiciary could assume a privileged role in
this deracinated conflict. He believed that "the soul of a government
of laws is the judicial function, and that function can only exist if adjudication is understood by our people to be, as it is, the essentially
disinterested, rational, and deliberate element of our society."[32] If the
rationality of bureaucracy was for Brennan tainted with organizational
self-interest, he viewed the reason of courts, in contrast, as detached
and trustworthy. Courts were somehow distinct from government. Because they embodied disinterested reason, they could be trusted to
mediate the conflict between government and individuals.[33]

The application of disinterested reason was for Brennan immensely
important. "I do not think there can be any challenge," he said, "to the
proposition that the ultimate protection of individual freedom is found
in court enforcement of . . . constitutional guarantees."[34] Public interest
litigation was thus for Brennan "a form of political expression" designed to make manifest and effective the principles of equality and
individualism. Indeed, "under the conditions of modern government,
litigation may well be the sole practicable avenue open to a minority
to petition for redress of grievances."[35]

These considerations prompted Brennan to give great priority to enlarging litigants' access to federal courts. He took the lead in the Warren Court in devising doctrinal strategies that would undo or circumvent prior restrictions on that access. He wrote the court's opinion in *Fay v. Noia,* for example, which radically revised the rules governing federal *habeas corpus* and made federal relief available in numerous instances where it theretofore would have been barred. Brennan rested his conclusion on a recognition of "the unceasing contest between personal liberty and government oppression" and on the necessity that "in a civilized society, government must always be accountable to the judiciary for a man's imprisonment." He specifically rejected "the exigencies of federalism" as a countervailing consideration, holding that these should not "be permitted to defeat the manifest federal policy that federal constitutional rights of personal liberty shall not be denied without the fullest opportunity for plenary judicial review."[36] Other examples of Brennan's determination to open up the federal courts during the Warren Court era include *Dombrowski v. Pfister,*[37] which increased the availability of federal injunctive relief, *Henry v. Mississippi,*[38] which limited the adequate state-ground doctrine, and *England v. Medical Examiners,*[39] which limited the grounds of federal court abstention.[40]

In this regard *Baker v. Carr* is of course exemplary. Although the decision is, on the surface, narrowly focused on a seemingly technical question of justiciability, in fact the question entails the whole issue of the enforceability of the substantive principles of individualism and equality. Because state courts could not be expected to adopt the nationalist perspectives these principles implied, the substantive agenda of the Warren Court would simply lie fallow if litigants were not afforded meaningful access to the power and detached reason of federal courts.

The increasing authority with which Brennan's opinions in retrospect have come to stand as definitive of the Warren Court stems from the fact that Brennan, more than any other single justice, most fully assimilated the full jurisprudential consequences of the Warren Court's revolutionary new vision of the American polity. He grasped, with comprehensive clarity and coherence, the relationship between individualism and equality, the bureaucratization of government, and the correspondingly augmented functions of the federal judiciary. He firmly discerned that individualism required opposition both to the communitarianism of traditional federalism and to the statism that has since come to dominate the Court through the opinions of Chief Justice Rehnquist and Justice Scalia.[41] He was able, with what seemed almost effortless ease, to create apt and convincing doctrinal structures to express these new understandings.

One can of course disagree with the substantive vision that underlies and supports this doctrine. One can question, for example, whether it too hastily denies the possibility of meaningful forms of social life intermediate between individuals and the bureaucratic state. One can also question the extent to which courts can truly embody the "disinterested" reason which for Brennan grounds their legitimacy. But there can be no disagreement with the lucid and consistent manner in which Brennan's opinions unfolded this vision and revealed its legal implications.

II

If Brennan's contribution to the logic of individualism ultimately lay in his ability to perfect the more inchoate perceptions of his colleagues, his contribution to the distinctively pragmatic conception of constitutional law that emerged from the Warren Court was of an entirely different magnitude. Brennan came to the Court from a career as a state judge in New Jersey, where he had acquired national prominence as an expert in judicial administration. His concern was to reform the law's actual functioning. This focus affected his entire approach to law and led him to formulate a constitutional jurisprudence based upon process rather than power. This jurisprudence has become one of the most important legacies of the Warren Court.

The jurisprudence is most clearly displayed in Brennan's interpretation of the First Amendment. When Brennan joined the Court, its members were embroiled in a vigorous but ultimately unproductive debate as to whether First Amendment freedoms were "absolutes," or whether they should be "weighed" against competing government interests in regulation.[42] Both sides of the debate viewed government interests and individual rights as locked in an indissoluble and paralyzing tension. Both sides viewed the question as one of ultimate government power. Brennan's distinctive and momentous contribution was to push the Court beyond this debate by introducing an entirely different focus on legal processes and procedures.

The origins of this perspective can be precisely attributed to Brennan's opinion in *Speiser v. Randall*,[43] which for this reason can be said to "stand among the most important constitutional cases of modern times."[44] *Speiser*, written during Brennan's second term on the Court, concerned a property tax exemption that California granted to those World War II veterans who executed a loyalty oath that they did not "advocate the overthrow of the Government of the United States or of the State of California by force or violence or other unlawful means."[45] Significantly, Brennan did not approach the case in terms of California's constitutional power to proscribe the advocacy of violent revolution; he was willing to assume that California had that power.

Instead Brennan focused his analysis on the procedures California used to distinguish between veterans who would and would not receive the tax emption. He interpreted California law as placing upon veterans the burden of demonstrating that they had not engaged in unlawful speech. Brennan concluded that this was unconstitutional because it created too great a danger that lawful speech would be adversely affected:

> The vice of the present procedure is that, where particular speech falls close to the line separating the lawful and unlawful, the possibility of mistaken fact finding—inherent in all litigation—will create the danger that the legitimate utterance will be penalized. The man who knows that he must bring forth proof and persuade another of the unlawfulness of his conduct necessarily must steer far wider of the unlawful zone than if the State must bear these burdens. This is especially to be feared when the complexity of the proof and the generality of the standards applied . . . provide but shifting sands on which the litigant must maintain his position.[46]

It is no exaggeration to observe that this paragraph marks a major innovation in American constitutional law, one which would lastingly reshape the very landscape of First Amendment jurisprudence.

By focusing attention on the way in which California law actually operated, rather than upon the abstract power that could be said to sustain it, *Speiser* required the Court to conceive law as a real, pragmatic instrument for social ordering instead of a transparently ideal set of commands or regulations. In *Speiser*, Brennan succeeded in bringing his colleagues to understand the material effects of the California regulatory scheme on speech that all conceded was legitimate and constitutionally protected. This perception of law as concretely embedded in particular procedural settings was nothing less than revolutionary.

In the years following *Speiser,* Brennan rapidly harvested the implications of his insight and in the process created the framework of First Amendment doctrine as we now know it. Brennan's focus in many of these decisions was narrowly on the procedural aspects of adjudication. In *Freedman v. Maryland,*[47] for example, he explored the consequences for prior restraint of the timing and burden of proof at judicial hearings. In *Marcus v. Search Warrants*[48] he explored these same issues in the context of the procedures for issuing search warrants.

In other ultimately more significant decisions, Brennan took the radical step of using the theory of *Speiser* to generate substantive law. Only two years after *Speiser,* for example, in *Smith v. California,* Brennan considered the constitutionality of a Los Angeles ordinance that imposed criminal penalties on booksellers for the mere possession of obscene writings. Although he invalidated the ordinance, Brennan assumed that obscene speech could be proscribed. He argued, however, that the absence of a *scienter* provision would have the effect of inhibiting the sale of "books that were not obscene," for "if the bookseller is criminally liable without knowledge of the contents, . . . he will tend to restrict the books he sells to those he has inspected; and thus the State will have imposed a restriction upon the distribution of constitutionally protected as well as obscene literature."[49]

In *NAACP v. Button* Brennan generalized the point, arguing that the logic of *Speiser* required that "precision of regulation must be the touchstone" in the regulation of speech. In a passage of immense influence, he coined the term *overbreadth* to describe an important way in which statutes could have the unacceptable consequence of inhibiting freedom of speech:

> The objectionable quality of vagueness and overbreadth does not depend upon absence of fair notice to a criminally accused or upon unchanneled delegation of legislative powers, but upon the danger of tolerating, in the area of First Amendment freedoms, the existence of a penal statute susceptible to sweeping and improper application. . . . These freedoms are delicate and vulnerable, as well as supremely precious in our society. The threat of sanctions may deter their exercise almost as potently as the actual

application of sanctions. Cf. *Smith v. California* . . . ; *Speiser v. Randall*. . . . Because First Amendment freedoms need breathing space to survive, government may regulate in the area only with narrow specifity.[50]

The logic of *Speiser* also led Brennan to develop a full-blown theory of First Amendment vagueness. Like all his colleagues, Brennan had earlier understood vagueness as a requirement of due process that set only the broadest limits on government power. Indeed, in *Roth v. United States*[51] he had argued that a "lack of precision" in the definition of obscenity was not "offensive to the requirements of due process" because "all that is required is that the language 'conveys sufficiently definite warning as to the proscribed conduct when measured by common understanding and practices.'"[52] But within a year the insights of *Speiser* would lead Brennan to a very different account of vagueness. In *Keyishian v. Board of Regents*, for example, he would argue "the defect of vagueness" was intolerable in the context of the regulation of speech, for "when one must guess what conduct or utterance may lose him his position, one necessarily will 'steer far wider of the unlawful zone . . .'*Speiser v. Randall*."[53]

The most important of *Speiser*'s progeny is, of course, *New York Times Co. v. Sullivan*. At issue in *Sullivan* was the Alabama law of libel, which permitted a public official to recover damages for defamatory statements unless the speaker could prove that the statements were true. Reasoning from the premises of *Speiser* and *Button*, Brennan had little difficulty concluding that Alabama's allocation of the burden of proof was unconstitutional, because it "dampens the vigor and limits the variety of public debate" by inducing "self-censorship."[54] In *Sullivan*, however, Brennan took the unusual step of crafting a constitutional standard that would permit unprotected speech to be regulated, while ensuring that "freedoms of expression" will "have the 'breathing space' that they 'need to survive.'"[55] He concluded that defendants could not be liable for damages for defamatory speech about public officials unless a plaintiff could prove with "convincing clarity" that the defamation had been "made with 'actual malice'—that is, with knowledge that it was false or with reckless disregard of whether it was false or not."[56]

The "actual malice" standard made no pretension of distinguishing constitutionally protected from constitutionally valueless speech. It was instead "designed solely as an instrument of policy, to attain the specific end of minimizing the chill on legitimate speech."[57] As such, the standard epitomizes the pragmatic conception of constitutional law, a conception whose articulation and development can authoritatively be traced to Brennan.[58]

That conception, of course, has its disadvantages: it severs the connection between law and cultural norms.[59] It rests on psychological assumptions about the relationship between law and behavior that are difficult to predict and to verify.[60] As a consequence, these assumptions are also subject to strategic manipulation. The attraction of the pragmatic focus introduced by Brennan was in part due to its apparent accommodation of governmental interests in regulation, for by sidestepping issues of ultimate power it appeared to invite states to reformulate their laws with more precision and accuracy. This posture of accommodation offered distinct advantages for an activist Court. In fact, however, this posture was at root illusory. Because the empirical predicates of the "chilling effect" are always vague, the exact degree of constitutionally mandated precision and clarity can never be specified, and they can therefore without explicit justification be loosened to uphold some government regulations and tightened to strike down others.

These disadvantages having been noted, however, it remains true that the pragmatic focus introduced by Brennan to the Warren Court has forever altered the face of American constitutional law. The most significant aspect of this change is the understanding of law as a process, rather than merely as an abstract command of power. The implications of this understanding extend well beyond the confines of First Amendment jurisprudence. To pick only an outstanding example, Brennan's focus on the actual process of law enabled him to fatally undermine the right-privilege distinction.

The Warren Court joined by Brennan was still using this distinction to decide cases.[61] In *Speiser*, therefore, California had argued that the tax exemption was a "privilege" bestowed at the pleasure of the state, and that it could for this reason also be withdrawn by the state for any reason.[62] But Brennan could effectively brush aside this argument because the focus of his analysis was not California's power to enact the tax exemption but rather the manner in which it had chosen to do so.

In *Sherbert v. Verner* Brennan consolidated this implication of *Speiser*.

In *Sherbert* the Court considered a South Carolina law that denied un-employment compensation benefits to a Seventh-Day Adventist who refused for religious reasons to work on Saturday. The state claimed that the benefits were not a "'right' but merely a 'privilege.'" Brennan rejected this argument and, citing *Speiser,* concluded that "conditions on public benefits cannot be sustained if they so operate, whatever their purpose, to inhibit or deter the exercise of First Amendment free-doms."[63] In this way Brennan's focus on the actual operation of the law enabled him to undercut the right-privilege distinction and to make possible such important non–First Amendment decisions as *Shapiro v. Thompson*[64] and *Goldberg v. Kelly.*[65]

Brennan's pragmatic conception of law had yet another, and perhaps even more important, consequence. It provided a natural and doctrin-ally legitimate avenue through which such values as empathy, compas-sion, and justice could influence the practice of constitutional law. By scrutinizing the actual operation of the law, Brennan could make visi-ble and give legal significance to the misery and suffering caused by the welfare regulations at issue in *Shapiro* or *Goldberg.* The pragmatic conception of law thus allowed the Warren Court to give legal recogni-tion "to the concrete human realities at stake" in a case.[66]

The human acknowledgment of these realities stands, of course, as one of the Warren Court's great achievements. If it has proved tragi-cally ephemeral, as recent decisions like *Employment Division, Oregon Department of Human Resources v. Smith*[67] suggest, it has nevertheless remained as the ghost at the constitutional banquets of the Burger and Rehnquist Courts. It has called us to our consciences.

III

Justice Brennan's retirement truly marked the end of an era. The techni-cal (as opposed to ethical) innovations of his legal pragmatism will, I think, remain as an enduring legacy. But the individualist values in whose service he employed that pragmatism are now fast dissolving. They are threatened by a resurgent communitarianism and by a rein-vigorated statism. One can discern the former in the many controver-sies over the regulation of speech to ensure civility, in the increasingly powerful attempts to ban flag burning, obscenity, pornography, racist speech, indecency in the broadcast media, artistic blasphemy, and so forth. One can discern the latter in the distrust of judicial reason and the fear of "anarchy" apparent in a decision like *Smith*.[68] In fact, submission to the bureaucratic dominion of the administrative state is likely to become the definitive feature of the contemporary Rehnquist Court.

It is traditional in writing about Brennan to stress the personal qualities of the man. He is the leprechaun, the Irish pol, the master negotiator, the charming compromiser, the twinkling, irresistible advocate. There is truth in all these characterizations, and there can be no doubt that the attraction of Brennan's personality enhanced his immense influence on the Warren Court. Emphasis on these personal characteristics, however, obscures the hard, intellectual vision that Brennan has bequeathed to us. His eminence in American law ultimately will depend not upon the inspiration of his charismatic presence, but rather upon the challenge of that vision, a challenge we cannot escape.

PART **III**

THE SECOND

GENERATION

8 *WILLIAM E. NELSON*

Justice Byron R. White

A Liberal of 1960

 $\mathbf{T}$ his chapter challenges the "conventional wisdom," chronicled by a sympathetic former law clerk, suggesting "that Justice White has been a disappointment because he did not turn out to be the 'liberal' that many expected of President John F. Kennedy's first appointee."[1] Byron R. White was indeed appointed to the Supreme Court because he was a Kennedy liberal. Contrary to the conventional wisdom, however, although the justice grew marginally more conservative during his nearly three decades on the bench, he on the whole adhered faithfully to the liberal values that led to his appointment. The considerable divergence that exists between White's voting record and the voting patterns of other liberal justices emerged almost entirely during the first decade of White's judicial tenure—his decade on the Warren Court. That divergence resulted less from changes in the views of Byron White than from a transformation in the content of liberalism in the mid to late 1960s.

This reinterpretation of Justice White's place on the Warren Court has value for two reasons. First, it corrects the received wisdom that the justice was not an adherent of a coherent jurisprudential perspective, and that "his separateness and isolation, his competitiveness and aloofness, all contribute to a studied unpredictability."[2] Second, the reinterpretation furthers our understanding of the Warren Court by helping us to see that its constitutional jurisprudence was not driven by a single, coherent objective called liberalism. On the contrary, the Warren Court's jurisprudence had several discrete objectives.

In his chapter in this volume on Justice Brennan, Robert C. Post argues that the Warren Court strove to reconstruct constitutional law on a threefold basis of individualist principles, egalitarian values, and a pragmatic conception of legal rules.[3] Post's analysis is enormously helpful in thinking not only about the career of Justice Brennan—the paradigmatic liberal in the Warren Court—but about the career of Justice White as well, and this chapter accordingly uses that analysis as its skeleton. It shows that Justice White was the same sort of pragmatist and egalitarian as Justice Brennan and that the only issue on which White and Brennan split was individualism. It shows, moreover, that the two justices had overlapping attitudes even toward individualism, with the distinction between them being that Brennan's individualism assumed an antistatist cast whereas White's did not. Any definition of liberalism which counts Justice Brennan but not Justice White as a liberal, as most contemporary definitions do, treats antistatism as the core element of liberalism. The members of the Kennedy administration who knew Justice White best in the early 1960s considered him a liberal. Thus, if he was no longer a liberal by 1970, the meaning of liberalism had changed: liberalism at the start of the 1960s, as Laura Kalman observes elsewhere in this volume, had been broad and diffuse enough to include within its ranks both those who "placed their faith in positive action by the state to protect the powerless" and those who distrusted government and accordingly "worked to protect the rights" of individuals "to be protected from the state."[4] By the decade's end, in contrast, antistatism had come to lie at liberalism's core, and a man like Byron White who continued to place his faith in the affirmative use of government power to achieve social change and justice would no longer be counted as liberal.

I

Byron White, who served as deputy attorney general from 1961 to 1962, was very much a part of the Kennedy team in the Department of Justice; in fact, he as much as anyone put the team together.[5] Thus, even in the absence of direct evidence, there is every reason to believe that White shared the Kennedy administration's liberal values.

What were those values? Surely one was a faith in the pragmatic use of law to resolve social problems and facilitate social change. Members of the administration had "an abiding faith in man as a rational being committing rational acts"[6] in order to resolve genuine social problems. As is shown by Robert Kennedy's two weeks of telephone conversations with Governor Ross Barnett of Mississippi concerning the registration of James Meredith at the university, Kennedy and his cohorts assumed that confrontational stands on the basis of theoretical principles should be avoided, that compromise was preferable to polemics, and that reasonable people could always work things out.[7] They understood that law, administered in a practical and sympathetic fashion by evenhanded officials, was essential to producing such compromises.

As an attorney in private practice during the 1950s, Byron White had seemed to his partners to be "a pragmatic problem solver,"[8] and he adhered to his pragmatism upon joining the Kennedy Justice Department. His pragmatism in the Justice Department is evidenced by a key episode in the Kennedy years—the appointment of Burke Marshall as assistant attorney general for civil rights. White, who played an active role in the appointment, "thought that the Administration ought to locate the primary leadership in the civil rights fight outside the Department of Justice. . . so that initiative, aggressive action, [and] education"—that is, efforts to articulate the theoretical foundations of equality—"should emanate from a different source than the Department." He viewed the department solely as "a law enforcement agency . . speaking for law and order," positioning itself neutrally in the midst of controversy, and thereby enjoying everyone's respect in its efforts to get the law obeyed. He feared that if the department "mix[ed] law enforcement with other things . . , the two together . . [would become] less effective."[9]

Robert Kennedy agreed. For that reason, he "didn't want to have someone in the Civil Rights Division who was dealing not from fact but was dealing from emotion . . [or] in the interest of a Negro or a group of Negroes or a group of those who were interested in civil rights."[10] White expressed the same idea when he commented that "it would be more interesting to get a first-class lawyer who would do the job in a technically proficient way that would be defensible in court—

that Southerners would not think of as a vendetta, but as an even-handed application of the law."[11] As an aide to Kennedy added, "As Bob and White looked ahead to the role the Justice Department would play in the gathering struggle over civil rights .. they felt the only proper course for the Department would be to proceed in strict accordance with the law, avoiding any appearance of pitting one social point of view against another."[12] Such an approach might not lead to a triumphant victory for any theoretical principle of equality, but it would produce practical advances toward equal civil rights.

All of this is not to claim that Robert Kennedy and Byron White did not favor the cause of civil rights; they clearly did favor it. As Robert Kennedy understood it, one of his two main duties in life was to "be kind to others that are less fortunate than we,"[13] and therefore he and White searched for someone "sensitive .. to the cause of equal rights," even though "not identified with it."[14] But while Kennedy and White believed in the moral good of equality, they did not understand that lawyers had the role of attaining that good; law, it seems, was something more practical than and ultimately at odds with morality. Thus, if the civil rights movement was to attain the moral good of equality, it would have to attain that good through the political process, not through the law.

Robert Kennedy decided early on that the best way he and the Justice Department could help the civil rights cause was to enforce the federally guaranteed right of African-Americans to vote. As he explained, he "felt strongly that this was where the most good could be accomplished. . . From the vote .. flow all other rights far, far more easily," and much "could be accomplished internally within a state if the Negroes participated in elections and voted." For this reason, the attorney general encouraged civil rights leaders to focus their equality drive on voting rights and assisted them by a sixfold increase in the number of voter registration suits which the Justice Department filed.[15]

Promoting the right of African-Americans to vote was consistent with a broader faith in the right to vote and the democratic process in general. The Kennedy team was quite sympathetic, for example, with the one person–one vote line of cases growing out of the 1961 precedent of *Baker v. Carr*.[16] The most hesitant member of the team was Solicitor General Archibald Cox, but the rest of the Department of Justice team pushed him hard to urge judicial enforcement of equal voting rights. Byron White supported this effort during his stay in the department, arguing with Cox that the government had to take an amicus posture in favor of the result to which the Court ultimately came in *Baker.*[17] White also took a stand in favor of the free functioning of the democratic process when he wrote President Kennedy a memo urging that strict limits be placed on invocations of the doctrine of executive privilege. He maintained that the "needs of Congress for the information" should be taken into account in order to make "meaningful investigation" possible and thereby counteract the "tendency" of the executive branch "to hide its errors."[18]

In short, the Department of Justice team that Byron R. White assembled on behalf of Attorney General Robert F. Kennedy fully shared two of the characteristics that Professor Post associates with Justice Brennan's liberalism—pragmatism and egalitarianism. White himself, of course, was a strong proponent at Justice of both these values. Moreover, both White and the Kennedy Justice Department were strong proponents of a third value—democratization of the electoral process and democratic decision making by the legislative branch—which Post has linked to Justice Brennan's individualism. Thus, at least at the time of his brief stint in Justice, Byron R. White was a liberal reliably cast in the Brennan mold.

When Charles E. Whittaker resigned from the Supreme Court in the spring of 1962, Byron R. White was appointed to replace him because everyone who participated in the nomination process perceived him as a liberal and as a loyal member of the liberal Kennedy team. There were two other serious candidates for the position—William H. Hastie and Paul Freund—but Chief Justice Earl Warren and Justice William O. Douglas found both of them too conservative and hence objectionable. As Warren said of Hastie, "He's not a liberal, and he'll be opposed to all the measures that we are interested in." The opposition of Warren and Douglas killed the Hastie and Freund appointments, and when Senator Richard Russell threatened to bring a delegation to the White House to seek the appointment of a conservative, President Kennedy moved quickly to appoint to the Court his liberal deputy attorney general, Byron R. White.[19]

II

Upon ascending the Supreme Court bench, Justice White continued to make judgments about the substance of the law not on grounds of abstract philosophical theory or technical legal doctrine but on the basis of "a pragmatic estimate as to how effective" his choice "would be."[20] As he wrote in his 1965 dissent in *Miranda v. Arizona,* constitutional decisions could "not rest alone on syllogism, metaphysics or some ill-defined notions of natural justice"; the Supreme Court and each of its justices had a continuing duty "to inquire into the advisability of its end product in terms of the long-range interest of the country."[21] Or, as he maintained a decade later with a quotation from the writings of Benjamin N. Cardozo, "The juristic philosophy of the common law is at bottom the philosophy of pragmatism... The rule that functions well produces a title deed to recognition."[22]

Justice White's concern with "the actual functioning of the law"[23] rather than with theory and technicality is so clear and so widely accepted that no need exists to dwell on it at length. Just a few examples will suffice. One example from the Warren Court era was his concurring opinion in *Griswold v. Connecticut,* where the justice refused to join in the opinions proclaiming a constitutional right to privacy and debating its source; instead, he decided the case on the wholly practical ground that he could not "see how the ban on the use of contraceptives by married couples in any way reinforce[d] the State's ban on illicit sexual relationships."[24] Similarly, Justice White wrote his 1965 opinion in *Swain v. Alabama*[25] not because he felt compelled by precedent but because he wanted to give a practical warning to "prosecutors that using peremptories to exclude blacks [from juries] on the assumption that no black juror could fairly judge a black defendant would violate the Equal Protection Clause"; and when he learned that *Swain* was not giving that warning, he did not feel that precedent or legal theory precluded him from joining in overruling it.[26] In a final example drawn from shortly after the Warren era, White in *Furman v. Georgia* relied upon "common sense and experience" to hold the death penalty unconstitutional, since "its imposition" had become a "pointless and needless extinction of life with only marginal contributions to any discernible social or public purpose."[27]

In short, Justice White like Justice Brennan was part of a generation trained in legal realism and sociological jurisprudence, and as such, he was far more interested in the practical ramifications than the theoretical soundness of Supreme Court opinions. White thereby fit into a long line of liberals, beginning with Louis D. Brandeis, who were willing to ignore precedent and alter doctrine in the interest of progressive social change.

III

The justice's views in racial equality cases during the Warren years were also consistent with the views of Justice Brennan and other liberals. In leading cases like *Goss v. Board of Education of Knoxville*,[28] *Griffin v. County School Board of Prince Edward County*,[29] and *Green v. County School of Board of New Kent County*,[30] Justice White joined a unanimous Court in its efforts to begin making the promise of school desegregation real, and in two important cases in which state and local governments adopted legislation making housing integration more difficult, he authored important five-to-four and eight-to-one opinions striking the legislation down.[31] When the Court began to divide during the early Burger years, White remained on the side of the prointegration forces in all the main constitutional cases—*Swann v. Charlotte-Mecklenburg Board of Education*,[32] *Palmer v. Thompson*,[33] *Milliken v. Bradley*,[34] *Arlington Heights v. Metropolitan Housing Corp.*,[35] and *University of California Regents v. Bakke*[36]—although now, sometimes, in dissent. His position, first articulated in *Palmer* and then adopted by the Court in *Washington v. Davis*[37] and the Columbus[38] and Dayton[39] school desegregation cases, was that "official denigrations" of African-Americans and "expression[s] of official policy that Negroes are unfit to associate with whites" were "at war with the Equal Protection Clause"[40] and justified full-scale remedial intervention by the courts.[41]

White also remained strongly committed on the Court to the position he had held earlier at the Justice Department in respect to equal voting rights. In *Gray v. Sanders*,[42] in *Wesberry v. Sanders*,[43] and ultimately in *Reynolds v. Sims*,[44] White joined a series of majority opinions that produced the one man–one vote rule in legislative apportionment cases. Later in the Warren years he joined a Brennan majority opinion which required states to "make a good-faith effort to achieve precise mathematical equality" in congressional districting[45] and wrote another majority opinion which extended the equal representation requirement to units of local government.[46]

The justice failed to commit himself to a broad reading of the egalitarian principle in only two major cases during the Warren years:

Swain v. Alabama,[47] where he wrote the majority opinion, and *Jones v. Alfred H. Mayer Co.*, where he joined Justice Harlan's dissent. Perhaps White's position in *Jones* rested on the pragmatic theory, stated in the dissent, that in view of the recent congressional adoption of fair-housing legislation, it was unnecessary to reinterpret the Thirteenth Amendment in ways that would cast much existing Supreme Court doctrine into doubt.[48] His position in *Swain*, however, appears simply to be an extension of his view as deputy attorney general that "the occurrence of crime" would not alone "be a sufficient reason to displace local law enforcement officials" with federal authorities; to warrant displacement, there would need to be "some solid evidence that local law enforcement people were not going to live up to their responsibilities."[49] Similarly, the statistical showing in *Swain* that African-Americans were underrepresented on juries did not alone convince White that they were subjects of purposeful discrimination, and thus he was not prepared to limit prosecutorial use of peremptory challenges against prospective black jurors. Nonetheless, he adhered to the basic antidiscrimination principle in *Swain* that use of "peremptories to exclude blacks on the assumption that no black juror could fairly judge a black defendant would violate the Equal Protection Clause," and when prosecutors failed to abide by the principle, White subsequently "agree[d] with the Court that the time ha[d] come" for the case to be overruled.[50]

Justice White's two departures from the egalitarian agenda of progressives—in a statutory construction case and in a criminal procedure case that he later joined in overruling—are trivial, however, in comparison with the vast areas of the law—school desegregation, affirmative action, voting rights, and reapportionment—where the justice consistently supported the equality principle. These two departures did not keep him, during the years when he and Chief Justice Earl Warren sat together on the Court, from being a part of the liberal majority striving to use the judiciary's power to achieve practical progressive reforms in the direction of greater equality.

IV

In his chapter on Justice Brennan, Professor Post urges that the jurisprudence of the Warren Court was propelled by a principle of individualism linked to and derived from the principle of equality. "Individualism and equality," Post writes, "are linked because the institution of democracy creates pressure to measure equality in terms of persons."[51] The doctrine of *Baker v. Carr,* he continues, by resting legislative apportionment on population rather than historic political boundaries constitutes not only an acceptance of the democratic notion that government derives its legitimacy from the equal political power of individuals but, even more, a rejection of the competing notion that power emerges from historic local communities. Post's concept of an individualism tied to democracy and equality rests ultimately on a view of the United States as a nation of "We, the People" rather than of "We, the States."

If individualism is so interpreted, then Justice White, like Justice Brennan, must be perceived as an individualist. Like Brennan but unlike justices Felix Frankfurter and John M. Harlan, White showed little sympathy for states' rights, which "is a form of cultural pluralism that valorizes the diversity of local cultures," and generally found it "incomprehensible to appeal" to states' rights "as a reason not to protect individual rights."[52] Like Brennan but unlike Frankfurter and Harlan, Justice White has been a consistently ardent nationalist.

White first expressed his nationalism in a dissenting opinion in an important 1963 preemption case, *Florida Lime & Avocado Growers, Inc. v. Paul.*[53] More significantly during the Warren Court era, he joined majority opinions authored by Justice Brennan in three cases that had a profound nationalizing impact: *New York Times Co. v. Sullivan,*[54] which nationalized the law of libel; *Fay v. Noia,*[55] which removed bars to habeas corpus proceedings in federal courts instituted by prisoners in state custody; and *Dombrowski v. Pfister,*[56] which expanded federal jurisdiction in civil rights cases. As another scholar has observed, "Justice White consistently has supported broad-ranging federal authority and vigorous institutions of national government" and "has attached great importance to national unification, and the supremacy *and* uniformity of federal law."[57]

Justice White, in short, consistently strove to undermine aberrant, localistic policies obstructing the advancement of individuals. In pursuit of this individualistic goal, he wrote and joined opinions limiting the power of local communities and enhancing the power of the nation. He also supported apportionment schemes that destroy the power of localities as such in the legislative process and instead give equal voice to every individual. He worked to make the political branches of government effective institutions for the advancement of individual well-being.

Thus, White, like Brennan, has been an individualist. But he has not been a complete individualist. There is another side to Justice Brennan's individualism—his opposition to "statism"[58]—that Justice White never shared. It is the side that arises when the interests of a particular individual come into conflict with the interests of those individuals who have effectively gained control of the instruments of government. In cases of such conflict, Justice Brennan generally created individual rights that trump government authority. Justice White, in contrast, never adopted Brennan's antiauthoritarian stance.

It is important to understand, however, that Byron White's rejection of the use of individual rights as trumps did not change since he first entered government and then came to the Court. The Kennedy Justice Department, of which Byron White was so central a part, had an unfavorable record toward individual rights in two key areas—the rights of individuals accused of crime and the rights of protesters. Byron White probably shared at least some responsibility for the department's policies during his year of service there, and, on the whole, he continued to vote consistently with those policies upon his ascension to the bench.

The Kennedy Justice Department showed little enthusiasm for expanding the constitutional rights of persons accused of crime. Indeed, Robert Kennedy himself had built his early reputation as counsel to the Senate's Select Committee on Improper Labor Activities, where he had vigorously pursued the likes of Dave Beck and Jimmy Hoffa[59] and "attack[ed] organized criminals with weapons and techniques as effective as their own." In particular, critics of Kennedy's techniques accused him of "badgering .. witnesses," of treating "the plea of self-incrimination [a]s tantamount to a confession of guilt," and of holding "hearings for the sole purpose of accusing, judging and condemning people." Even Arthur Schlesinger, Jr., Kennedy's sympathetic biographer, agreed that Kennedy "had displayed an excess of zeal" and "was a man driven by a conviction of righteousness, a fanaticism of virtue, [and] a certitude about guilt that vaulted over gaps in evidence."[60] This tough attitude toward racketeering and other crime, and a corresponding tendency to construe the law of criminal constitutional procedure narrowly, continued after Kennedy became attorney general, when he proposed that the administration support legislation to permit wiretapping when authorized by a federal judge. Byron White as deputy attorney general strongly supported Kennedy's proposal.[61]

The Kennedy administration's reluctance to take an antistatist stance on the side of people outside government power structures also emerged in its attitude toward the right of African-Americans—or, for that matter, anyone else—to protest. In retrospect, the members of the Kennedy Justice Department did not understand the function of protest or how to deal with it, and accordingly the department did a terrible job of providing federal protection for civil rights demonstrators in the South. The Justice Department took the position that state government had the duty to protect citizens—including African-American citizens—from violence, and accordingly the department routinely sought to negotiate with state and local officials to provide protection rather than use the FBI or the army for that purpose. Officials like Burke Marshall "were very concerned about the complex .. problems implied in the use of federal force," even when they "could have written an executive order permitting an occupation" of a southern state by the military. They found use of the military "as a practical matter .. impossible" and as "a policy matter .. undesirable." Nicholas Katzenbach thought it "all very well to move troops in" but then wondered "how do you get them out," while Byron White's close friend Lou Oberdorfer thought that "civilian authority ought to avoid the use of troops like the plague." Troops were "an insult to the people" and set "a precedent for some less civilized President to use in a tyrannical way."[62]

As a result, death and mayhem came to many civil rights workers, and the "unbelievable position of confidence" which the Kennedy Justice Department had had "in the minds of the oppressed" rapidly eroded. When several African-American leaders, including Jerome Smith, a CORE official who had been bludgeoned by southern police, met in 1963 with Robert Kennedy and Burke Marshall, they reported that begging for federal protection while fighting for the American dream of equal rights made them "nauseous,"[63] while Smith acknowledged he would "never"[64] serve in a war on behalf of the United States. When Kennedy reported his shock at these statements, the African-American leaders, in turn, "were shocked that he was shocked."[65] From that point on the meeting deteriorated into a "violent, emotional verbal assault" on Kennedy with the African-Americans stating that Kennedy could not "understand what this young man is saying" and

Kennedy feeling that the African-American leaders "didn't want to talk" about facts but were "all emotion, hysteria—they stood up and orated—they cursed—some of them wept and left the room."[66] In his years as attorney general, Robert Kennedy simply could not understand what this fear and distrust of government was about.

Once he was on the Supreme Court, Justice White continued to adhere to the attitudes on criminal procedure and radical protest that had been prevalent in the Justice Department during his brief stint as deputy attorney general. As a result, those who had hoped that the justice, as President Kennedy's first appointee to the Supreme Court, would regularly side with Chief Justice Earl Warren in important criminal procedure cases were quickly disillusioned. A mere two months after his appointment, he wrote his first major dissent to an opinion of a Warren majority. The case that provoked White's dissent was *Robinson v. California*, which held that the states could not make addiction a crime. In response, the new justice, wanting not to impede local police efforts to stamp out narcotics abuse, accused the majority of "writ[ing] into the Constitution its own abstract notions of how best to handle the narcotics problem."[67]

Justice White's string of dissents from some of the major criminal procedure opinions of the Warren Court continued. He dissented in *Escobedo v. Illinois*,[68] which invalidated a confession obtained at a police station from a defendant who had asked to see his lawyer, who was present in another room in the station house; in *Malloy v. Hogan*,[69] which held the Fifth Amendment binding on the states through the Fourteenth Amendment; in *Miranda v. Arizona*,[70] which prohibited all custodial interrogation in the absence of an attorney; in *Berger v. New York*,[71] which invalidated New York legislation authorizing wiretapping upon issuance of a judicial warrant; and in *United States v. Wade*,[72] which prohibited the holding of postindictment lineups in the absence of counsel.

In his dissents White expressed a concern similar to that held by Robert Kennedy and the Kennedy Justice Department about the effectiveness of law enforcement. In *Miranda*, for instance, he wrote that the majority's rule would "slow down the investigation and apprehension of confederates" and "return a killer, a rapist or other criminal to the streets . . to repeat his crime." He worried about the rule's "impact on those who rely on the public authority for protection and who without it can engage only in violent self-help."[73] Similarly in *Berger v. New*

York, where the majority struck down a statute not unlike one that White would have supported as deputy attorney general, the justice argued that "official eavesdropping and wiretapping . . are needed for the enforcement of criminal laws," especially in view of the "interrelation between organized crime and corruption of government officials" and "the enormous difficulty of eradicating both forms of social cancer."[74]

At the same time, though, Justice White did not prove to be totally conservative. Thus he joined the Court's opinion in *Gideon v. Wainwright,*[75] requiring appointment of counsel for all indigents accused of felonies, and wrote a concurring opinion in *Spinelli v. United States,*[76] a five-to-three decision requiring strict guidelines for the issuance of search warrants based on informants' tips. In 1967 he wrote two leading decisions applying the Fourth Amendment to administrative searches,[77] and in the years following Earl Warren's retirement as chief justice, White joined in two important pro–civil liberties decisions: *Bivens v. Six Unknown Named Agents,*[78] which authorized judicial implication of civil remedies for violation of the Constitution, and *Furman v. Georgia*[79] which temporarily suspended use of the death penalty. In the 1980s he even dissented on occasion from majority opinions upholding warrantless searches in criminal cases,[80] and in Justice Brennan's last term on the Court he provided the fifth vote for a five-to-four Brennan majority saving the exclusionary rule from further erosion.

What is most noteworthy, however, about Justice White's criminal procedure jurisprudence is that it has never been tied to the old Frankfurter-Harlan concern for state autonomy. Thus, Justice White was never an opponent during the Warren years of the application of the Bill of Rights to the states; indeed, he wrote *Duncan v. Louisiana,*[81] a leading incorporation opinion. When White dissented from the Warren criminal procedure cases, he did so on the merits—with reasons applicable in federal as well as state prosecutions—because he thought the majority was too severely restricting the power of all levels of government by creating individual rights.

Justice White's views on issues of constitutional criminal procedure accordingly do not follow a discernible pattern embraced by other members of the Court. His views, indeed, appear somewhat mixed, even though he on the whole leaned, especially in his early years on the Court, toward refusing to grant defendants rights as individuals that would trump the judgments of government authorities. A comparably mixed but ultimately antiindividualist pattern emerges from White's votes and opinions in a series of freedom of expression cases that came before the Court during the mid and late 1960s as a result of protests against racial discrimination and the Vietnam War.

In the first two of these cases, the justice did vote to protect the protestors' rights of expression. Thus in *Edwards v. South Carolina* he joined an opinion of the Court reversing breach of peace convictions of 187 African-American students who had marched along the grounds of the state capitol to protest against racial discrimination; the Constitution, according to the Court, did "not permit a State to make criminal the peaceful expression of unpopular views," especially when the convictions were not the product of "the evenhanded application of a precise and narrowly drawn regulatory statute."[82] Similarly in *Brown v. Louisiana,* involving the conviction of five young African-Americans for refusing to leave a segregated reading room of a public library, White found it "difficult to avoid the conclusion that petitioners were asked to leave the library because they were Negroes,"[83] and therefore he concurred in reversing the convictions. He was also willing to concur in the result of *Tinker v. Des Moines Independent Community School District,*[84] which permitted high school students to wear black armbands in protest against the Vietnam War.

But when protest began to threaten the power structure or to offend public sensibilities, White pulled back from a broad reading of the First Amendment. In *Cox v. Louisiana*[85] he wanted to affirm the conviction of a minister who had led a march on the third-floor jail in a local courthouse to protest arrests in demonstrations against segregated lunch counters. In Justice White's view the marchers had obstructed public passageways and, by marching on a courthouse, had threatened the independence and integrity of the judiciary. The next year he became part of a five-to-four majority affirming the convictions of African-American students who had demonstrated on the premises of a jail,[86] and two years after that case, he joined another majority that affirmed a conviction of an antiwar protester who had burned his draft card.[87] Arguably, demonstrations in a jail yard and public burnings of draft cards somehow threaten the ability of government agencies—the prison system and the Selective Service System—to carry out their functions, and perhaps these slim threats to the functioning of government account for Justice White's narrow reading of the First Amendment in the *Adderley* and *O'Brien* cases. A year after *O'Brien,* however,

the justice made it clear that he would permit the prosecution of protesters even when their protests did not threaten the power structure:
in his dissent in *Street v. New York*[88] and his later refusal to join the
majority in *Cohen v. California*,[89] he signaled his view that offensive protest, such as burning the flag or including four-letter expletives in political speeches, was not entitled to constitutional protection.

Justice White's views about the inappropriateness of threatening
and offensive protest probably were shared by most Americans in the
early 1960s. His views certainly were shared by his colleagues in the
Kennedy Justice Department: recall, for instance, the 1963 meeting between department officials and African-American activists at which
Robert Kennedy was shocked by the statement of a young African-
American activist that he would not fight for the nation in a war.[90] By
the late 1960s, however, many liberals had changed their views: Robert
Kennedy himself, after attending a June 1968 meeting with African-
American militants in Oakland, California, where he was abused with
statements such as "We don't want to hear none of your shit. What the
goddamned hell are you going to do, boy," told an aide that he was
"glad" he had gone to the meeting, since the militants "need to know
someone who'll listen." He knew that many African-Americans have
"got a lot of hostility and lots of reasons for it" and that "when they
get somebody like me, they're going to take it out on me." He also
knew that "after all the abuse the blacks have taken through the centuries, whites are just going to have to let them get some of those feelings
out." As one biographer has commented, Robert Kennedy had taken a
"long journey" from his first meeting with African-American militants
nearly five years earlier.[91] Justice White, having gone to the Court,
never took that journey and so had remained in a world where rational
discourse rather than emotion was the essence of political expression
in a free society.

V

The late 1960s wrought a substantial change in the goals of many
American liberals. In the early 1960s the goal of liberals—and the primary goal of the Warren Court—was the use of national power, including the judiciary's power, to facilitate pragmatic social change, especially in the areas of racial equality and legislative apportionment. For
this purpose the government was to be trusted and its power en-

hanced, not impaired. When he was appointed to the Court in 1962, Justice White agreed with this liberal agenda of nationalism, democracy, equality, and pragmatic social reform. Even today a majority of the Court probably would join Justice White to sustain efforts a democratically chosen Congress might undertake to remedy social inequality and injustice. Notably, having voted with the conservatives to strike down a local affirmative action program, White voted with the liberals to uphold a congressionally mandated one.[92] This much of the Warren Court agenda seems secure.

But the Warren Court had a second goal—the enhancement of individual rights and the consequent restriction of governmental authority. Justice White has never signed onto this antistatist program. When White came to the Court in the early 1960s, it was a subsidiary part of the Warren agenda. But as first the racial protests, then the Vietnam War and the antiwar protests, and finally the misfeasance of the Nixon years convinced many Americans that government often cannot be trusted, the goal of creating individual rights to restrict governmental power assumed increasing centrality for the liberal wing on the Court, coming to fruition in cases like *Roe v. Wade*[93] and the dissents in *Bowers v. Hardwick*.[94] Justice White disagreed. As he suggested in his *Bowers* majority opinion, the judiciary's recognition of antistatist, individual rights will not create a better world for the weak and powerless today any more than antistatist property rights jurisprudence did in the 1930s. Only the power of government can, in White's view, improve the world. While in my heart I disagree, I still must concede that Justice White may be right.

9
LAURA KALMAN

Abe Fortas

Symbol of the Warren Court?

The battle over whether Abe Fortas should succeed Earl Warren as chief justice in 1968 indicates how Fortas's judicial career helped to define the Warren Court.[1] The question is simple: Did the Senate reject Fortas because of his identification with the Warren Court and/or liberalism, or did it have other reasons?

I

Fortas did indeed share the Warren Court's liberalism. On a personal level, for Fortas, as for Warren, liberalism after World War II meant social reform at home and globalism abroad to preserve capitalism, democracy, and individual rights. Few who knew Fortas doubted the intensity of his beliefs. Asked what Fortas cared most about, Clark Clifford immediately answered: "The liberal cause. He was a deep-seated dyed-in-the-wool one-hundred-percent liberal. . . . He was a true-blue [Franklin D. Roosevelt liberal]."[2] The tension between two fundamental values at the core of liberalism, the state as agent of social reform and individual rights, was particularly acute in an area to which Fortas devoted much serious thought—symbolic speech. Liber-

als placed their faith in positive action by the state to protect the powerless, but they also worked to expand the rights of the powerless to
be protected from the state. In its blurring of the boundary between
law and politics, symbolic speech also involves an aspect of Fortas's
career which was representative of the Warren Court and especially of
Warren himself. Both Warren and Fortas, as Richard Nixon once
pointed out, were "political men," and their symbolic speech opinions
reflected that orientation.[3]

Put most charitably, Fortas's position on symbolic speech zigzagged.
When civil rights activists turned from litigation to direct action in
their drive to desegregate the South, Fortas was all for them. As a
Jew, he considered them fellow outsiders. In the 1966 case of *Brown v.
Louisiana,* he wrote the plurality opinion for the Court, which Warren
declared himself "happy to join."[4] It reversed the convictions of five
African-Americans for violating Louisiana's breach of peace statute
after they sat in at a public library to challenge its segregation policies.
Fortas privately admitted that he probably should interpret the Court's
earlier decision in *Cox v. Louisiana* to mean that the breach of peace
statute at issue in *Brown* was unconstitutional on its face. But he did
not want to do so. Anxious to protect legitimate state interests at the
same time that he promoted individual civil liberties, he believed that
considerations of social policy required him to uphold the breach of
peace statute under consideration in *Brown.* "I believe that there is a
permissible and constitutional office for this kind of breach-of-the-
peace statute—and it would be difficult to distinguish the Louisiana
statute from the statutes in a number of different states," Fortas told
his brethren.[5] At the same time, Fortas did not want breach of peace
statutes used to oppress demonstrators such as Brown. In a sentence
in his draft which he deleted from his final opinion, Fortas explained
that instead of summarily reversing because of *Cox,* "we have to consider this case *in extenso* because of the importance in light of the situation in Louisiana and perhaps elsewhere incident to the current process of racial adjustment, of unmistakable clarity providing direction
which should terminate the use of statutes of this sort for unlawful
arrests and convictions."[6]

In his published opinion in *Brown,* Fortas declared the breach of
peace statute constitutional but said that Brown and his friends had
engaged in nondisruptive conduct and that there was "no evidence"
they had violated the statute.[7] Even if the demonstrators had violated

the statute by disturbing the peace, Fortas continued, they could not be convicted because conviction would have violated their constitutional protections. To Fortas, "the barebones of the problem" was that the demonstrators had been arrested for exercising their First Amendment rights of free speech and assembly.[8]

As the number of protesters swelled to include those who demanded an end to the war in Vietnam, the issue of First Amendment guarantees arose in increasingly difficult contexts. At the time, deciding when violence or a challenge to authority justified curtailing freedom was always a tough call. It was especially difficult for Fortas. He publicly distinguished the "Gandhi type of protest" in which Martin Luther King engaged "from the adolescent antics of kids who break into the Pentagon."[9] And in a sense he was right to do so, for there were real differences between civil rights protesters and antiwar demonstrators. King and his colleagues expected arrest and viewed it as part of their witnessing. Many of the protesters against the war, however, considered arrest unjustified and were engaging not in civil disobedience but in criticism of the state. Fortas was not moved by this conceptual distinction alone. Personal convictions also explained why he proved so much less tolerant of those who opposed the war than those who challenged racial prejudice. "For all his liberalism on other issues," one of Fortas's clerks recalled, whenever "anything that could be viewed as criticism of the Vietnam war of Johnson in particular or even the Executive [Branch] in general [arose] . . . , Fortas was probably the most conservative judge on the Court."[10]

By the summer of 1967, Fortas was counseling Johnson on how to manage the antiwar demonstrators who poured into Washington. Fortas advised Johnson to find a basis for closing off the sidewalks adjacent to the White House.[11] Though he could have foreseen that the Court would consider the constitutionality of ordinances regulating demonstrations against the war, he still advised the White House how to draft one. Fortas may have reasoned that no advice he gave as presidential counselor bound him to any decision as a justice. But like his private advice to Johnson, his public actions also revealed a retreat from the sensitivity to symbolic speech and dissident minorities he had displayed in *Brown*.

In *United States v. O'Brien*, for example, Fortas joined Warren's majority opinion upholding a 1965 law prohibiting the destruction of draft cards which Congressman L. Mendel Rivers had introduced as "answer" to those who protested the war by burning their draft cards.[12] Warren displayed little patience for David O'Brien's claim that in burning his draft card, he had engaged in symbolic speech. "We cannot accept the view that an apparently limitless variety of conduct can be labeled 'speech' whenever the person engaging in the conduct intends thereby to express an idea," the chief justice noted. Even assuming O'Brien had engaged in symbolic speech when he burned his draft card, Warren continued, the law prohibiting the destruction of draft cards furthered a substantial governmental interest in assuring the availability of draft cards, and the restriction on First Amendment freedoms was no greater than was essential to the furtherance of that interest.[13]

By the time Warren announced the Court's decision in *O'Brien* in May 1968, demonstrators had closed down Columbia University. Fortas was completing a pamphlet entitled *Concerning Dissent and Civil Disobedience*, which placed most student protest out of the limits of permissible dissent.[14] Supreme Court justices generally do not engage in such overtly political acts. As Fred Graham noted at the time: "Fortas's strong condemnation of some of the current student tactics has been noteworthy, not only because justices rarely speak out on events that could eventually reach the high court, but also because he has impeccable liberal credentials as one of the court's most consistent civil libertarians."[15]

Fortas maintained in his pamphlet that civil disobedience was morally, politically, and legally unacceptable when it involved violation of constitutional, valid laws merely to dramatize dissent. To illustrate his point, he compared the library sit-ins at issue in *Brown* with the draft-card burning involved in cases such as *O'Brien*. In doing so, he reinterpreted his opinion in *Brown* in such a way as to indicate his diminishing tolerance for dissent. "In the library sit-in case the protesters violated a segregation ordinance," Fortas now claimed in his pamphlet. "The ordinance was unconstitutional and its violation could not be constitutionally punished." According to Fortas, draft-card burning might prove another matter entirely. "If the law forbidding the burning of a draft card is held to be constitutional and valid, the fact that the card is burned as a result of noble and constitutionally protected motives is no help to the defender," he explained.[16] While Fortas was now saying that the demonstrators in *Brown* had been protesting an unconstitutional segregation ordinance, in fact a breach of peace statute had been at issue in *Brown*. Fortas had gone out of his way to declare that statute constitutional before saying that the demonstrators had not violated it. He had also expressly said that even if the protesters in *Brown* actually had violated this constitutional statute, their conduct still would have represented a valid exercise of First Amendment rights.[17]

That Fortas was wavering in his commitment to symbolic speech became clearer in 1969 when the Court considered the legitimacy of flag burning in *Street v. New York*.[18] Street was a World War II veteran who burned the flag he usually displayed on national holidays when he heard that racists had ambushed civil rights worker James Meredith on his march from Memphis to Jackson. Though the case involved a civil rights protest, by the late 1960s flag burning closely resembled draft-card burning in its frequent use to protest the war in Viet Nam, and Fortas surely viewed the case in the context of protest against the war rather than protest against racism. Here Fortas vacillated. In the beginning he intended to concur in John Harlan's majority opinion reversing Street's conviction.[19] Though Harlan's opinion carefully evaded the issue of whether flag burning constituted symbolic speech, Fortas still could not bring himself to side with the majority.[20] In the end he decided to dissent, as did Warren, Black, and White. Though Fortas expressly indicated his agreement with Warren's dissent,[21] he filed a separate dissent setting forth the reasons that state and federal governments could prevent flag desecration. In words which Chief Justice Rehnquist would quote twenty years later in his dissent in *Texas v. Johnson*,[22] Fortas contended that a flag was "a special kind of personalty" and that though Street might have owned his flag, ownership was subject to "special burdens and responsibilities."[23] Read alongside his reinterpretation of his opinion in *Brown* and his reflections on draft-card burning in *Concerning Dissent and Civil Disobedience*, Fortas's dissent in *Street* suggested he was losing his enthusiasm for symbolic speech.

Yet around the same time that Fortas was writing his dissent in *Street*, he delivered his majority opinion in *Tinker v. Des Moines School District*, which Warren and four other members of the Court joined.[24] Here Fortas displayed the strong support of symbolic speech he had shown in *Brown* three years earlier, arguing that students who wore black armbands to show their opposition to the war were engaging in symbolic speech and could not be suspended from school. What was going on?

One clue is in Fortas's repeated classification of the Tinkers' conduct as nondisruptive in his opinion.[25] His personal correspondence provided another clue. Soon after the Court announced its decision in *Tinker,* Fortas received a letter from his old friend Jaime Benitez. As president of the University of Puerto Rico, Benitez criticized Fortas's position in *Tinker* on the grounds that the behavior the Court tolerated there would interfere with university life. The letter irked Fortas, who greatly respected Benitez. "This amazes me, coming from you; because I am sure you know that this Court . . . [has] drawn a stern and sharp line between speech and disruptive conduct—whether or not the latter is accompanied by speech," Fortas replied. That was the point, Fortas said, of both *Concerning Dissent and Civil Disobedience* and his opinion in *Tinker.* "The question is not just of primarily the rule of law," Fortas lectured Benitez. "The question is one of policy strategy and tactics for the governing authorities." Fortas had tried publicly to indicate "the deep sympathy that I feel for school administrators confronted with this problem; and my profound belief that what is effective and rational for them to do in one situation may be extremely disrupting in another. To put it specifically what may be an appropriate response in a situation confronting American University here in Washington . . . may be entirely inappropriate or inadequate in Puerto Rico."[26]

As his letter suggested, Fortas had come to his reading of the relationship between the First Amendment and symbolic speech not because of the "rule of law" but because of his political intention to fashion a test which would protect both the right to dissent and the authority of the state in the context of the troubled late 1960s. Fortas explained to another friend that he had written *Concerning Dissent and Civil Disobedience* after he had spent two years visiting the nation's college campuses and had determined that "faculties in the besieged schools are very largely demoralized and at their wits' end. My object was really to try to provide the balanced members of the faculties (not all of them are in this category by a long shot) with a constructive and reasoned theoretical basis upon which they could communicate with their students."[27] That also seemed to be his aim in *Tinker.*

While his intentions were good, Fortas's solution was arcane. In the context of the late sixties, Fortas's emphasis on and definition of non-disruptive conduct seemed as anachronistic as the unenforced antievolution statute he insisted on invalidating in *Epperson v. Arkansas*.[28] If the protest was not particularly dramatic, like wearing a black armband, he would permit it, but if it was dramatic enough to drive a point home, like burning a draft card, Fortas would not tolerate it. Writing in the 1968 *Harvard Law Review*, Louis Henkin, hardly a radical, maintained that in burning his draft card, O'Brien had made a speech and that he "deserved a better opinion." The opinions of Fortas and his colleagues increasingly resembled exercises in linedrawing as they struggled to extend protection to one form of symbolic speech that they personally did not consider threatening and could label "nondisruptive" and to remove it from another which they did find threatening and therefore "disruptive." While virtually all judicial opinions are exercises in linedrawing, Henkin reminded his readers that the lines must be "rational." If they were not, he warned, "the law and legal process become less rational and lose the confidence of those they serve."[29]

Fortas's position on symbolic speech, which was similar to Warren's, helped to erode confidence in the Court. Few on the right seemed to realize Fortas agreed that in many situations, state interests might outweigh First Amendment rights. One person displeased with *Tinker* informed Fortas that he was a "decadent, unethical, immoral, debased and odious practitioner of the Far Left" who "represented the permissive wing of permissive Jewry."[30] Students would soon be wearing signs proclaiming "join Abe Fortas and the S.D.S.," another predicted.[31] An envelope addressed to "Marxist Justice Fortas, Judicial Star Chamber, . . . Division for Marxist Sociology" suggested where most of Fortas's critics thought he belonged.[32]

The left wanted no part of Fortas either. "For students who have experienced the Free Speech Movement at Berkeley, the march on the Pentagon, the Democratic National Convention in Chicago, the rebellion at Columbia and the confrontation over People's Park in Berkeley—to say nothing of the countless number of demonstrations, protest and draft resistance movements that have struck almost every campus in the country—the refusal of the law to accord the same degree of constitutional protection to symbolic conduct that it has conferred upon conventional speech is an insistence that lawful speech be lifeless speech," Paul Savoy observed in a contemporary article on the "new politics of legal education."[33] And as Fortas recognized, the left hardly welcomed his pamphlet setting out his views on dissent and civil disobedience. "Feeling on many campuses in this country is so strong that most of the letters that I have received from students and faculty . . . about my pamphlet . . . [are] critical of my position because it insists that disruption of classes . . . is lawlessness and is not protected by the purpose that the students may have—however noble they may consider that [purpose] to be," Fortas observed.[34] Howard Zinn's *Disobedience and Democracy*, for example, attacked Fortas's pamphlet, pointing to "nine fallacies on law and order" it expressed. "For the crisis of our time, the slow workings of American reform [and] the limitations on protest and disobedience set by liberals like Justice Fortas are simply not adequate," Zinn maintained.[35]

In their own way, Fortas's ideas about symbolic speech proved a metaphor of the problems many "liberals" faced as the war in Vietnam, the rise of the new left, and demands for black power unraveled their ideology and political base.[36] Like the Great Society, "the Warren Court can be seen . . . as the culmination and perhaps the end, of . . . twentieth-century liberal sensibility."[37] Given its centrist style and its embrace of two contradictory values—affirmative action by government to protect the powerless and the rights of minorities against the state—perhaps liberalism was bound to become unpopular in the 1960s. Reviled by the right for providing too much affirmative government, liberals were condemned by the left for not doing enough to protect dissident minorities. Much of the power of modern American liberalism during Lyndon Johnson's first years in office had derived from the hope that the reforms its proponents had been promising since the New Deal would stem radicalism, but the changes Fortas, Warren, and others had brought about seemed only to spark radicalism. Perhaps liberals had forfeited their leadership by suggesting insufficient reforms. Alternatively, perhaps their reforms had been so successful that they had stimulated the new left with visions of what might be possible at the same time that they mobilized a new right by threatening the traditional vision of the good society. For whatever the reason, the revolution was occurring by 1968-69, and it was directed against Fortas, Warren, Lyndon Johnson, and other centrist reformers as their attempts to walk a careful middle line between the state and the individual increasingly satisfied no one.

II

By the summer of 1968, when Johnson nominated Fortas to succeed Warren as chief justice, it was clear that liberals on the Supreme Court and in the White House were on the defensive. Johnson's hold on the presidency had become so tenuous that he had decided against seeking reelection. African-Americans no longer protested inequality through peaceful sit-ins at libraries; the ghettos were in flames. Students all over the country were defying Earl Warren by burning their draft cards while the right dreamed of his impeachment.

If Fortas helps to define the Warren Court in the sense of espousing a liberalism similar to Warren's, should the Senate rejection of his nomination to be chief justice be viewed as a rejection of the Warren Court's liberalism? Though the left stayed out of the nomination battle, Fortas became a vehicle for the right's attack on the Court's civil rights and civil liberties decisions. When Johnson nominated Fortas as chief justice, both Fortas's opponents and supporters treated him as an exemplar of the Warren Court. Senate Judiciary Committee chair James Eastland reported that he "had never seen so much feeling against a man as against Fortas."[38] For Louisiana's Russell Long, Fortas was "'one of the dirty five' who sides with the criminal." Judiciary Committee member Sam Ervin told the White House that "considering what the Supreme Court has done to the Constitution, I'll have to read Fortas's decisions before I can decide [on him]."[39] And a note from Thurgood Marshall typified the support Fortas received from Warren Court liberals:

> You are still "my man!"
> You are still "my leader!"
> I still love you!
> OH what I could say about the opposition![40]

At the time Fortas privately blamed most of his problems on his relationship to the Warren Court. "Primarily the bitter response mirrors the opposition to what has happened with respect to the racial question and the general revolution of human dignity [as] reflected by our decisions," he wrote William O. Douglas during the confirmation hearings. "Every decent constitutional decision in the last three years, and for some years prior thereto, has been denounced."[41]

Surely the ideological reaction against the Warren Court was an important factor in explaining the hostility to Fortas. One thinks of Strom Thurmond taking Fortas to task for Warren Court opinions such as *Mallory v. United States.* "Mallory—I want that name to ring in your ears," Thurmond shouted at Fortas. "Mallory! Mallory, a man who raped a woman, admitted his guilt, and the Supreme Court turned him loose on a technicality. Is not that the type of decision calculated to encourage people to commit more rapes and serious crimes?"[42] While *Mallory* was a 1957 decision handed down eight years before Fortas joined the Court, many joined Thurmond in blaming Fortas for such decisions. Animosity toward the Warren Court gave his enemies the impetus to make an issue out of Fortas's nomination.

Still, had Johnson appointed another individual as closely identified jurisprudentially in the public mind with the Warren Court majority as Fortas—Brennan or Goldberg, for example—that person almost certainly would have been confirmed. Even Senator Robert Griffin, one of Fortas's most vociferous opponents, declared himself ready to accept Arthur Goldberg as chief justice, and Goldberg viewed Fortas as a kindred jurisprudential spirit.[43] To be sure, there had been rumblings of dissatisfaction with the Warren Court in Thurgood Marshall's 1967 confirmation hearings. Senator John McClellan, for example, had asked Marshall whether there were times when "an individual, in his role as an integral member of society, must . . . sacrifice a portion of his individual rights for the collective security and safety of all?"[44] But Marshall had been confirmed with relatively little difficulty and by a vote of sixty-nine to eleven, though he might have been expected to become a member of the Warren Court majority. Despite all of the furor over the Warren Court during Fortas's confirmation hearings, obviously other factors were involved.

Clearly one of those additional factors was Fortas's closeness to Lyndon Johnson. It was well known that Fortas had a private line to the While House in his chambers. "Everyone talked about it around town," one of his colleagues said. It made some of the other justices "uncomfortable."[45] Another colleague believed Fortas was "distracted" as a justice.[46] Others at the Court recalled that Fortas acted as if he could fulfill his judicial duties "with the back of his hand." He seemed to think he could "take twenty minutes . . . between appointments at the White House . . . [and] write a few paragraphs that . . . [would] put . . . reapportionment . . . in context," one clerk remembered. That clerk knew he could take naps in Fortas's chambers because Fortas spent so little time there.[47] Perhaps understandably, Fortas was more engaged by acting as a channel between Johnson and the Israelis during the Six-Day War and by coping with the Detroit riots than he was by some of the issues that come before the Court. Given the fact that he had to sandwich his Court duties between summonses to the White House, Fortas's judicial performance was truly impressive. But Congress did not see it that way. Justices had long counseled presidents, but it was Fortas's misfortune to have his advisory role exposed at a time when there was increasing anxiety over the growth of presidential power. To senators, that fear made it more important than ever to maintain the sanctity of separation of powers, a point they raised repeatedly in railing against the Fortas nomination.[48]

While separation of powers implies a concern with the structure of American government, that was not really what was at stake. It was not the idea of justices counseling presidents that bothered members of Congress so much—though they certainly pretended it did—as the idea of a justice counseling this particular president. Fortas's relationship with Johnson meant that Congress associated him with the liberalism of both the Warren Court and Lyndon Johnson. Though Earl Warren supported the war in Vietnam and the Court declined to rule on its constitutionality, virtually no one attributed the war in Vietnam to the Warren Court. Opponents held Johnson responsible for the Warren Court, but they did not blame the Warren Court for Johnson. Like Johnson, Fortas had to answer for the executive and judicial branches, for the consequence of domestic reform and globalism. The freight of political liberalism and Warren Court liberalism, which was the jurisprudential analogue of political liberalism, may have been just too heavy for any one individual to bear in 1968.

Still, the old Lyndon Johnson might have been able to pull it off for Fortas. An alternative explanation for the nomination's defeat is that Johnson badly mishandled it. When Earl Warren told the President in June 1968 that he intended to resign as chief justice, Johnson followed his usual practice when he was confronted with a difficult decision. He called in Clark Clifford and Abe Fortas and asked them what he should do. As Johnson requested, Clifford came early. At that point Johnson informed Clifford that he wanted to make Fortas chief justice and to name Homer Thornberry—a federal judge, former member of Congress, and old friend from Texas—to replace Fortas.

Clifford was alarmed. The President had become a lame duck when he made his March 31 announcement that he would not seek reelection, but Clifford had noted that Johnson was "really not conscious of how much his power had diminished." Now Clifford tried to tell him. He warned Johnson that Thornberry would be viewed as a crony of the president's and would detract from Fortas. Oddly, Clifford did not worry that Fortas would be viewed as a Johnson intimate. He considered Fortas's qualifications for the chief justiceship outstanding. Clifford begged Johnson to couple Fortas's nomination as chief justice with that of a respected, nonpartisan Republican such as Albert Jenner, the Chicago lawyer who headed the American Bar Association's standing committee on the federal judiciary. If the Senate knew it would get a good, solid moderate Republican along with Fortas, he argued, it would buy the package.[49]

Johnson, however, remained fixated on Thornberry. He was certain that Thornberry's nomination would strengthen Fortas's chances of Senate confirmation. He knew that Senator Richard Russell of Georgia would applaud Thornberry, and he believed that Russell would support Fortas to get Thornberry. The president thought that enough of Russell's southern colleagues would follow his lead to preclude a Senate filibuster directed at Fortas. Thus Johnson reasoned that although they might consider Fortas too liberal, southern senators would approve him to clear a place for their old friend and colleague in Congress, Homer Thornberry. When Fortas arrived at the White House, he sided with Johnson against Clifford.[50]

Now Johnson, having decided on Fortas and Thornberry, swung into action and courted Senator Russell and Senate minority leader Everett Dirksen.[51] Accustomed to the mores of the Senate in his day, the president assumed that the support of both men guaranteed victory. But the Senate of 1968 was a different place from the Senate of Lyndon Johnson's day, when junior senators unquestioningly followed senior senators. Neither Russell nor Dirksen had as much power as Johnson assumed, and in the end both jumped ship. Dirksen could not even convince his son-in-law Howard Baker of Tennessee to vote for Fortas, a fellow Tennessean.[52]

By the time Dirksen deserted Fortas, the public had learned that Fortas had accepted $15,000 in lecture fees for teaching a course at American University, and some blamed Fortas's defeat in large part on that revelation.[53] The money had been raised by Fortas's former partner, Paul Porter, from five heads of corporations, three of whom had been Fortas's clients.[54] Porter knew that Fortas felt strapped. At $39,000, a Supreme Court justice's salary was a fraction of the $173,274 Fortas had earned practicing law the year before he joined the Court.[55] But Porter also knew that Fortas was restless on the Court and would be intrigued by the idea of teaching a course on law and social policy.[56] And since Supreme Court justices were commonly paid lecture fees and sometimes taught, Porter saw nothing wrong with arranging the course. Although he wrote several of the donors that he had told Fortas they contributed,[57] that was just blarney. In fact, Porter refused to tell Fortas who had contributed, apparently because he did not want to compromise Fortas.[58] Yet although no one could show that Fortas had known who the donors were, the arrangement seemed suspicious when it was revealed near the end of the confirmation hearings. Over and over again, hostile senators pointed out that Fortas's former partner had raised the money by going to Fortas's former clients.[59] And Fortas had made an error in judgment. Though he did not know who the donors were, he should have realized that Porter would raise the money from clients. Even Fortas's most ardent supporters agreed that Fortas and Porter should have been more alert to the appearance of impropriety. One friend thought Porter had unwittingly "put a knife in Abe's back."[60]

Still, by the time the lecture fees became public knowledge, the nomination was doomed. Dirksen, for example, knew by that time that he had to desert Fortas to retain some remnants of his power. The lecture fees were nails in the coffin, not knives in the back. Fortas's acceptance of lecture fees had almost nothing to do with the defeat of his nomination.

III

In the end there are two explanations, both equally plausible, for Fortas's failure to be confirmed. His defeat can be attributed to his dual identification with the Warren Court and Lyndon Johnson. In that event, his failure to be confirmed represented a repudiation of American liberalism, though not necessarily of the Warren Court. And it is just as conceivable that Fortas was rejected because the president had been too clever by half. "Johnson just outsmarted himself," Nicholas Katzenbach recalled. "He thought that Homer Thornberry was so much liked by the Congress ... that in order to put him on the Supreme Court, they would let Fortas be Chief Justice, and he ... miscalculated."[61] Even the president's staff thought that the appointment of Johnson's two dear friends, Fortas and Thornberry, resembled "old crony week."[62] Fortas might well have become chief justice had the president followed Clifford's advice and nominated an unquestionably qualified Republican as associate justice.[63] His attempt to appoint both Fortas and Thornberry and his reliance on Dirksen and Russell as the keys to his strategy suggested that Johnson had lost his touch by the summer of 1968.

The tragedy of this is that Fortas, who shared Warren's values, would have made an outstanding chief justice. Having been managing partner of Arnold, Fortas & Porter and having built it into a great law firm, he was eminently qualified to manage the Court. Scholars have focused on two kinds of leadership that chief justices can provide. "Task leadership serves to complete the court's work in the most efficient manner, while process leadership provides a friendly environment to facilitate the conduct of judicial business. According to this model, Chief Justices are successful to the extent they are able to combine both functions or recruit allies capable of playing the role they themselves reject."[64] In terms of task leadership, Fortas might have become the best chief justice in the Court's history. He was an extraordinarily efficient lawyer. But he lacked Earl Warren's presence and reputation for collegiality, and process leadership might have proven more difficult for Fortas. In that event, if his past was a reliable guide, Fortas would have counted on someone such as William Brennan to provide the process leadership that he had encouraged his gregarious partners, Thurman Arnold and Paul Porter, to provide at his law firm. And had Fortas become chief justice, the Warren Court era might have lasted longer then it did.

There is something sad about the possibility that a simple misstep altered the course of history. There is something equally sad, but somehow appropriate, about Fortas and Warren leaving the Court at the same time. The two men, who never stopped believing in the Great Society and the Warren Court, can remind us how powerful the appeal of their liberalism was, however flawed their position on symbolic speech suggests liberalism may sometimes have been.

NOTES

BIBLIOGRAPHY

INDEX

Chapter 1

1. The papers of Earl Warren and William Douglas, covering the entire span of Warren's tenure, are available at the Library of Congress. William Brennan's papers are available there with restrictions. John Marshall Harlan's papers are available at Princeton University. In addition, intensified journalistic attention to the Supreme Court, which is related to developments I discuss below, has produced a substantial body of apparently accurate anecdotal information on the internal and external politics of the Supreme Court. For samplings, see O'Brien, *Storm Center;* Woodward and Armstrong, *The Brethren.*

2. For a brief comment on the present-mindedness in recent comprehensive histories of the Supreme Court, see Tushnet, "Book Review."

3. This section of the essay is the most speculative, and I am sure that ultimately its argument will have to be elaborated and qualified substantially. I believe, though, that it will be useful to set out the argument to provoke discussion.

4. 347 U.S. 483 (1954).

5. For a discussion of the Court's deliberations in *Brown* supporting this statement, see Tushnet, "What Really Happened."

6. "Introduction," in Robinson and Sullivan, *New Directions,* p. 2.

7. 358 U.S. 1 (1958).

8. 350 U.S. 985 (1956).

9. A memorandum from Justice Frankfurter to his colleagues made these points explicitly. The memorandum is reprinted in Hutchinson, "Unanimity and Desegration," pp. 95–96.

10. Dennis v. United States, 341 U.S. 494 (1951).

11. Yates v. United States, 354 U.S. 298 (1957).

12. See, e.g., Watkins v. United States, 354 U.S. 178 (1957); Sweezy v. New Hampshire, 354 U.S. 234 (1957).

13. Jencks v. United States, 353 U.S. 657 (1957).

14. For an analysis of the decisions, Congress's reaction, and the Court's response, see Murphy, *Congress and the Court.*

15. Barenblatt v. United States, 360 U.S. 109 (1959); Uphaus v. Wyman, 360 U.S. 72 (1959); Scales v. United States, 367 U.S. 203 (1961).

16. For a muted statement of skepticism, see Kalven, *Worthy Tradition,* pp. 224–25; for a stronger one, see Murphy, *Congress and the Court,* p. 229.

17. Communist Party v. Subversive Activities Control Board, 367 U.S. 1 (1961).

18. For a statistical study showing sharpening divisions during the 1960 term and a substantial change in the liberal direction during the 1961 term (attributable to Whittaker's retirement and Frankfurter's stroke before the term ended), see Segal and Spaeth, "Decisional Trends."

19. NAACP v. Button, 371 U.S. 415 (1963); Gibson v. Florida Legislative Investigation Committee, 372 U.S. 539 (1963). For detailed discussions of the cases, see Tushnet, *Making Civil Rights Law*; Schwartz, *Super Chief,* pp. 450–53.

20. Schwartz, *Super Chief,* pp. 450–52; 372 U.S. at 578–83.

21. For a discussion of the Court's deliberations in the sit-in cases, see Schwartz, *Super Chief,* pp. 479–86, 508–25.

22. Lombard v. Louisiana, 373 U.S. 267 (1963).

23. Bouie v. City of Columbia, 378 U.S. 347 (1964).

24. Schwartz, *Super Chief,* p. 512.

25. Shapiro, "Fathers and Sons."

26. Mikva, "Role of Theorists," p. 455.

27. United States v. Carolene Products, 304 U.S. 144, 152 n. 4 (1938).

28. For a forceful elaboration of political malfunction as the guiding theory of the late Warren Court, see Ely, *Democracy and Distrust.*

29. Brown v. Mississippi, 297 U.S. 278 (1936); Chambers v. Florida, 309 U.S. 227 (1940); Powell v. Alabama, 287 U.S. 45 (1932).

30. Griswold v. Connecticut, 381 U.S. 479 (1965). It might be argued that the persistence of the statute on the books reflected the undue influence Roman Catholics had on Connecticut's political process, but converting that into an argument that the political process was flawed is almost certainly impossible.

31. For an argument that political process approaches were sufficient to justify the Court's actions, see Klarman, "Puzzling Resistance."

32. The lines of the argument were laid out in Adamson v. California, 332 U.S. 46 (1947).

33. Reed v. Reed, 404 U.S. 71 (1971); Roe v. Wade, 410 U.S. 113 (1973).

34. Edsall and Edsall, *Chain Reaction,* pp. 107–13, connects the "rights revolution" associated with the Warren Court and the conservative ascendance in national politics.

35. United States v. O'Brien, 391 U.S. 367 (1968).

36. Street v. New York, 394 U.S. 576 (1969).

37. For essays surveying the possible definitions, see Halpern and Lamb, *Supreme Court Activism and Restraint.*

38. 384 U.S. 436 (1966).

39. For an account along these lines, linking these descriptions of *Miranda* to the Warren Court's action in *Brown,* see Seidman, "*Brown* and *Miranda.*"

40. 367 U.S. 643 (1961).

41. For a good statement of this tension, see Tigar, "Disquiet in the Citadel."

42. 392 U.S. 1 (1968).

43. 392 U.S. 514 (1968).

44. Schwartz, *Super Chief*, pp. 693–94.

45. 380 U.S. 202 (1965).

46. Tushnet, "What Really Happened."

47. 349 U.S. 294 (1955).

48. For a discussion of the role of law clerks in the modern era, see O'Brien, *Storm Center*, pp. 122–35.

49. See White, *Earl Warren*, p. 229, describing Warren's use of bench memos and stating that Warren "regarded conferences as an opportunity to see where others stood."

50. As the Court has become more ideologically coherent, these processes may change. Or the justices may continue to communicate in the modern bureaucratic way, via memoranda, rather than in the old-fashioned way, via personal contacts. I thank Vicki Jackson for this suggestion.

51. See "Reliving the Watergate Years with Some New Tapes," *Newsweek*, June 17, 1991, p. 32.

52. Technically Souter was a federal judge when he was appointed to the Supreme Court, but he had not heard any cases as a federal judge.

53. I thank Bill Eskridge for this final point.

54. The citations for these articles are *University of Chicago Law Review* 47 (1979): 57–80; "Vermont Yankee, the APA, the D.C. Circuit, and the Supreme Court," *Supreme Court Review* 1978 (1978): 345–409; *UCLA Law Review* 20 (1973): 899–982; *Duke Law Journal* 1971 (1971): 319–66. He had also published a number of extremely short comments, mostly in his capacity as head of the Administrative Conference or as chair of a bar association on administrative law.

55. For discussions of how little the Court departed from Warren Court approaches after 1969, see the essays collected in Blasi, *Burger Court;* Dorsen, "Trends and Prospects."

56. I am indebted to Mike Seidman for this point, and for many others in this chapter.

57. 411 U.S. 1 (1973).

58. Maher v. Roe, 432 U.S. 464 (1977); Harris v. McRae, 448 U.S. 297 (1980).

59. Hutchinson, "Book Review."

60. Schwartz, *Super Chief*, pp. 295–97.

61. Tushnet, "Optimist's Tale."

Chapter 2

1. When Robert Jackson was appointed an associate justice by Franklin Roosevelt in 1941, he and others anticipated that he would be a justice of great influence among his New Deal colleagues (he had been both attorney general and solicitor general under Roosevelt) and a strong candidate for the next chief justiceship. Jack-

son, however, was not temperamentally suited for close collegial decision making and consequently alienated some of his colleagues, notably Hugo Black and William O. Douglas, who reportedly threatened to resign from the Court in 1946 should then President Truman select Jackson to replace Chief Justice Harlan Stone. For more detail on Jackson's career, see White, *American Judicial Tradition.*

2. 323 U.S. 214 (1944).

3. 390 U.S. 39 (1968).

4. For details, see Howard, *Mr. Justice Murphy.*

5. Kurland, "Earl Warren."

6. White, "Earl Warren as Jurist."

7. 347 U.S. 483 (1954).

8. 377 U.S. 533 (1964).

9. 384 U.S. 436 (1966).

10. See Kluger, *Simple Justice;* Schwartz, *Super Chief.*

11. 369 U.S. 186 (1962).

12. See Heck, "Justice Brennan."

13. See, e.g., Hutchinson, "Hail to the Chief"; Tushnet, "Revisionist History."

14. Brennan's role on the Burger and Rehnquist Courts was increasingly that of preserving extant Warren Court majority decisions in the face of attack or of deploring, in dissent, the abandonment of assumptions on which such decisions were based. In this role his philosophical convictions came more clearly to the surface, and the depth as well as the facility of his constitutional interpretations became more apparent.

15. 347 U.S. 497 (1954).

16. See White, *Marshall Court,* pp. 504–24.

17. The episode is described in White, *Earl Warren,* pp. 15–16.

18. Posner, "Decline of Law."

19. See White, *Marshall Court,* p. 167.

Chapter 3

1. Interview with Jerome Cohen, July 2, 1974; Kaufman, "The Justice and His Law Clerks."

2. Quoted in Freund, "Felix Frankfurter"; Brown, "The Uniform of Justice."

3. Interview with Al Sacks, July 15, 1974.

4. Rodell, "Felix Frankfurter—Conservative."

5. Interview with Al Sacks, July 15, 1974.

6. Interview with Jerome Cohen, July 2, 1974.

7. Quoted in Schwartz, *Super Chief,* pp. 261, 35, 257. When a new Frankfurter law clerk asked his predecessor why Earl Warren had begun to vote more often with Hugo Black in the late 1950s he was told: "Because Felix irritates, while Hugo soothes" (interview with Jerome Cohen, July 2, 1974).

8. Kanin, "Trips to Felix," pp. 34–35; Lash, *Diaries of Felix Frankfurter*, p. 30.

9. Josephson, "Jurist—III"; Kanin, "Trips to Felix," p. 41; Brown, "Frankfurter: The Past Is Prologue"; Schwartz, *Super Chief*, p. 241.

10. Rodell, "Felix Frankfurter—Conservative," p. 459; Allen and Shannon, *Truman Merry-Go-Round*, p. 373; Bickel, "Justice Frankfurter at Seventy-Five."

11. Mapp v. Ohio, 367 U.S. 643 (1961).

12. Baker v. Carr, 369 U.S. 186 (1962).

13. A major exception during the Warren era was in the area of searches and seizures. In Chimel v. California, 395 U.S. 752 (1969), the Court accepted Frankfurter's dissenting views in United States v. Rabinowitz, 339 U.S. 56 (1950), and Harris v. United States, 331 U.S. 145 (1947), to narrow the limits of permissible searches conducted without a warrant incident to a lawful arrest.

14. 369 U.S. 832 (1962), ordering reargument; 372 U.S. 144 (1963).

15. 369 U.S. 367 (1962), ordering reargument on merits; 372 U.S. 144 (1963).

16. Russell v. United States, 369 U.S. 749 (1962).

17. Gibson v. Florida Legislative Investigation Committee, 372 U.S. 539 (1963).

18. Before his stroke Frankfurter had voted in another case, Wood v. Georgia, 370 U.S. 375 (1962), to sustain a contempt citation against a Georgia sheriff who accused a local judge of intimidating African-American voters and stirring up racial hatred.

19. In addition to the search and seizure cases noted above, see Frankfurter's dissenting opinions in Everson v. Board of Education of Ewing Township, 330 U.S. 1 (1947), and Zorach v. Clauson, 343 U.S. 306 (1952).

20. See, for example, Mendelson, "Influence of James B. Thayer," p. 75; Snowiss, *Judicial Review*, pp. 216–17, 188–89.

21. Burt, *Two Jewish Justices*, pp. 129, 123. See also Hirsch, *Enigma of Felix Frankfurter*.

22. 309 U.S. 227 (1940).

23. 367 U.S. 568 (1961).

24. Id. at 620–21.

25. 328 U.S. 463 (1946).

26. 342 U.S. 524 (1952).

27. 355 U.S. 115 (1957).

28. Quoted in Schwartz, *Super Chief*, pp. 266–67.

29. Compare Buck v. Bell, 274 U.S. 200 (1927), with Skinner v. Oklahoma, 316 U.S. 535 (1942).

30. Minersville School District v. Gobitis, 310 U.S. 586 (1940), and West Virginia State Board of Education v. Barnette, 319 U.S. 624 (1943).

31. Beauharnais v. Illinois, 343 U.S. 250 (1952).

32. See especially Schneiderman v. United States, 320 U.S. 118 (1943), Perez v. Brownell, 356 U.S. 44 (1958), and Trop v. Dulles, 356 U.S. 86 (1958).

33. 339 U.S. 460 (1950).

34. 368 U.S. 157 (1961).

35. Quoted in Schwartz, *Super Chief,* p. 404. Although felled by illness before the final decision in NAACP v. Button, 371 U.S. 415 (1963), Frankfurter was prepared to sustain the Virginia law that forbade solicitation of clients by an agent of an organization that litigates a case in which it is not a party and has no pecuniary interest. The law was aimed at the NAACP and other civil rights groups that advised persons about legal redress. Arguing that "there's no evidence . . . this statute is aimed at Negroes as such," Frankfurter concluded, "I can't imagine a worse disservice than to continue being the guardians of Negroes." See Schwartz, *Super Chief,* p. 450.

36. The exception is Mark Silverstein's penetrating study *Constitutional Faiths.*

37. 261 U.S. 525 (1923).

38. Quoted in Bickel, *Unpublished Opinions of Mr. Justice Brandeis,* p. 221.

39. New State Ice Co. v. Liebman, 285 U.S. 262, 311 (1932).

40. Frankfurter, *Public and Its Government,* pp. 151–55.

41. Quoted in Lasch, *True and Only Heaven,* pp. 415–16.

42. Frankfurter, *Public and Its Government,* p. 164.

43. See United States v. South-Eastern Underwriters Assn., 322 U.S. 533 (1944), and California v. United States, 332 U.S. 19 (1947).

44. Hood v. DuMond, 336 U.S. 525 (1949).

45. See, for example, New York v. United States, 326 U.S. 572 (1946).

46. Brown v. Gerdes, 321 U.S. 178 (1944).

47. Flournoy v. Wiener, 321 U.S. 253, 264 (1944).

48. He did vote to curb such contempts in Quinn v. United States, 349 U.S. 155 (1955); Emspak v. United States, 349 U.S. 190 (1955); Watkins v. United States, 354 U.S. 178 (1957); and Sweezy v. New Hampshire, 354 U.S. 234 (1957).

49. Communist Party v. Subversive Activities Control Board, 367 U.S. 1 (1961).

50. 349 U.S. 155 (1955).

51. 349 U.S. 190 (1955).

52. Quoted in Schwartz, *Super Chief,* p. 179.

53. After Frankfurter's retirement the Court defanged the registration provisions of the McCarran Act when applied to specific individuals. See Aptheker v. Secretary of State, 378 U.S. 500 (1964), and Albertson v. Subversive Activities Control Board, 382 U.S. 70 (1965).

54. Offutt v. United States, 348 U.S. 11 (1954). In addition to *Offutt,* notable exceptions are Nye v. United States, 313 U.S. 33 (1941), and Judge Medina's contempt citations in Sacher v. United States, 343 U.S. 1 (1952).

55. See especially Times-Mirror Co. v. Superior Court of California, 314 U.S. 252 (1941); Craig v. Harney, 331 U.S. 367 (1947).

56. See United States v. United Mine Workers, 330 U.S. 258 (1947), and Frankfurter's views on the first sit-in cases quoted in Schwartz, *Super Chief,* pp. 402–4.

57. Bolt, *Man for All Seasons,* pp. 37–38.

58. Beale, "A Man for All Seasons," pp. 18–19.

59. Quoted in Schwartz, *Super Chief,* p. 278.

60. Wolf v. Colorado, 338 U.S. 25, 27 (1949).

61. Quoted in Schwartz, *Super Chief,* p. 409.

62. Mapp v. Ohio, 367 U.S. 643 (1961); Gideon v. Wainwright, 372 U.S. 335 (1963); Miranda v. Arizona, 384 U.S. 436 (1966).

63. See Harlan's concurring opinion in Griswold v. Connecticut, 381 U.S. 479 (1965), and Blackmun's opinion for the majority in Roe v. Wade, 410 U.S. 113 (1973).

64. Bickel, *Supreme Court and the Idea of Progress.*

Chapter 4

1. For Douglas's life, see Simon, *Independent Journey,* as well as the three volumes of autobiography, *Of Men and Mountains, Go East, Young Man,* and *The Court Years.*

2. The subcommittee of the House Judiciary Committee assigned to look into the charges found them all lacking in substance. See *Associate Justice William O. Douglas. Final Reports of Special Subcommittee on Impeachment Resolutions,* 91st Cong., 2d sess. (1970).

3. Eisenberg, *Nature of the Common Law,* pp. 15, 17.

4. For a discussion of these qualities of Frankfurter and how they affected his jurisprudence, see Urofsky, *Felix Frankfurter.*

5. Learned Hand to Felix Frankfurter, Feb. 6, 1944, Felix Frankfurter Papers, Library of Congress. See Urofsky, "Conflict among the Brethren," pp. 84ff.; Simon, *The Antagonists,* chap. 3.

6. Thomas Reed Powell to William O. Douglas, March 28, 1944, Thomas Reed Powell Papers, Harvard Law School Library, Cambridge, Mass.

7. "It is the very essence of a government of laws that the predilections of judges not carry the day, and that the law as written by the lawmakers be applied equally to all. This I had assumed to be elementary" (Douglas, "On Misconception of the Judicial Function").

8. Rogat, review of Douglas, *The Anatomy of Liberty* and *Freedom of the Mind,* in *New York Review of Books,* Oct. 22, 1964, pp. 5–6.

9. Wolfman, Silver, and Silver, *Dissent without Opinion,* pp. 4, 19.

10. Rosenberg v. United States, 346 U.S. 273 (1953).

11. Felix Frankfurter to John Marshall Harlan, October 23, 1956, quoted in Parrish, "Cold War Justice," p. 808.

12. Douglas, *Court Years,* pp. 78–82. There has been much controversy over the guilt or innocence of the Rosenbergs, as well as the fairness of the legal process that condemned them to death. See, for example, Schneir and Schneir, *Invitation to an Inquest,* and Nizer, *Implosion Conspiracy.*

13. Parrish, "Cold War Justice," p. 832; Simon, *Independent Journey,* p. 312.

14. Fortas, "William O. Douglas: An Appreciation."

15. See, for example, Countryman, "Justice Douglas and Freedom of Expression"; "The Contribution of the Douglas Dissent"; and "Even-Handed Justice." Countryman also edited a representative sampling of Douglas's Court work, *The Douglas Opinions.*

16. Cohen, "Justice Douglas and the *Rosenberg* Case," responds to Parrish, "Cold War Justice." Parrish answered in "Justice Douglas and the *Rosenberg* Case: A Rejoinder."

17. Maverick, "Douglas and the First Amendment"; Powe, "Justice Douglas after Fifty Years"; Strossen, "The Religion Clause Writings of Justice William O. Douglas"; Days, "Justice William O. Douglas and Civil Rights"; Adler, "Note: Toward a Constitutional Theory of Individuality"; Glancy, "Getting the Government Off the Backs of the People."

18. White, "The Anti-Judge"; a shorter version appears as chap. 15 in White, *American Judicial Tradition.* All citations are to the law review article.

19. Ibid., p. 18.

20. Ibid., p. 40.

21. Douglas, *Go East, Young Man,* p. 465; interviews with over a dozen former Douglas clerks, reported in Urofsky, "Getting the Job Done"; interview with Justice Lewis F. Powell, Jr., April 5, 1988, Charlottesville, Va. Justice William J. Brennan, on the other hand, does not believe that Douglas lost interest at the end (interview with Justice Brennan, May 17, 1988, Washington, D.C.).

22. White, "Anti-Judge," p. 43.

23. 307 U.S. 277 (1939). The challenge to the Revenue Act of 1932, 47 Stat. 169, rested on Art. III, sec. 1 of the Constitution, which forbids Congress to reduce a federal judge's salary during that judge's term of office.

24. Douglas, *Go East, Young Man,* pp. 466–68.

25. Ibid.

26. White, "Anti-Judge," p. 45.

27. Kalman, *Legal Realism.*

28. See, among their many writings, Llewellyn, "A Realistic Jurisprudence: The Next Step"; Frank, *Law and the Modern Mind;* and the classic Cardozo, *Nature of the Judicial Process.*

29. White, "Anti-Judge," pp. 46, 48, quoting Douglas, *Go East, Young Man,* p. 466.

30. See, for example, his opinions in Sunshine Anthracite Coal Co. v. Adkins, 310 U.S. 381 (1940), and Murdock v. Pennsylvania, 319 U.S. 105 (1943), which Professor White agrees meet his criteria, but which he considers as exceptions to the rule (White, "Anti-Judge," p. 47 n.159).

31. White, "Anti-Judge," p. 65. For a different defense of Douglas's actions in the case, see Cohen, "Justice Douglas and the *Rosenberg* Case."

32. White, "Anti-Judge," p. 65.

33. 383 U.S. 663 (1966).

34. White, "Anti-Judge," p. 65 n.228.

35. 316 U.S. 535 (1942).

36. 381 U.S. 479 (1965).

37. White, "Anti-Judge," p. 66 n.229.

38. Ibid., pp. 70–71.

39. Cox, "Constitutional Adjudication," pp. 95–96.

40. White, "Anti-Judge," p. 80.

41. M. White, *Social Thought in America*, p. 65. I do not wish to imply that Professor G. Edward White calls for, or holds up as an ideal, a rigid and doctrinaire form of analysis as the only legitimate means of constitutional interpretation. But when he charges Douglas with "reject[ing] both of the principal twentieth-century devices to constrain subjective judicial lawmaking: fidelity to constitutional text or doctrine, and institutional deference" (White, "Anti-Judge," p. 18), I believe that White has imposed a formalistic standard akin, in its belief in a "right" way, to that rejected by Holmes.

42. Holmes, *The Common Law*.

43. "The Theory of Legal Interpretation."

44. "The Path of the Law."

45. White, "Anti-Judge," p. 8.

46. Holmes, *Common Law*, p. 5.

47. Rodriguez v. Bethlehem Steel Corp., 525 P.2d 669 (Cal. 1974).

48. See the discussion of this issue in Eisenberg, *Common Law*, chap. 4.

49. Foley v. Interactive Data Corporation, 254 Cal. Rptr. 211, 255 (Cal. 1988).

50. Corbin, "The Offer of an Act," pp. 771–72.

51. 309 U.S. 331 (1940). The case involved a taxpayer who created a short-term trust over which he exercised full control as trustee, although the income went to his wife. The commissioner of revenue ruled that the taxpayer had established the trust merely to avoid taxes and in effect had retained full control of the assets, for which he must therefore bear the tax consequences. Section 61(a) of the Revenue Act of 1934 did not address the issue of short-term trusts with great clarity, and Douglas ruled that as a result the trier of fact could determine whether a trustee had as a practical matter rights associated with ownership and, if so, the accruing tax liability. There are only a few citations to prior cases in the decision, but Douglas's analysis of what property rights and ownership mean is by no means fanciful or far-fetched.

52. "Foreword," in Wolfman, *Dissent without Opinion*, pp. x–xi.

53. 316 U.S. 535 (1942).

54. 381 U.S. 479 (1965).

55. White, "Anti-Judge," p. 66.

56. Buck v. Bell, 274 U.S. 200, 208 (1927).

57. 300 U.S. 379 (1937).

58. 316 U.S. at 541–42.

59. White, "Anti-Judge," p. 68.

60. Griffin v. Illinois, 351 U.S. 12 (1956) (requiring indigent defendants be furnished with trial transcripts; Justice Black wrote the Court's opinion utilizing an equal protection analysis); Douglas v. California, 372 U.S. 353 (1963). In the latter case Douglas wrote the Court's brief opinion requiring states to appoint counsel for indigent defendants at the first appeal stage; he cited *Griffin* for the equal protection analysis involving poverty as an invidious distinction.

61. One might note here that Douglas did not invent the idea of a penumbral doctrine. *Black's Law Dictionary* traces it to an early federal eminent domain decision, Kohl v. United States, 91 U.S. 367 (1875). Holmes used the notion of "the penumbra of the 4th and 5th amendments " in his dissent in the wiretap case, Olmstead v. United States, 277 U.S. 438, 469 (1928). See Glancy, "Douglas's Right to Privacy: A Response to His Critics," pp. 161–62, for a discussion of penumbral doctrine in prior legal reasoning.

62. 381 U.S. at 486.

63. White, "Anti-Judge," pp. 70–71.

64. D'Souza, "The New Liberal Censorship," p. 13; Robert Bork, Foreword to Gary McDowell, *Constitution and Contemporary Constitutional Theory*, p. x; Emerson, "Nine Justices," p. 230;

65. Olmstead v. United States, 277 U.S. 438, 478 (1928) (Brandeis, J., dissenting).Kauper, "Penumbras, Peripheries, Emanations," p. 253. However, see Glancy, "Douglas's Right of Privacy," for a defense of Douglas's reasoning and its ties to prior Court decisions and reasoning. See also Adler, "Toward a Constitutional Theory of Individuality."

66. See then Judge Warren E. Burger's dissent in In re President of Georgetown College, 331 F.2d 1000, 1015 (D.C. Cir. 1964).

67. 391 U.S. 68, 70–71 (1968). In a companion case Douglas also wrote for the Court in holding another Louisiana statute violative of the equal protection clause when it denied a mother recovery for the wrongful death of an illegitimate child while allowing recovery in the deaths of legitimate children. Glona v. American Guarantee & Liability Insurance Co., 391 U.S. 73 (1968).

68. 401 U.S. 532, 538–39 (1971). Since then the Court has followed what might at best be called a wavering line in cases involving the rights of illegitimate children. See, for example, Weber v. Aetna Casualty & Insurance Co., 406 U.S. 164 (1972), which followed *Levy*, and Mathews v. Lucas, 427 U.S. 495 (1976), which followed *Labine*, down to Mills v. Habluetzel, 456 U.S. 91 (1982), in which Justice Rehnquist wrote for the Court applying equal protection analysis to differential time limits imposed on claims for child support for legitimate and illegitimate offspring.

69. Perhaps Frankfurter's strongest statement on the limits of judicial competence can be found in his plurality opinion in Colegrove v. Green, 328 U.S. 549 (1946).

70. In Gunther, *Constitutional Law,* perhaps the most widely used text in its field, the author includes nine Douglas opinions for the Court among his principal cases, and only one written by Frankfurter. In nonprincipal cases Douglas opinions are also referred to far more frequently than Frankfurter's. In criminal procedure, which has changed so rapidly, a major text, Saltzburg, *American Criminal Procedure,* includes two majority opinions by Douglas among the principal cases, both considered valid. The sole Frankfurter opinion included involves the Fourth Amendment, on which Frankfurter considered himself the Court's leading authority. That case, Wolf v. Colorado, 338 U.S. 25 (1949), held that the exclusionary rule did not apply to the states; that holding was overruled in Mapp v. Ohio, 367 U.S. 643 (1961). Douglas never claimed any special expertise in criminal procedure, but according to one scholar, he had an enormous impact on criminal procedure (Duke, "William O. Douglas and the Rights of the Accused"). Duke notes a number of decisions which are still valid law, and which are part and parcel of the Warren Court's "due process revolution." These include Douglas v. California, 372 U.S. 353 (1963); Griffin v. California, 380 U.S. 609 (1965); Boykin v. Alabama, 395 U.S. 238 (1969); Papachristou v. Jacksonville, 405 U.S. 156 (1972); and Argersinger v. Hamlin, 407 U.S. 25 (1972).

71. Frank v. Maryland, 359 U.S. 360 (1959).

72. Interview with Charles Miller, Washington, D.C., March 2, 1989. The Douglas dissent is at 359 U.S. at 374.

73. Camara v. Municipal Court of San Francisco, 387 U.S. 523 (1967); See v. Seattle, 387 U.S. 541 (1967).

74. This, of course, was one of Brandeis's essential ideas in understanding the law. See Mason, *Brandeis: A Free Man's Life,* p. 69.

75. Glancy, "Douglas's Right of Privacy," pp. 161–62; Warren and Brandeis, "The Right to Privacy." Professor Jan Deutsch of Yale Law School clerked for Potter Stewart in the October 1962 term, and he reports how frustrated he would often be with Douglas's opinions. He would meet with Douglas's clerk, Jerome Falk, and say "Jerry, it doesn't work. *It does not work!*" Then Falk would show him that it did work, because Douglas did not take just the bare holdings but all the glosses that went with earlier opinions, and from those he wove his own conclusions. "Most legal scholars at Yale do not think that glossing matters," Deutsch concluded, "but do you know how hard it is to do what Douglas did and produce a coherent opinion" (interview with Jan Deutsch, June 28, 1988, New Haven).

76. Countryman, "Scholarship and Common Sense," p. 1409. Countryman, in response to a question about Douglas never developing his argument, said: "Well, I've heard that criticism all my life, and frankly I don't think there's a helluva lot to it. For instance, in the *Dennis* case [Dennis v. United States, 341 U.S. 494 (1951)], he didn't ring all the changes on the clear and present danger test, like Frankfurter would have done. He just said that anybody who thinks these birds are a clear and present danger is in the grip of hysteria. . . . That was all that needed to be said.

There had been enough changes rung on clear and present danger . . . so he didn't think it was necessary to run through the thing again" (interview with Vern Countryman, Aug. 29, 1988, San Francisco).

77. Radin, "The Theory of Judicial Decisions"; Countryman, "Scholarship and Common Sense," p. 1409 n.14. (Radin was a friend of Douglas's, and initially chose his law clerks for him.) Douglas told his friend Eric Sevareid that judges who write fifty-eight page opinions do so because they do not stick to the plain meaning of the Constitution and therefore have to justify their results (Glancy, "Douglas's Right of Privacy," p. 163 n.58).

78. Meese, "Construing the Constitution." As an example, Justice Hans Linde of the Oregon Supreme Court, a former law clerk to Douglas, believes that the Constitution must be strictly interpreted, and that a common-law approach is much too elastic (conversation with Justice Linde, April 16, 1989, Seattle).

79. Erie Railroad Co. v. Tompkins, 304 U.S. 64 (1938).

80. I am indebted to Professor Robert Post of Boalt Hall for reminding me of this fact.

81. Semonche, *Charting the Future.*

82. West Virginia Board of Education v. Barnette, 319 U.S. 624, 639 (1943).

83. 163 U.S. 537 (1896). For Frankfurter's reluctance to proceed in Brown v. Board of Education, 347 U.S. 483 (1954), see Kluger, *Simple Justice,* chap. 25. Frankfurter asked his law clerk Alexander Bickel to see if the *Brown* result could be justified in terms of history and original intent, and it could not be. Bickel later published the result of his research as "The Original Understanding and the Segregation Decision."

84. Douglas, "Memorandum for the File," in Urofsky, *The Douglas Letters,* pp. 165–67.

85. Colegrove v. Green, 328 U.S. 549 (1946).

86. Baker v. Carr, 369 U.S. 186 (1962).

87. Reynolds v. Sims, 377 U.S. 533 (1964).

88. Gray v. Sanders, 372 U.S. 368 (1963).

89. Id. at 382, 384.

90. Powe, "Evolution to Absolutism"; Emerson, "Justice Douglas' Contribution to the Law," p. 356.

91. Transcript of CBS Reports, "Mr. Justice Douglas," Sept. 6, 1972, quoted in Glancy, "Douglas's Right of Privacy," p. 164.

92. Douglas, *Court Years,* pp. 55–56.

93. Powe, "Justice Douglas after Fifty Years," p. 270. Chief Justice Rehnquist believes that some of the opinions Douglas wrote earlier in his career regarding corporate finance and securities regulation show that he was a master not only of the law in those areas but of the businesses involved, inside and out (interview with William H. Rehnquist, May 17, 1988, Washington, D.C.).

94. Douglas, *Almanac of Liberty,* p. vii.

95. Holmes to Nina Gray, March 2, 1903, quoted in Novick, *Honorable Justice,* p. 256.

96. Kaufman, "Helping the Public Understand." This is not to say that only short and simplistic opinions can do this. Louis Brandeis wrote to educate his brethren, and his opinions, both in the majority and in dissent, are considered models of judicial craftsmanship and analysis. But as his law clerk Paul Freund recalled, often after extensive work on an opinion Brandeis would say, "Now I think the opinion is persuasive, but what can we do to make it more instructive?" (Freund, "Justice Brandeis: A Law Clerk's Remembrance," p. 11).

97. See the analysis of Douglas's obscenity case opinions in this light in Campbell, "How Opinions Can Persuade." Douglas, however, seems to have consciously eschewed taking on the role of teacher. His clerk for the October 1951 term, Marshall Small, recalled that in a tax case Douglas wrote a very brief opinion. Small suggested that he might want to expand it and noted how Harlan Fiske Stone had always made an effort to elucidate the reasoning in tax cases. Douglas very abruptly snapped: "I don't write law review articles" (interview with Marshall Small, Aug. 26, 1988, San Francisco.)

98. "Transcript," cited by Glancy, "Douglas's Right of Privacy," p. 175 n.66; Douglas, "Stare Decisis," p. 746. One might point here to one of the great common-law decisions of this century, Judge Cardozo's opinion in Macpherson v. Buick Motor Co., 217 N.Y. 382 (1916), which eliminated the need for privity and brought product liability law into the twentieth century. To do this, Cardozo, whom many consider the greatest common-law judge of this century, had to ignore precedent and write an innovative opinion in order to reach what everyone agrees was the right result.

99. Karst, "Dedication."

100. Interview with Justice William J. Brennan, Jr., May 17, 1988, Washington, D.C.

101. Simon, *Independent Journey,* p. 250.

102. Interview with Jerome Falk, Aug. 26, 1988, San Francisco.

103. Karst, "Dedication," p. 511.

104. Holmes, *Common Law.*

105. *Harvard Law Record,* Feb. 8, 1980, quoted in Karst, "Dedication," p. 511 n.1. The *Law Record* does not identify the disciple.

106. Jaffe, "Was Brandeis an Activist?" p. 1003.

107. Hurtado v. California, 110 U.S. 516, 530 (1884).

Chapter 5

1. The works on the Warren Court, Justice Black, and their changing image are extensive. Useful introductions are: Schwartz, *Super Chief;* Yarbrough, *Black and His Critics;* Dunne, *Hugo Black;* Freyer, *Black and the Dilemma of American Liberalism.* See

also White, *American Judicial Tradition*, pp. 317–68. For a full bibliography on Black which includes many references to his place on the Warren Court and the Court generally, see Freyer, *Black and Modern America*, pp. 330–62. The statement attributed to William H. Rehnquist is as quoted in Kluger, *Simple Justice*, p. 609.

2. Yarbrough, *Black and His Critics*, provides the most comprehensive treatment not only of the range of criticism but also of its varied philosophical, theoretical, or epistemological basis. A critic whose thoroughgoing study supports Yarbrough's conclusions concerning the consistency and sophistication of Black's constitutional faith and its influence, while nonetheless disagreeing with both, is Snowiss, "The Legacy of Justice Black."

3. Compare my *Black and the Dilemma of American Liberalism* to Yarbrough's *Black and His Critics*. See also Simon, *The Antagonists*, who, like Yarbrough and myself, uses manuscript sources unavailable to Dunne, *Black and the Judicial Revolution*. In addition, there are the materials collected in Freyer, *Black and Modern America*.

4. As quoted in Meador, *Black and His Books*, pp. 30, 31. For more extensive treatment of this point, see Freyer, *Black and the Dilemma of American Liberalism*.

5. As quoted in Simon, *Antagonists*, p. 237.

6. William Brennan, "Remarks on the Occasion of the Justice Hugo L. Black Centennial," in Freyer, *Black and Modern America*, pp. 171–72.

7. As quoted in Simon, *Antagonists*, p. 249.

8. Freyer, *Hugo Black and the Dilemma of American Liberalism*, pp. 1–13. See also Hamilton, *Hugo Black: The Alabama Years*.

9. Black and Black, *Memoirs*, p. 8.

10. Ibid., pp. 1–64; and for this and the following four paragraphs, see also note 8 above.

11. Black to Hugo Black, Jr., Nov. 1949, Hugo L. Black Papers, box 3, Library of Congress.

12. Freyer, *Black and the Dilemma of American Liberalism*, pp. 14–47.

13. Ibid., for this and the following paragraph.

14. *New York Times*, Sept. 26, 1971, p. 76, col. 1 (interview with Justice Black; transcript is located in Special Collections, University of Alabama School of Law).

15. Black to Hugo L. Black, Jr., Jan. 18, 1945, and Black to Sterling Black, April 1, 1944, Black Papers, box 3.

16. Bell, "Interest-Convergence Dilemma"; Hutchinson, "Unanimity and Desegregation"; Freyer, *Black and the Dilemma of American Liberalism*, pp. 122–52.

17. Black to Hugo Black, Jr., Jan. 18, 1945, Black Papers, box 3; Freyer, *Black and the Liberal Dilemma*, p. 119.

18. Black to Edna Street Barnes, Nov. 14, 1962, Black Papers, box 1.

19. Hutchinson, "Unanimity and Desegregation."

20. The statements are as quoted in Kluger, *Simple Justice*, pp. 593–94.

21. Hutchinson, "Unanimity and Desegregation," pp. 34–44, 50–59; Freyer, *Black and the Liberal Dilemma*, pp. 122–37.

22. Hutchinson, "Unanimity and Desegregation," p. 48.

23. Ibid., pp. 60–96; Freyer, *Black and the Liberal Dilemma*, pp. 122–37. The quotation is from Brown v. Board of Education, 349 U.S. 294, 301 (1955). On Frankfurter's contact with his former clerk concerning the "deliberate speed" phrase, see Elman, "The Solicitor General's Office."

24. Hutchinson, "Unanimity and Desegregation," pp. 73–85; Freyer, *Little Rock Crisis*, pp. 156–57.

25. Schwartz, *Super Chief*, pp. 402–4, 479–87, 508–26, 606–8; Branch, *Parting the Waters*, pp. 272–92; Bell, "Epistolary Exploration."

26. Black and Black, *Mr. Justice and Mrs. Black*, p. 105.

27. Ibid.

28. Schwartz, *Super Chief*, pp. 404, 481, 510–25, quotation at p. 510.

29. Ibid.; Bell v. Maryland, 378 U.S. 226, 339 (1964).

30. Schwartz, *Super Chief*, p. 525.

31. Ibid., pp. 595–602; Gomillion v. Lightfoot, 364 U.S. 339 (1960).

32. Freyer, *Black and the Dilemma of American Liberalism*, pp. 143–47.

33. South Carolina v. Katzenbach, 383 U.S. 301 (1966).

34. 383 U.S. 663, 670–74 (1966).

35. Black and Black, *Mr. Justice and Mrs. Black*, pp. 112, 121; Black to Hugo Black, Jr., Nov. 29, 1949, Black Papers, box 3.

36. Frank, "Hugo L. Black," pp. 12, 19; Freyer, *Black and the Dilemma of American Liberalism*, pp. 45, 50–51.

37. Frank, "Hugo L. Black," pp. 16, 39, 49–52.

38. Kurland, "Justice Robert H. Jackson"; Coleman, Jr., "Mr. Justice Felix Frankfurter"; Countryman, "Justice Douglas."

39. Barenblatt v. U.S., 360 U.S. 109, 151 (1959); Brandenberg v. Ohio, 395 U.S. 444 (1969).

40. Freyer, *Black and the Dilemma of American Liberalism*, pp. 138–52.

41. Transcript of interview located in Special Collections, University of Alabama School of Law.

42. 379 U.S. at 575.

43. 385 U.S. 39 (1966).

44. Tinker v. Des Moines Community School District, 393 U.S. 503, 524–25 (1969). For fuller discussion and citation, see Freyer, "Introduction."

45. 393 U.S. at 524–25.

46. Cox v. Louisiana, 379 U.S. 559, 584 (1965).

47. 370 U.S. 421, 431–32 (1962).

48. Everson v. Board of Educ., 330 U.S. 1, 18 (1947).

49. The dissent appears in Board of Educ. v. Allen, 392 U.S. 236, 250 (1968). For the criticism, see Freyer, *Black and the Dilemma of American Liberalism*, pp. 116–17, 149–50.

50. See text accompanying notes 2 and 3.

51. 332 U.S. 46, 89 (1947).

52. Yarbrough, *Black and His Critics*, pp. 115–125.

53. Black, *Constitutional Faith*, p. 34.

54. Dunne, *Black and the Judicial Revolution*, pp. 184–86; Palko v. Connecticut, 302 U.S. 319 (1937).

55. Freyer, *Black and the Dilemma of American Liberalism*, pp. 79–87, 117–18.

56. 351 U.S. 12 (1956).

57. 352 U.S. 432, 440 (1957).

58. 367 U.S. 643 (1961); 378 U.S. 478 (1964); 377 U.S. 201 (1964); 372 U.S. 335 (1963).

59. Benton v. Maryland, 395 U.S. 784 (1969); Yarbrough, *Black and His Critics*, pp. 210–26.

60. 381 U.S. 479, 507 (1961).

61. As quoted in Freyer, *Black and the Dilemma of American Liberalism*, pp. 141–42.

62. Black and Black, *Mr. Justice and Mrs. Black*, p. 154.

63. Meador, *Black and His Books*, as quoted, p. 30.

64. Dunne, *Black and the Judicial Revolution*, as quoted, p. 409.

65. As quoted in Freyer, *Black and the Dilemma of American Liberalism*, p. 151.

66. Transcript of interview located in Special Collections, University of Alabama School of Law.

67. As quoted in Freyer, *Black and the Dilemma of American Liberalism*, p. 141.

Chapter 6

1. Warren, "Mr. Justice Harlan," pp. 370–71; Friendly, "Mr. Justice Harlan," p. 384. For other expressions, see Freund, "Foreword," pp. xiii-xiv; Wright, "Hugo L. Black," pp. 3–4; Lewin, "Justice Harlan"; Lewis Powell, annual dinner address, May 15, 1986, American Law Institute, *Remarks and Addresses at the 63rd Annual Meeting, May 13–16, 1986*. The first full biography of Justice Harlan is Yarbrough, *John Marshall Harlan*.

2. Cox, *Warren Court*, p. 6.

3. 369 U.S. 186 (1962).

4. 377 U.S. 533 (1964).

5. Avery v. Midland County, 390 U.S. 474, 486 (1968) (Harlan, J., dissenting); Hadley v. Junior College Dist., 397 U.S. 50, 59 (1970) (Harlan, J., dissenting).

6. Reynolds v. Sims, 377 U.S. at 615.

7. Harper v. Virginia State Board of Elections, 383 U.S. 663, 680 (1966) (Harlan, J., dissenting); Kramer v. Union Free School Dist., 395 U.S. 621, 634 (1969) (Harlan, J., joining Stewart, J., dissenting); Oregon v. Mitchell, 400 U.S. 112, 152 (1970) (Harlan, J., concurring in part and dissenting in part).

8. 351 U.S. 12, 29, 34 (1956) (Harlan, J., dissenting).

9. 372 U.S. 353, 360 (1963) (Harlan, J., dissenting).

10. Shapiro v. Thompson, 394 U.S. 618, 655 (1969) (Harlan, J., dissenting). See also Levy v. Louisiana, 391 U.S. 68, 76 (1968), where Harlan in dissent took the view that a state law granting children the right to sue for wrongful death of their mother could validly be interpreted to deny this right to nonmarital children who lived with and were dependent on her.

11. See, e.g., Duncan v. Louisiana, 391 U.S. 145 (1968). On the changes, see generally Kamisar, *Police Interrogation and Confessions.*

12. Mapp v. Ohio, 367 U.S. 643, 672 (1961) (Harlan, J., dissenting); Malloy v. Hogan, 378 U.S. 1, 14 (1964) (self-incrimination) (Harlan, J., dissenting); Miranda v. Arizona, 384 U.S. 436, 504 (1966) (Harlan, J., dissenting); Duncan v. Louisiana, 391 U.S. at 171 (Harlan, J., dissenting); Pointer v. Texas, 380 U.S. 400, 408 (1965) (Harlan, J., concurring in the result) (confrontation); Benton v. Maryland, 395 U.S. 784, 801 (1969) (Harlan, J., dissenting) (double jeopardy). See also Harlan's separate opinion in Williams v. Florida, 399 U.S. 78, 117 (1970), noting that the necessary consequence under incorporation of the holding that a twelve-person jury is not required in state criminal trials is, through a "backlash," the application of the same lesser standard in federal cases.

13. See Benton v. Maryland, 395 U.S. 784, 801 (1969) (Harlan, J., dissenting); Desist v. United States, 394 U.S. 244, 256 (1969) (Harlan, J., dissenting).

14. 384 U.S. 641, 659 (1966) (Harlan, J., dissenting).

15. 383 U.S. 745, 762 (1966) (Harlan, J., concurring in part and dissenting in part).

16. Perez v. Brownell, 356 U.S. 44 (1958) (Harlan, J., joining Frankfurter, J., dissenting); Trop v. Dulles, 356 U.S. 86 (1958); Afroyim v. Rusk, 387 U.S. 253, 268 (1967) (Harlan, J., dissenting).

17. Rowoldt v. Perfetto, 355 U.S. 115, 121 (1957) (Harlan, J., dissenting).

18. 357 U.S. 116 (1958).

19. 378 U.S. 500 (1964).

20. Barenblatt v. United States, 360 U.S. 109 (1959); Konigsberg v. State Bar, 366 U.S. 36 (1961); Scales v. United States, 367 U.S. 203 (1961). Another, particularly harsh, decision was Flemming v. Nestor, 363 U.S. 603 (1960), which upheld the denial of Social Security benefits to an alien who was deported because he had been a member of the Communist party many years before.

21. Lerner v. Casey, 357 U.S. 468 (1958), overruled by Malloy v. Hogan, 378 U.S. 1 (1964); Hoyt v. Florida, 368 U.S. 57 (1961), overruled by Taylor v. Louisiana, 419 U.S. 522 (1975). For discussion of these themes, see Wilkinson, "Justice John Marshall Harlan"; Caplan, "Questioning *Miranda.*"

22. See *John Marshall Harlan, 1899–1971* (memorial addresses delivered at a meeting of the Association of the Bar of the City of New York by Justice Potter Stewart, former attorney general Herbert Brownell, and Professor Paul Bator), cited in Gunther, "In Search of Judicial Quality," p. 1004 n.23.

23. 349 U.S. 294 (1955).

24. 358 U.S. 1 (1958).

25. 347 U.S. 483 (1954).

26. E.g., Goss v. Board of Education, 373 U.S. 683 (1963) (school case); Griffin v. County School Board, 377 U.S. 218 (1964) (same); Heart of Atlanta Motel v. United States, 379 U.S. 241 (1964) (public accommodations); Peterson v. City of Greenville, 373 U.S. 244 (1963) (same); Watson v. City of Memphis, 373 U.S. 526 (1963) (recreational facilities).

27. 372 U.S. 335, 349 (1963).

28. 401 U.S. 371 (1971).

29. Giordenello v. United States, 357 U.S. 480 (1958) (defective search warrant); Jones v. United States, 357 U.S. 493 (1958) (no probable cause to search); Katz v. United States, 389 U.S. 347, 360 (1967) (Harlan, J., concurring). But see Berger v. New York, 388 U.S. 41, 89 (1967) (Harlan, J., dissenting) (opposing application of exclusionary rule where state engaged in electronic eavesdropping).

30. In re Gault, 387 U.S. 1, 65 (1967) (Harlan, J., concurring in part and dissenting in part).

31. Marchetti v. United States, 390 U.S. 39 (1968).

32. 357 U.S. 449 (1958).

33. 376 U.S. 254 (1964).

34. E.g., St. Amant v. Thompson, 390 U.S. 727 (1968); Garrison v. Louisiana, 379 U.S. 64 (1964). But see Rosenblatt v. Baer, 383 U.S. 75, 96 (1966) (Harlan, J., concurring in part and dissenting in part).

35. Bond v. Floyd, 385 U.S. 116 (1966); Brandenburg v. Ohio, 395 U.S. 444 (1969).

36. Street v. New York, 394 U.S. 576 (1969).

37. 351 U.S. 536 (1956). See also Vitarelli v. Seaton, 359 U.S. 535 (1959); Service v. Dulles, 354 U.S. 363 (1957) (security discharges in both cases invalid because agency failed to follow prescribed procedures).

38. Yates v. United States, 354 U.S. 298 (1957); Lewis, "Earl Warren."

39. Nowak v. United States, 356 U.S. 660 (1958); Maisenberg v. United States, 356 U.S. 670 (1958).

40. Abington School Dist. v. Schempp, 374 U.S. 203 (1963); Engel v. Vitale, 370 U.S. 421 (1962); Torcaso v. Watkins, 367 U.S. 488 (1961).

41. Board of Educ. v. Allen, 392 U.S. 236 (1968); Lemon v. Kurtzman, 403 U.S. 602 (1971).

42. Sherbert v. Verner, 374 U.S. 398, 418 (1963) (Harlan, J., dissenting).

43. Welsh v. United States, 398 U.S. 333, 357 (1970) (Harlan, J., concurring in the result).

44. Board of Educ. v. Allen, 392 U.S. at 249.

45. Ibid.

46. Greenawalt, "Enduring Significance," p. 984.

47. Poe v. Ullman, 367 U.S. 497, 522 (1961).

48. 381 U.S. 479, 499 (1965) (Harlan, J., concurring).

49. 405 U.S. 438 (1972).

50. 410 U.S. 113 (1973).

51. See, e.g., FTC v. Procter & Gamble Co., 386 U.S. 568, 581 (1967) (Harlan, J., concurring); United States v. Continental Can Co., 378 U.S. 441, 467 (1964) (Harlan, J., dissenting); Brown Shoe Co. v. United States, 370 U.S. 294 (1962) (Harlan, J., concurring in part and dissenting in part); Klor's, Inc. v. Broadway-Hale Stores, Inc., 359 U.S. 207 (1959) (Harlan, J., concurring in result). An informed discussion of Harlan's time at the bar is Wood, "John M. Harlan."

52. Graham Greene, *Human Factor,* pp. 148, 149.

53. 49 *ABA Journal* 943 (1963).

54. Dorsen, "The Second Mr. Justice Harlan," p. 271.

55. Ibid., p. 254.

56. 369 U.S. 186, 330 (1962) (Harlan, J., dissenting).

57. 377 U.S. 533, 589 (1964) (Harlan, J., dissenting). See also Wesberry v. Sanders, 376 U.S. 1, 20 (1964), in which Harlan dissented at length from a ruling that in congressional elections "as nearly as is practicable one man's vote . . . is to be worth as much as another's" (id. at 7–8).

58. 380 U.S. 479, 498 (1965) (Harlan, J., dissenting).

59. 372 U.S. 391, 448 (1963) (Harlan, J., dissenting).

60. 379 U.S. 443, 457 (1965) (Harlan, J., dissenting).

61. 392 U.S. 83, 116 (1968) (Harlan, J., dissenting).

62. 367 U.S. 497, 522 (1961).

63. 357 U.S. 449 (1958).

64. Engel v. Vitale, 370 U.S. 421 (1962).

65. Powell v. McCormack, 395 U.S. 486 (1969).

66. Another Harlan opinion that adopted a broad view of standing is Parmelee Transp. Co. v. Atchison, Topeka & Santa Fe R. Co., 357 U.S. 77 (1958).

67. Monroe v. Pape, 365 U.S. 167, 192 (1961) (Harlan, J., concurring).

68. J. I. Case Co. v. Borak, 377 U.S. 426 (1964).

69. Dorsen, "The Second Mr. Justice Harlan," p. 257.

70. E.g., Afroyim v. Rusk, 387 U.S. 253, 268 (1967) (Harlan, J., dissenting from the overruling of Perez v. Brownell, 356 U.S. 44 [1958]); Mapp v. Ohio, 367 U.S. 643, 672 (1961) (Harlan, J., dissenting from overruling of Wolf v. Colorado, 338 U.S. 25 [1949]).

71. 316 U.S. 455 (1942), overruled by Gideon v. Wainwright, 372 U.S. 335 (1963).

72. 390 U.S. 39 (1968), overruling United States v. Kahriger, 345 U.S. 22 (1953), and Lewis v. United States, 348 U.S. 419 (1955).

73. 382 U.S. 111, 116 (1965), overruling in part Kesler v. Department of Public Safety, 369 U.S. 153 (1962), an opinion by Justice Frankfurter in which Harlan had

joined. Other cases where Harlan was willing to overrule obsolete precedents are Lear, Inc. v. Adkins, 395 U.S. 653 (1969); Walker v. Southern Ry., 385 U.S. 196, 199 (1966) (Harlan, J., dissenting).

74. See, e.g., Coolidge v. New Hampshire, 403 U.S. 443, 490 (1971) (Harlan, J., concurring) (following Mapp v. Ohio, 367 U.S. 643 [1961], and Ker v. California, 374 U.S. 23 [1963]); Ashe v. Swenson, 397 U.S. 436, 448 (1970) (Harlan, J., concurring) (following Benton v. Maryland, 395 U.S. 784 [1969]); Burns v. Richardson, 384 U.S. 73, 98 (1966) (Harlan, J., concurring in the result) (following Reynolds v. Sims, 377 U.S. 533 [1964]).

75. 355 U.S. 184 (1957) (Harlan, J., joining Frankfurter, J., dissenting); see also id. at 330.

76. 395 U.S. 711, 744, 751 (1969) (Harlan, J., concurring in part and dissenting in part). See also Usner v. Luckenbach Overseas Corp., 400 U.S. 494, 503–4 (1971) (Harlan, J., dissenting).

77. Veterans of the Abraham Lincoln Brigade v. Subversive Activities Control Board, 380 U.S. 513, 514 (1965).

78. See note 20 above, and accompanying text.

79. Stamler v. Willis, 393 U.S. 217 (1968), appeal dismissed from 287 F. Supp. 734 (N.D. Ill., 1968). See also Wiseman v. Titicut Follies, 398 U.S. 960, 960 (1970) (Harlan, J., dissenting from denial of writ of certiorari).

80. Massachusetts v. Laird, 400 U.S. 886 (1970).

81. Among many other examples that could be cited, despite Harlan's strong commitment to racial equality, he did not believe (1) that a state was responsible for discrimination by a privately owned and operated restaurant open to the general public, even though it was located in a municipal parking facility that was constructed with public funds, was tax exempt, and flew the state flag (Burton v. Wilmington Parking Authority, 365 U.S. 715 [1961]); or (2) that land bequeathed in trust to a Georgia city as a "park and pleasure ground" for white people was unconstitutionally administered because a state court replaced public trustees with private ones and the park was municipally maintained (Evans v. Newton, 382 U.S. 296 [1966]); or (3) that a state constitutional amendment, adopted by referendum, that protected the right of private parties to exercise total rights over real property, including the ability to discriminate on the ground of race, was invalid because the state was thereby encouraging the discrimination (Reitman v. Mulkey, 387 U.S. 369 [1967]). And in a nonracial context Harlan dissented from a holding that a privately owned shopping mall was the equivalent of a company town so as to bar peaceful picketing of a supermarket in the mall. Amalgamated Food Employees Union v. Logan Valley Plaza, 391 U.S. 308 (1968).

82. See Friendly, "Mr. Justice Harlan," p. 388.

83. Dandridge v. Williams, 397 U.S. 471, 489 (1970) (Harlan, J., concurring).

84. McKeiver v. Pennsylvania and In re Burrus, 403 U.S. 528, 557 (1971) (Harlan, J., concurring in the judgments); McGautha v. California, 402 U.S. 183 (1971).

85. Wyman v. James, 400 U.S. 309 (1971).

86. New York Times Co. v. United States, 403 U.S. 713, 752 (1971) (Harlan, J., dissenting).

87. Rosenbloom v. Metromedia, Inc., 403 U.S. 29, 62 (1971) (Harlan, J., dissenting); Baird v. State Bar, 401 U.S. 1 (1971); In re Stolar, 401 U.S. 23 (1971).

88. Law Students Civil Rights Research Council v. Wadmond, 401 U.S. 154 (1971); United States v. Reidel, 402 U.S. 351, 357 (1971) (Harlan, J., concurring).

89. Palmer v. Thompson, 403 U.S. 217 (1971); James v. Valtierra, 402 U.S. 137 (1971). But see Adickes v. Kress & Co., 398 U.S. 144 (1970).

90. Adickes v. Kress & Co., 398 U.S. 144 (1970); Northcross v. Board of Educ., 397 U.S. 232 (1970).

91. Griggs v. Duke Power Co., 401 U.S. 424 (1971).

92. See note 33 above, and accompanying text.

93. See, e.g., "The Supreme Court, 1970 Term," pp. 104–13. But see Tribe, *American Constitutional Law*, pp. 1462–63, 1639–40. See also Goldberg v. Kelly, 397 U.S. 254 (1970), in which Harlan joined Justice Brennan's pathbreaking opinion granting welfare recipients pretermination procedural rights.

94. Williams v. Illinois, 399 U.S. 235 (1970); Tate v. Short, 401 U.S. 395, 401 (1971) (Harlan, J., concurring in the judgment).

95. Coolidge v. New Hampshire, 403 U.S. 443, 490 (1971) (Harlan, J., concurring).

96. In re Winship, 397 U.S. 358, 368 (1970) (Harlan, J., concurring).

97. Cohen v. California, 403 U.S. 15 (1971).

98. E.g., Bivens v. Six Unknown Named Agents, 403 U.S. 388, 398 (1971) (Harlan, J., concurring in the judgment); Welsh v. United States, 398 U.S. at 344 (Harlan, J., concurring in the result, statutory case); Moragne v. States Marine Lines, Inc., 398 U.S. 375 (1970) (Harlan, J., common-law [admiralty] case).

99. Hart and Sacks, *The Legal Process*, pp. 715–16, 4–5. *The Legal Process* is not a work of constitutional law, and "the authors regarded constitutional problems as distinct sorts of issues" (Dorsen, "In Memoriam," p. 13 n.12). Nevertheless, many judges and scholars adapted legal process themes to constitutional cases. See, e.g., Ely, *Democracy and Distrust*.

Chapter 7

1. Hutchinson, "Hail to the Chief," p. 924.

2. 347 U.S. 483 (1954).

3. Brennan, "The Equality Principle," pp. 673–74.

4. 358 U.S. 1 (1958). On Brennan's role in the drafting of the *Cooper per curiam* opinion, see Schwartz, *Super Chief*, pp. 295–301. Schwartz concludes that the "chief credit" for *Cooper* "must go to Brennan" (ibid., p. 301).

5. 391 U.S. 430 (1968).

6. Tocqueville, *Democracy in America* 2: 99–103.

7. Wechsler, *Principles, Politics, and Fundamental Law,* pp. 46–47.

8. Tocqueville, *Democracy in America* 2: 104.

9. For a discussion of the difference between orienting law toward groups as compared to individuals, see Post, "Cultural Heterogeneity and Law," pp. 299–305.

10. See City of Richmond v. J. A. Croson Co., 488 U.S. 469 (1989); compare Wygant v. Jackson Board of Educ., 476 U.S. 267, 281 n. 8 (1986) (opinion of Powell, J.), with id. at 309 (Marshall, J., dissenting).

11. See, e.g., Metro Broadcasting, Inc. v. FCC, 497 U.S. 547 (1990).

12. 369 U.S. 186 (1962).

13. Warren, *Memoirs,* p. 309.

14. 328 U.S. 549 (1946).

15. "The United States shall guarantee to every State in this Union a Republican Form of Government." U.S. Const. Art. IV, sec. 4.

16. 369 U.S. at 223, 226, 237.

17. Id. at 300 (Frankfurter, J., dissenting).

18. Warren, "Mr. Justice Brennan," p. 2.

19. Brennan, "My Encounters with the Constitution," *Judges Journal* 26, no. 3 (Summer 1987): 10. Brennan wrote of Warren that "he strongly believed that individual human dignity was the primary value fostered and protected by the Constitution" (*Tribute to Chief Justice Earl Warren,* Fairmont Hotel, San Francisco, April 8, 1989, p. 3).

20. 377 U.S. 533 (1964).

21. 369 U.S. at 332.

22. See Post, "Cultural Heterogeneity and Law," pp. 301–5.

23. Brennan, "Some Aspects of Federalism," p. 954.

24. Ibid., p. 960.

25. Brennan, "Reason, Passion, and 'The Progress of the Law,'" pp. 18–19.

26. Brennan, "The Bill of Rights and the States," pp. 535–36.

27. See, e.g., Mapp v. Ohio, 367 U.S. 643 (1961) (Fourth Amendment); Robinson v. California, 370 U.S. 660 (1962) (Eighth Amendment); Gideon v. Wainwright, 372 U.S. 335 (1963) (Sixth Amendment); Malloy v. Hogan, 378 U.S. 1 (1964) (Fifth Amendment); Pointer v. Texas, 380 U.S. 400 (1965) (Sixth Amendment); Klopfer v. North Carolina, 386 U.S. 213 (1967) (Sixth Amendment); Parker v. Gladden, 385 U.S. 363 (1966) (Sixth Amendment); Washington v. Texas, 388 U.S. 14 (1967) (Sixth Amendment); Duncan v. Louisiana, 391 U.S. 145 (1968) (Sixth Amendment); Benton v. Maryland, 395 U.S. 784 (1969) (Fifth Amendment).

Of these opinions, only *Malloy* was written by Brennan himself. Brennan has recounted with pride, however, that *Malloy* was the first of these decisions to decide a case "in explicitly incorporationist terms": "The Court's opinion in *Malloy* made clear that the rights and prohibitions nationalized in the past were now considered to apply to the states with full federal regalia intact" (Brennan, "Bill of Rights and the States," pp. 543–44).

28. Brennan, "Bill of Rights and the States," p. 536 (quoting Schwartz, "The Amendment in Operation," p. 30.

29. 394 U.S. 618 (1969). On the fascinating genesis and history of the *Shapiro* opinion, see Schwartz, *Unpublished Opinions of the Warren Court,* pp. 304–93.

30. 394 U.S. at 651 (Warren, J., dissenting).

31. Id. at 634, 638.

32. Brennan, "Justice Thurgood Marshall," p. 395.

33. Seven years later Brennan would argue that courts could not rely on "reason alone" but must instead display "the passion that understands the pulse of life beneath the official version of events" (Brennan, "Reason, Passion, and 'The Progress of the Law,'" p. 22).

34. Brennan, "Some Aspects of Federalism," p. 954.

35. NAACP v. Button, 371 U.S. 415, 429, 430 (1963).

36. 372 U.S. 391, 401–02, 415, 424 (1963).

37. 380 U.S. 479 (1965).

38. 379 U.S. 443 (1965).

39. 375 U.S. 411 (1964).

40. Brennan's concern with expanding access to federal courts persisted into the Burger Court era, in decisions like Steffel v. Thompson, 415 U.S. 452 (1974), which increased access to federal declaratory relief, and Bivens v. Six Unknown Named Agents, 403 U.S. 388 (1971), which pioneered the concept of the implied federal cause of action.

It should be noted that in this respect, more than in any other, the Burger and Rehnquist Courts have been successful in undoing Brennan's work. Although the concept of federalism has not yet been resurrected as an argument to limit the interpretation of substantive federal rights (see Sandalow, "Federalism and Social Change"), the Court after the Warren era has used the concept to limit access to federal fora. Exemplary is Younger v. Harris, 401 U.S. 37 (1971), which used the notion of "Our Federalism" sharply to delimit *Dombrowski,* and Teague v. Lane, 489 U.S. 288 (1989), whose deference to the finality of state decision making processes sealed the demise of *Fay v. Noia,* formally overruled in Coleman v. Thompson, 111 S.Ct. 2546 (1991).

41. For a recent example, particularly pertinent to Brennan's constitutional legacy, see Employment Div., Dept. of Human Res. v. Smith, 494 U.S. 872 (1990).

42. See, e.g., Konigsberg v. State Bar of California, 366 U.S. 36, 50–51 (1961).

43. 357 U.S. 513 (1958).

44. Schauer, "Fear, Risk, and the First Amendment," p. 701. See also Anastaplo, "Justice Brennan, Due Process and the Freedom of Speech."

45. 357 U.S. at 515.

46. Id. at 525–26.
47. 380 U.S. 51 (1965).
48. 367 U.S. 717 (1961).
49. 361 U.S. 147, 152–53 (1959).
50. 371 U.S. 415, 438, 432–33 (1963).
51. 354 U.S. 476 (1957).
52. Id. at 491 (quoting United States v. Petrillo, 332 U.S. 1, 7–8 [1947]).
53. 385 U.S. 589, 599, 604 (1967).
54. 376 U.S. 254, 279 (1964).
55. Id. at 272 (quoting NAACP v. Button, 371 U.S. 415, 433 [1963]).
56. Id. at 285–86, 279–80.
57. Post, "Defaming Public Officials," p. 553.
58. The other Warren Court opinion to epitomize the pragmatic conception of law is Miranda v. Arizona, 384 U.S. 436 (1966), written by Chief Justice Warren. On Brennan's assistance to Warren in clarifying the logic of pragmatic law in *Miranda*, see Schwartz, *Super Chief*, pp. 590–91.
59. See Post, "Defaming Public Officials," p. 554.
60. Recent empirical evidence suggests, for example, that rather than protecting defendants from unwarranted litigation, the "actual malice" rule may paradoxically "encourage plaintiffs to sue for libel and provide an ironic sanctuary even for frivolous claims" (Bezanson, "Libel Law," p. 227).
61. See Barsky v. Board of Regents, 347 U.S. 442 (1954).
62. 357 U.S. at 518.
63. 374 U.S. 398, 404, 405 (1963).
64. 394 U.S. 618 (1969).
65. 397 U.S. 254 (1970).
66. Brennan, "Reason, Passion, and 'The Progress of the Law,'" p. 20.
67. 494 U.S. 872 (1990).
68. Id. at 888.

Chapter 8

1. O'Donnell, "Common Sense and the Constitution," p. 436. I am indebted to Norman Dorsen, Christopher Eisgruber, John Gibbons, Laura Kalman, Eben Moglen, and Robert Post for their comments and ideas.
2. Price, "White: A Justice of Studied Unpredictability."
3. See Robert C. Post, "William J. Brennan and the Warren Court," in this volume.
4. Laura Kalman, "Abe Fortas: Symbol of the Warren Court?" in this volume.
5. See Navasky, *Kennedy Justice*, p. 163; Schlesinger, *Robert Kennedy and His Times*, p. 237.
6. Halberstam, *Best and the Brightest*, p. 233.

7. See Navasky, *Kennedy Justice*, pp. 164–65. Navasky reports the conversations on pp. 165–234.

8. Hoaglund, "Byron White as a Practicing Lawyer," p. 367.

9. Quoted in Navasky, *Kennedy Justice*, p. 161.

10. Guthman and Shulman, *Robert Kennedy in His Own Words*, pp. 78–79.

11. Quoted in Navasky, *Kennedy Justice*, p. 162. On White's role in the Marshall appointment, see Schlesinger, *Kennedy and His Times*, pp. 288–89.

12. Quoted in Navasky, *Kennedy Justice*, p. 52.

13. Quoted in Schlesinger, *Kennedy and His Times*, p. 612. The other duty was to "love our country" (Ibid.).

14. Quoted in Navasky, *Kennedy Justice*, p. 162.

15. See Guthman and Shulman, *Kennedy in His Own Words*, pp. 102–3; Schlesinger, *Kennedy and His Times*, pp. 290–91; Navasky, *Kennedy Justice*, pp. 188, 204.

16. 369 U.S. 186 (1962).

17. See Navasky, *Kennedy Justice*, pp. 297–322, esp. pp. 301–2.

18. Quoted in Schlesinger, *Kennedy and His Times*, p. 381.

19. See Guthman and Shulman, *Kennedy in His Own Words*, pp. 115–16; Schlesinger, *Kennedy and His Times*, pp. 376–78.

20. Nelson, "Deference and the Limits to Deference," p. 348.

21. 384 U.S. 436, 526, 531–32 (1966).

22. Gertz v. Robert Welch, Inc., 418 U.S. 323, 403 (1974) (dissenting opinion, quoting Benjamin N. Cardozo, *Selected Writings*, ed. Margaret E. Hall [New York: Fallon Publications, 1947], 149).

23. Post, "William J. Brennan and the Warren Court," in this volume.

24. 381 U.S. 479, 502, 505 (1965).

25. 380 U.S. 202 (1965).

26. Batson v. Kentucky, 476 U.S. 79, 100–101 (1986) (concurring opinion).

27. 408 U.S. 238, 312 (1972).

28. 373 U.S. 683 (1963).

29. 377 U.S. 218 (1964).

30. 391 U.S. 430 (1968).

31. See Reitman v. Mulkey, 387 U.S. 369 (1967); Hunter v. Erickson, 393 U.S. 385 (1969).

32. 402 U.S. 1 (1971). *Accord,* Missouri v. Jenkins, 495 U.S. 33 (1990).

33. 403 U.S. 217, 240 (1971) (White, J., dissenting).

34. 418 U.S. 717, 762 (1974) (White, J., dissenting).

35. 429 U.S. 252, 272 (1977) (White, J., dissenting).

36. 438 U.S. 265, 324 (1978) (Brennan, J., White, J., Marshall, J., and Blackmun, J., concurring in part and dissenting in part). *But see* City of Richmond v. J. A. Croson Co., 488 U.S. 469 (1989), where White joined an opinion by Justice O'Connor giving local governments a narrower latitude to formulate affirmative action remedies than the opinion he had joined in *Bakke* had given to the states.

37. 426 U.S. 229 (1976).

38. Columbus Board of Education v. Penick, 443 U.S. 449 (1979).

39. Dayton Board of Education v. Brinkman, 443 U.S. 526 (1979).

40. Palmer v. Thompson, 403 U.S. 217, 240–41 (White, J., dissenting).

41. See generally Nelson, "Deference and the Limits to Deference," pp. 355–58.

42. 372 U.S. 368 (1963).

43. 376 U.S. 1 (1964).

44. 377 U.S. 533 (1964).

45. Kirkpatrick v. Preisler, 394 U.S. 526, 530–31 (1969).

46. Avery v. Midland County, 390 U.S. 474 (1968).

47. 380 U.S. 202 (1965).

48. 392 U.S. 409, 477–79 (1968) (Harlan, J., dissenting). Having joined an opinion giving a narrow construction to the Civil Rights Act of 1866, he has continued to support a narrow construction of that act; see Patterson v. McLean Credit Union, 491 U.S. 164 (1989), as well as of other federal civil rights legislation. See also Wards Cove Packing Co. v. Atonio, 490 U.S. 642 (1989).

49. Deposition of Justice Byron R. White, in Peck v. United States, 76 Civ. 93 (CES), S.D.N.Y., Dec. 6, 1982, pp. 8–9.

50. Batson v. Kentucky, 476 U.S. 79, 101–2 (1986) (White, J., concurring).

51. Post, "Justice Brennan."

52. Ibid.

53. 373 U.S. 132, 159 (1963).

54. 376 U.S. 254 (1964).

55. 372 U.S. 391 (1963). *But cf.* Teague v. Lane, 489 U.S. 288, 316–17 (1989), where White concurred in a judgment of the Court creating new bars to habeas relief.

56. 380 U.S. 479 (1965).

57. Varat, "White and Federal Authority."

58. Post, "Justice Brennan."

59. Schlesinger, *Kennedy and His Times,* pp. 141–69.

60. See generally ibid., pp. 137–169 (quotations from pp. 149, 169, 188, 189).

61. See Navasky, *Kennedy Justice,* pp. 74–75; Schlesinger, *Kennedy and His Times,* pp. 270–71.

62. See Navasky, *Kennedy Justice,* pp. 119–20, 164–67, 198–99.

63. Quoted, ibid., pp. 204, 113.

64. Quoted in Schlesinger, *Kennedy and His Times,* p. 332.

65. Quoted in Navasky, *Kennedy Justice,* p. 113.

66. Quoted in Schlesinger, *Kennedy and His Times,* pp. 332–34.

67. 370 U.S. 660, 689 (1962).

68. 378 U.S. 478, 495 (1964).

69. 378 U.S. 1, 33 (1964).

70. 384 U.S. 436, 526 (1966).

71. 388 U.S. 41, 107 (1967).

72. 388 U.S. 218, 250 (1967).

73. 384 U.S. at 544.

74. 388 U.S. at 116–17.

75. 372 U.S. 335 (1963).

76. 393 U.S. 410, 423 (1969). White continued to adhere to his *Spinelli* opinion into the 1980s. See Illinois v. Gates, 462 U.S. 213, 246, 254–67 (1983) (concurring opinion), where White joined a judgment of the Court overruling *Spinelli* on the ground that the exclusionary rule should not apply to evidence obtained by the police in good faith even though in violation of the Fourth Amendment; White, however, agreed with three dissenters that the substantive Fourth Amendment principles elaborated in *Spinelli* should not be overruled.

77. See Camara v. Municipal Court, 387 U.S. 523 (1967); See v. City of Seattle, 387 U.S. 541 (1967).

78. 403 U.S. 388 (1971).

79. 408 U.S. 238 (1972).

80. See Varat, "White and Federal Authority," p. 406.

81. 391 U.S. 145 (1968).

82. 372 U.S. 229, 236–37 (1963).

83. 383 U.S. 131, 151 (1966) (White, J., concurring).

84. 393 U.S. 503, 515 (1969) (White, J., concurring). For later majority and dissenting opinions by White upholding the rights of high school students, see Ingraham v. Wright, 430 U.S. 651, 683 (1977) (dissenting opinion); Goss v. Lopez, 419 U.S. 565 (1975).

85. Two opinions exist for this case, at 379 U.S. 536 (1965) and 379 U.S. 559 (1965).

86. Adderley v. Florida, 385 U.S. 39 (1966).

87. United States v. O'Brien, 391 U.S. 367 (1968).

88. 394 U.S. 576, 610 (1969).

89. 403 U.S. 15, 28 (1971).

90. See text accompanying note 40 above.

91. Schlesinger, *Kennedy and His Times,* pp. 908–9.

92. Compare City of Richmond v. J. A. Croson, Inc., 488 U.S. 469 (1989), with Metro Broadcasting, Inc. v. Federal Communications Commision, 497 U.S. 547 (1990).

93. 410 U.S. 113 (1973).

94. 478 U.S. 186, 199 (Blackmun, J., dissenting), 214 (Stevens, J., dissenting) (1986).

Chapter 9

1. I thank Morton Borden, W. Randall Garr, David Rabban, Rayman Solomon, and Mark Tushnet for their comments on this chapter.

2. Interview with Clark Clifford, July 1985.

3. Garment, "Annals of Law."

4. Earl Warren to Fortas, Jan. 12, 1966, Abe Fortas Supreme Court Papers, Yale University Archives.

5. Fortas, Memorandum for the Brethren, Re: No. 41—*Brown* v. *Louisiana,* December 1965, ibid.; Schwartz, *Super Chief,* p. 608.

6. Fortas, draft, *Brown* v. *Louisiana,* Dec. 30, 1965, Fortas Supreme Court Papers.

7. Brown v. Louisiana, 383 U.S. 131 (1966). For a critique of Fortas's use of the "no evidence" doctrine, see "The Supreme Court, 1965 Term," pp. 152–53.

8. 383 U.S. at 139.

9. Fortas, Meiklejohn Lecture, University of Wisconsin, Abe Fortas Papers. A portion of these papers, which are privately held, is being transferred to the Yale University Archives.

10. Confidential interview no. 1. To protect the anonymity of interviewees, I have assigned those interviews numbers. Readers can use the numbers to link an individual's various comments.

11. Fortas to Marvin Watson, Aug. 1, 1969, Fortas Papers.

12. See generally Alfange, "Free Speech and Symbolic Conduct," pp. 3–10 (Rivers quoted at p. 5, n.20).

13. United States v. O'Brien, 391 U.S. 367, 376 (1968).

14. Fortas, *Concerning Dissent and Civil Disobedience.*

15. Fred Graham, "Fortas Hits Student Law Violations," *Atlanta Constitution,* May 24, 1968, clipping in Fortas Papers.

16. Fortas, *Concering Dissent and Civil Disobedience,* pp. 124–25, 94–95.

17. Tigar, "Book Review," pp. 513–14.

18. Street v. New York, 394 U.S. 576 (1969).

19. Fortas, draft concurrence, circulated Dec. 11, 1968, Fortas Supreme Court Papers.

20. Memorandum to the Conference, March 19, 1969, ibid.

21. 394 U.S. at 615.

22. Dissenting opinion of Chief Justice Rehnquist, Justice White and Justice O'Connor, Texas v. Johnson, 491 U.S. 397, 432 (1969).

23. 394 U.S. at 617.

24. Tinker v. Des Moines School District, 393 U.S. 503 (1969).

25. Id. at 506–9, 513.

26. Jaime Benitez to Fortas, April 21, 1969; Fortas to Benitez, April 25, 1969, Fortas Papers.

27. Fortas to Fred Lazarus, May 21, 1969, ibid.

28. Epperson v. Arkansas, 393 U.S. 97 (1968).

29. Henkin, "On Drawing Lines."

30. Charles Coleman to Fortas, Feb. 24, 1969, Fortas Supreme Court Papers.

31. Nick Pettenger to Fortas, Feb. 24, 1969, ibid.

32. Coleman to Fortas, Feb. 24, 1969, ibid.
33. Savoy, "Toward a New Politics of Legal Education," pp. 444, 450.
34. Fortas to Benitez, April 25, 1969, Fortas Papers.
35. Zinn, *Disobedience and Democracy*, p. 7.
36. See generally Matusow, *Unraveling of America*.
37. G. Edward White, *Earl Warren*, p. 344.
38. Warren Christopher to Larry Temple, Dec. 20, 1968, Memorandum on the Fortas and Thornberry Nominations, box 3, Special File Pertaining to Abe Fortas and Homer Thornberry, Lyndon B. Johnson Library, Austin, Texas.
39. Michael Manatos to Lyndon Johnson, 4:15 P.M., June 25, 1968, and 5:30 P.M., June 26, 1968, ibid.
40. Thurgood Marshall to Fortas, n.d., Fortas Papers.
41. Fortas to William O. Douglas, July 25, 1968, ibid.
42. U.S. Senate, 90th Cong., 2d sess., *Hearings before the Committee on the Judiciary, Nominations of Abe Fortas and Homer Thornberry*, July 11, 12, 16, 17, 18, 19, 20, 22, and 23, 1968, p. 191. See Mallory v. United States, 354 U.S. 449 (1957).
43. Interview with Robert Griffin by CBS Newsmen Nelson Benton, Bruce Morton, and Hal Walker, box B129, folder 29, Gerald R. Ford Library, Ann Arbor, Mich.; interview with Arthur Goldberg, Dec. 1983.
44. U.S. Senate, 90th Cong., 1st sess., *Hearings before the Committee on the Judiciary, Nomination of Thurgood Marshall*, July 13, 14, 18, 19, and 24, 1967, p. 7.
45. Confidential interview no. 2.
46. Confidential interview no. 3.
47. Confidential interview no. 1.
48. See, e.g., Fortas and Thornberry confirmation *Hearings*, p. 49.
49. Interview with Clifford; Johnson, *The Vantage Point*, p. 545.
50. Ibid.
51. See Murphy, *Fortas*, pp. 279–83, 292–99.
52. *Congressional Record* 114, pt. 15, 90th Cong., 2d sess., July 1, 1968, pp. 19543–44 (remarks of Senator Baker).
53. Thus the office of Fortas's opponent, Senator Robert Griffin, for example, "claim[ed] three switches against Fortas because of the $15,000" (memorandum written by Ernest Goldstein, box 3, Fortas-Thornberry File). Fortas's supporters, senators Dirksen and Mansfield, agreed that Fortas's fee for the American University seminar had been "hurtful, particularly since Paul Porter raised the money" (Michael Manatos to Lyndon Johnson, Sept. 16, 1968, 4:15 P.M., ibid.)
54. Porter had solicited the money from Maurice Lazarus of Federated Department Stores, Troy Post of Greatamerica Corporation, Paul Smith of Philip Morris, and investment bankers Gustave Levy and John Loeb. Lazarus, Post and Smith had been Fortas's clients.
55. I am indebted to Carolyn Agger Fortas for giving me a summary of Fortas's earnings for 1964 prepared by the accounting firm of Laventhol and Horwath.

56. Paul Porter to Gustave Levy, Feb. 2, 1968, to Benjamin Sonnenberg, Feb. 8, 1968, and to Maurice Lazarus, Feb. 9, 1968, Paul Porter Papers, box 5, Lyndon B. Johnson Library.

57. See, e.g., Paul Porter to Troy Post, Feb. 7, 1968, to Gustave Levy, Feb. 9, 1968, ibid. See also Porter to Maurice Lazarus, Feb. 9, 1968, to John Loeb, Feb. 14, 1968 (indicating he would tell Fortas of Lazarus's and Loeb's contributions), ibid.

58. Paul Porter to Fortas, Feb. 28, 1968, Fortas Papers.

59. Fortas and Thornberry confirmation *Hearings,* p. 1291. See also, e.g., *Congressional Record* 114, pt. 21, Sept. 25, 1968, p. 28119 (remarks of Senator Griffin).

60. Interview with Eugene Bogan, May 1985.

61. Interview with Nicholas Katzenbach, December 1983.

62. Quoted in Murphy, *Fortas,* p. 286.

63. See generally Masarro, "LBJ and the Fortas Nomination."

64. Parrish, "Little Daily Questions and Shooting Tiger."

BIBLIOGRAPHY

Adler, Sheldon S. "Note: Toward a Constitutional Theory of Individuality: The Privacy Opinions of Justice Douglas." *Yale Law Journal* 87 (1978): 1579–1600.

Alfange, Dean, Jr. "Free Speech and Symbolic Conduct: The Draft-Card Burning Case." *Supreme Court Review* (1968): 1–52.

Allen, Robert S., and William V. Shannon. *The Truman Merry-Go-Round.* New York: Vanguard Press, 1950.

Anastaplo, George. "Justice Brennan, Due Process, and the Freedom of Speech: A Celebration of *Speiser v. Randall.*" *John Marshall Law Review* 20 (1986): 7–27.

Beale, Sir Howard. "A Man for All Seasons." In *Felix Frankfurter: A Tribute*, ed. Wallace Mendelson, pp. 18–21. New York: Reynal, 1964.

Bell, Derrick. "Comment: *Brown v. Board of Education* and the Interest-Convergence Dilemma." *Harvard Law Review* 93 (1980): 518–33.

———. "An Epistolary Exploration for a Thurgood Marshall Biography." *Harvard Blackletter Journal* 6 (1989): 51–67.

Bezanson, Randall. "Libel Law and the Realities of Litigation: Setting the Record Straight." *Iowa Law Review* 71 (1985): 226–33.

Bickel, Alexander M. "Justice Frankfurter at Seventy-Five." *New Republic*, Nov. 18, 1957, p. 7.

———. "The Original Understanding and the Segregation Decision." *Harvard Law Review* 69 (1955): 1–65.

———. *The Supreme Court and the Idea of Progress.* New York: Harper & Row, 1970.

———. *The Unpublished Opinions of Mr. Justice Brandeis.* Chicago: Univ. of Chicago Press, 1957.

Black, Hugo L. *A Constitutional Faith.* New York: Knopf, 1968.

———. and Elizabeth Black. *Mr. Justice and Mrs. Black: Memoirs.* New York: Random House, 1986.

Blasi, Vincent, ed. *The Burger Court: The Counter-Revolution That Wasn't.* New Haven: Yale Univ. Press, 1983.

Bolt, Robert. *A Man for All Seasons.* New York: Random House, 1962.

Branch, Taylor. *Parting the Waters: America in the King Years 1954–1963.* New York: Simon & Schuster, 1988.

Brennan, William. "The Bill of Rights and the States: The Revival of State Constitutions as Guardians of Individual Rights." *New York University Law Review* 61 (1986): 535–53.

———. "The Equality Principle: A Foundation of American Law." *U.C. Davis Law Review* 20 (1987): 673–78.

——. "Justice Thurgood Marshall: Advocate for Human Need in American Jurisprudence." *Maryland Law Review* 40 (1981): 390–97.

——. "Reason, Passion, and 'The Progress of the Law.'" *Cardozo Law Review* 10
(1988): 3–23.

——. "Some Aspects of Federalism." *New York University Law Review* 39 (1964):
945–61.

Brown, John Mason. "Frankfurter: The Past Is Prologue." *Saturday Review,* Nov. 20,
1954, p. 17.

——. "The Uniform of Justice." *Saturday Review,* Oct. 30, 1954, p. 9.

Burt, Robert A. *Two Jewish Justices: Outcasts in the Promised Land.* Berkeley: Univ. of
California Press, 1988.

Campbell, J. L., III. "How Opinions Can Persuade: A Case Study of William O.
Douglas." *Federal Bar News and Journal* 29 (1982): 231–34.

Caplan, Gerald. "Questioning *Miranda.*" *Vanderbilt Law Review* 38 (1985): 1417–76.

Cardozo, Benjamin N. *The Nature of the Judicial Process.* New Haven: Yale Univ.
Press, 1921.

Cohen, William. "Justice Douglas and the *Rosenberg* Case: Setting the Record
Straight." *Cornell Law Review* 70 (1985): 211–52.

Coleman, William T., Jr. "Mr. Justice Felix Frankfurter: Civil Libertarian as Lawyer
and as Justice: Extent to Which Judicial Responsibilities Affected His Pre-
Court Convictions." In *Six Justices on Civil Rights,* ed. Ronald D. Rotunda, pp.
85–105. New York: Oceana Publications, 1983.

Corbin, Arthur. "The Offer of an Act for a Promise." *Yale Law Journal* 29 (1920):
767–72.

Countryman, Vern. "The Contribution of the Douglas Dissents." *Georgia Law Review*
10 (1976): 331–52.

——. "Even-Handed Justice." *Harvard Civil Rights–Civil Liberties Law Review* 11
(1976): 233–40.

——. "Justice Douglas and Freedom of Expression." *University of Illinois Law Review*
(1978): 301–27.

——. "Justice Douglas and Freedom of Expression." In *Six Justices on Civil Rights,*
ed. Ronald D. Rotunda, pp. 107–33. New York: Oceana Publications, 1983.

——. "Scholarship and Common Sense." *Harvard Law Review* 93 (1980): 1407–15.

——. ed. *The Douglas Opinions.* New York: Random House, 1977.

Cox, Archibald. "The Supreme Court, 1965 Term--Foreword: Constitutional Adjudication and the Promotion of Human Rights." *Harvard Law Review* 80
(1966): 91–122.

——. *The Warren Court: Constitutional Decision as an Instrument of Reform.* Cambridge: Harvard Univ. Press, 1968.

Days, Drew S. "Justice William O. Douglas and Civil Rights." In *"He Shall Not Pass
This Way Again": The Legacy of Justice William O. Douglas,* ed. Stephen L.
Wasby, pp. 109–20. Pittsburgh: Univ. of Pittsburgh Press, 1990.

Dorsen, Norman. "In Memoriam: Albert M. Sacks." *Harvard Law Review* 105 (1991): 11–14.

——. "The Second Mr. Justice Harlan: A Constitutional Conservative." *New York University Law Review* 44 (1969): 249–71.

——. "The United States Supreme Court: Trends and Prospects." *Harvard Civil Rights–Civil Liberties Law Review* 21 (1986): 1–26.

Douglas, William O. *An Almanac of Liberty.* Garden City, N.Y.: Doubleday, 1954.

——. "On Misconception of the Judicial Function and the Responsibility of the Bar." *Columbia Law Review* 59 (1959): 227–33.

——. *The Court Years.* New York: Random House, 1980.

——. *Go East, Young Man.* New York: Random House, 1974.

——. *Of Men and Mountains.* New York: Random House, 1950.

——. "Stare Decisis." *Columbia Law Review* 49 (1949): 735–58.

D'Souza, Dinesh. "The New Liberal Censorship." *Policy Review* 38 (Fall 1986): 8–15.

Duke, Steven. "William O. Douglas and the Rights of the Accused." In *"He Shall Not Pass This Way Again": The Legacy of Justice William O. Douglas,* ed. Stephen L. Wasby, pp. 133–48. Pittsburgh: Univ. of Pittsburgh Press, 1990.

Dunne, Gerald T. *Hugo Black and the Judicial Revolution.* New York: Simon & Schuster, 1977.

Edsall, Thomas Byrne, with Mary D. Edsall. *Chain Reaction: The Impact of Race, Rights, and Taxes on American Politics.* New York: Norton, 1991.

Eisenberg, Melvin Aaron. *The Nature of the Common Law.* Cambridge: Harvard Univ. Press, 1988.

Elman, Philip, interviewed by Norman Silber. "The Solicitor General's Office, Justice Frankfurter, and Civil Rights Litigation, 1946–60: An Oral History." *Harvard Law Review* 100 (1987): 817–52.

Ely, John Hart. *Democracy and Distrust.* Cambridge: Harvard Univ. Press, 1980.

Emerson, Thomas. "Justice Douglas' Contribution to the Law: The First Amendment." *Columbia Law Review* 74 (1974): 353–57.

——. "Nine Justices in Search of a Doctrine." *Michigan Law Review* 64 (1965): 219–34.

Fortas, Abe. *Concerning Dissent and Civil Disobedience.* New York: New American Library, 1968.

——. "William O. Douglas: An Appreciation." *Indiana Law Journal* 51 (1975): 3–5.

Frank, Jerome. *Law and the Modern Mind.* New York: Coward-McCann, 1935.

Frank, John P. "Hugo L. Black: Free Speech and the Declaration of Independence." In *Six Justices on Civil Rights,* ed. Ronald D. Rotunda, pp. 11–54. New York: Oceana Publications, 1983.

Frankfurter, Felix. *The Public and Its Government.* New Haven: Yale Univ. Press, 1930.

Freund, Paul. "Felix Frankfurter: Reminiscences and Reflections." *Harvard Law School Centennial Celebration,* Nov. 19, 1962, p. 6.

——. "Foreword." In *The Evolution of a Judicial Philosophy: Selected Opinions and*

Papers of Justice John M. Harlan, ed. David Shapiro, pp. xiii-xv. Cambridge: Harvard Univ. Press, 1969.

——. "Historical Reminiscence: Justice Brandeis: A Law Clerk's Remembrance." *American Jewish History* 68 (1978): 7–18.

Freyer, Tony. "The First Amendment and the Conference Commemorating the Centennial of Justice Hugo L. Black: An Introduction." *Alabama Law Review* 38 (1987): 215–21.

——. *Hugo L. Black and the Dilemma of American Liberalism.* Glenview, Ill.; Scott, Foresman / Little, Brown, 1990.

——. *The Little Rock Crisis.* Westport, Conn.: Greenwood Press, 1984.

——. ed. *Justice Hugo Black and Modern America.* Tuscaloosa: Univ. of Alabama Press, 1990.

Friendly, Henry. "Mr. Justice Harlan, as Seen by a Friend and Judge of an Inferior Court." *Harvard Law Review* 85 (1971): 382–89.

Garment, Leonard. "Annals of Law." *New Yorker,* April 17, 1989, p. 90.

Glancy, Dorothy J. "Douglas's Right of Privacy: A Response to His Critics." In *"He Shall Not Pass This Way Again": The Legacy of Justice William O. Douglas,* ed. Stephen L. Wasby, pp. 155–77. Pittsburgh: Univ. of Pittsburgh Press, 1990.

——. "Getting the Government Off the Backs of the People: The Right of Privacy and Freedom of Expression in the Opinions of Justice William O. Douglas." *Santa Clara Law Review* 21 (1981): 1047–67.

Greene, Graham. *The Human Factor.* Paperback ed. New York: Random House, Vintage Books, 1978.

Greenawalt, Kent. "The Enduring Significance of Neutral Principles." *Columbia Law Review* 78 (1978): 982–1021.

Gunther, Gerald. *Constitutional Law.* 11th ed. Mineola, N.Y.: Foundation Press, 1985.

——. "In Search of Judicial Quality on a Changing Court: The Case of Justice Powell." *Stanford Law Review* 24 (1972): 1001–35.

Guthman, Edwin O., and Jeffrey Shulman, eds. *Robert Kennedy in His Own Words: The Unpublished Recollections of the Kennedy Years.* New York: Bantam Books, 1988.

Halberstam, David. *The Best and the Brightest.* New York: Random House, 1972.

Halpern, Stephen C., and Charles Lamb. *Supreme Court Activism and Restraint.* Lexington, Mass.: Lexington Books, 1982.

Hamilton, Virginia Van der Veer. *Hugo Black: The Alabama Years.* Baton Rouge: Louisiana State Univ. Press, 1972.

Hart, Henry, and Al Sacks. *The Legal Process: Basic Problems in the Making and Application of Law.* Tentative ed. Cambridge: Harvard Law School, 1958.

Heck, Edward. "Justice Brennan and the Heyday of Warren Court Liberalism." *Santa Clara Law Review* 20 (1980): 841–87.

Henkin, Louis. "The Supreme Court, 1967 Term--Foreword: On Drawing Lines." *Harvard Law Review* 82 (1968): 63–92.

Hirsch, Harry N. *The Enigma of Felix Frankfurter*. New York: Basic Books, 1981.

Hoagland, Donald W. "Byron White as a Practicing Lawyer in Colorado." *University of Colorado Law Review* 58 (1987): 365–70.

Holmes, Oliver Wendell, Jr. *The Common Law*. Ed. Mark DeWolfe Howe. Cambridge: Harvard Univ. Press, 1963.

——. "The Path of the Law" (1897). In Oliver Wendell Holmes, Jr., *Collected Legal Papers*, pp. 167–202. New York: Harcourt, Brace & Co., 1920.

——. "The Theory of Legal Interpretation" (1899). In Oliver Wendell Holmes, Jr., *Collected Legal Papers*, pp. 203–9. New York: Harcourt, Brace & Co., 1920.

Howard, J. Woodford. *Mr. Justice Murphy: A Political Biography*. Princeton, N.J.: Princeton Univ. Press, 1968.

Hutchinson, Dennis. "Hail to the Chief: Earl Warren and the Supreme Court." *Michigan Law Review* 81 (1983): 922–30.

——. "Unanimity and Desegregation: Decisionmaking in the Supreme Court, 1948–1958." *Georgetown Law Journal* 68 (1979): 1–96.

Jaffe, Louis. "Was Brandeis an Activist? The Search for Intermediate Premises." *Harvard Law Review* 80 (1967): 986–1003.

Johnson, Lyndon. *The Vantage Point: Perspectives of the Presidency, 1963–1969*. New York: Holt, Rinehart and Winston, 1971.

Josephson, Matthew. "Jurist--III." *New Yorker*, Dec. 14, 1940, p. 34.

Kalman, Laura. *Legal Realism at Yale, 1927–1960*. Chapel Hill: Univ. of North Carolina Press, 1986.

Kalven, Harry. *A Worthy Tradition: Freedom of Speech in America*. New York: Harper & Row, 1988.

Kamisar, Yale. *Police Interrogation and Confessions*. Ann Arbor: Univ. of Michigan Press, 1980.

Kanin, Garson. "Trips to Felix." In *Felix Frankfurter: A Tribute*, ed. Wallace Mendelson, pp. 34–58. New York: Reynal, 1964.

Karst, Kenneth L. "Dedication: William O. Douglas, 1898–1980." *UCLA Law Review* 27 (1980): 511–13.

Kaufman, Andrew L. "The Justice and His Law Clerks." In *Felix Frankfurter: A Tribute*, ed. Wallace Mendelson, pp. 223–28. New York: Reynal, 1964.

Kaufman, Irving R. "Helping the Public Understand and Accept Judicial Decisions." *ABA Journal* 63 (1977): 1567–69.

Kauper, Paul. "Penumbras, Peripheries, Emanations, Things Fundamental, and Things Forgotten: The *Griswold* Case." *Michigan Law Review* 64 (1965): 235–58.

Klarman, Michael. "The Puzzling Resistance to Political Process Theory." *Virginia Law Review* 77 (1991): 747–832.

Kluger, Richard. *Simple Justice*. New York: Knopf, 1976.

Kurland, Philip. "Earl Warren: Master of the Revels." *Harvard Law Review* 96 (1982): 331–39.

——. "Justice Robert H. Jackson: Impact on Civil Rights and Civil Liberties." In *Six*

Justices on Civil Rights, ed. Ronald D. Rotunda, pp. 57–82. New York: Oceana Publications, 1983.

Lasch, Christopher. *The True and Only Heaven: Progress and Its Critics*. New York: Norton, 1991.

Lash, Joseph. *From The Diaries of Felix Frankfurter*. New York: Norton, 1975.

Lewin, Nathan. "Justice Harlan: 'The Full Measure of the Man.'" *ABA Journal* 58 (1972): 579–83.

Lewis, Anthony. "Earl Warren." In *The Warren Court: A Critical Analysis*, ed. Richard Sayler, Barry Boyer, and Robert Gooding, Jr., pp. 1–31. New York: Chelsea House, 1969.

Llewellyn, Karl. "A Realistic Jurisprudence: The Next Step." *Columbia Law Review* 30 (1930): 431–65.

McDowell, Gary. *The Constitution and Contemporary Constitutional Theory.* Cumberland, Va.: Center for Judicial Studies, 1985.

Masarro, John. "LBJ and the Fortas Nomination for Chief Justice." *Political Science Quarterly* 97 (1982–83): 603–21.

Mason, Alpheus T. *Brandeis: A Free Man's Life*. New York: Viking Press, 1946.

Matusow, Allen. *The Unraveling of America: A History of Liberalism in the 1960s*. New York: Harper and Row, 1984.

Maverick, Maury, Jr. "Douglas and the First Amendment: Visiting Old Battlegrounds." *Baylor Law Review* 28 (1976): 235–48.

Meador, Daniel J. *Mr. Justice Black and His Books*. Charlottesville: Univ. Press of Virginia, 1974.

Meese, Edwin, III. "Construing the Constitution." *University of California Davis Law Review* 19 (1985): 22–30.

Mendelson, Wallace. "The Influence of James B. Thayer upon the Work of Holmes, Brandeis, and Frankfurter." *Vanderbilt Law Review* 31 (1978): 71–87.

Mikva, Abner. "The Role of Theorists in Constitutional Cases." *University of Colorado Law Review* 63 (1992): 451–56.

Murphy, Bruce. *Fortas: The Rise and Ruin of a Supreme Court Justice*. New York: William Morrow, 1988.

Murphy, Walter. *Congress and the Court: A Case Study in the American Political Process*. Chicago: Univ. of Chicago Press, 1962.

Navasky, Victor S. *Kennedy Justice*. New York: Atheneum, 1971.

Nelson, William E. "Deference and the Limits to Deference in the Constitutional Jurisprudence of Justice Byron R. White." *University of Colorado Law Review* 58 (1987): 347–64.

Nizer, Louis. *The Implosion Conspiracy.* Garden City, N.Y.: Doubleday, 1973.

Note. "The Supreme Court, 1970 Term." *Harvard Law Review* 85 (1971): 38–353.

Note. "The Supreme Court, 1965 Term." *Harvard Law Review* 80 (1966): 125–272.

Novick, Sheldon. *Honorable Justice: The Life of Oliver Wendell Holmes*. Boston: Little, Brown, 1989.

O'Brien, David. *Storm Center: The Supreme Court in American Politics.* New York: Norton, 1986.

O'Donnell, Pierce. "Common Sense and the Constitution: Justice White and the Egalitarian Ideal." *University of Colorado Law Review* 58 (1987): 433–70.

Parrish, Michael. "Cold War Justice: The Supreme Court and the Rosenbergs." *American Historical Review* 82 (1977): 805–42.

——. "Justice Douglas and the *Rosenberg* Case: A Rejoinder." *Cornell Law Review* 70 (1985): 1048–57.

——. "Little Daily Questions and Shooting Tiger." In *Power and Responsibility: Case Studies in American Leadership,* ed. David Kennedy and Michael Parrish, pp. 141–70. New York: Harcourt, Brace and Jovanovich, 1986.

Posner, Richard. "The Decline of Law as an Autonomous Discipline, 1962–1987." *Harvard Law Review* 100 (1987): 761–80.

Post, Robert. "Cultural Heterogeneity and Law: Pornography, Blasphemy, and the First Amendment." *California Law Review* 76 (1988): 297–335.

——. "Review Essay: Defaming Public Officials: On Doctrine and Legal History." *American Bar Foundation Research Journal* (1987): 539–57.

Powe, Lucas A., Jr. "Evolution to Absolutism: Justice Douglas and the First Amendment." *Columbia Law Review* 74 (1974): 371–411.

——. "Justice Douglas after Fifty Years: The First Amendment, McCarthyism, and Rights." *Constitutional Commentary* 6 (1989): 267–87.

Price, Monroe E. "White: A Justice of Studied Unpredictability." *National Law Journal,* Feb. 18, 1980, p. 24.

Radin, Max. "The Theory of Judicial Decisions: or How Judges Think." *American Bar Association Journal* 11 (1925): 357–62.

Robinson, Armstead L., and Patricia Sullivan, eds. *New Directions in Civil Rights Studies.* Charlottesville: Univ. Press of Virginia, 1991.

Rodell, Fred. "Felix Frankfurter--Conservative." *Harper's Magazine* 183 (Oct. 1941): 456–57.

Saltzburg, Stephen A. *American Criminal Procedure: Cases and Commentary.* 3d ed. St. Paul: West Publishing Co., 1988.

Sandalow, Terrance. "Federalism and Social Change." *Law and Contemporary Problems* 43 (1980): 29–38.

Savoy, Paul. "Toward a New Politics of Legal Education." *Yale Law Journal* 79 (1970): 444–504.

Schauer, Frederick. "Fear, Risk, and the First Amendment: Unravelling the 'Chilling Effect.'" *Boston University Law Review* 58 (1978): 685–732.

Schlesinger, Arthur M., Jr., *Robert Kennedy and His Times.* Boston: Houghton Mifflin, 1978.

Schneir, Walter, and Miriam Schneir. *Invitation to an Inquest: Reopening the Rosenberg "Atom Spy" Case.* Garden City, N.Y.: Doubleday, 1965.

Schwartz, Bernard. "The Amendment in Operation: A Historical Overview." In *The*

Fourteenth Amendment, pp. 29–38, ed. Bernard Schwartz. New York: New York Univ. Press, 1970.

——. *Super Chief*. New York: New York Univ. Press, 1983.

——. *The Unpublished Opinions of the Warren Court*. New York: Oxford Univ. Press, 1985.

Shapiro, Martin. "Fathers and Sons: The Court, the Commentators, and the Search for Values." In *The Burger Court: The Counter-Revolution That Wasn't*, ed. Vincent Blasi, pp. 218–38. New Haven: Yale Univ. Press, 1983.

Segal, Jeffrey A., and Harold J. Spaeth. "Decisional Trends on the Warren and Burger Courts: Results from the Supreme Court Data Base Project." *Judicature* 73 (1989): 103–7.

Seidman, L. Michael. "*Brown* and *Miranda*." *California Law Review* 80 (1992): 673–753.

Semonche, John E. *Charting the Future: The Supreme Court Responds to a Changing Society, 1890–1920*. Westport, Conn.: Greenwood Press, 1978.

Silverstein, Mark. *Constitutional Faiths: Felix Frankfurter, Hugo Black, and the Process of Judicial Decision Making*. Ithaca, N.Y.: Cornell Univ. Press, 1984.

Simon, James F. *The Antagonists: Hugo Black, Felix Frankfurter, and Civil Liberties in Modern America*. New York: Simon & Schuster, 1989.

——. *Independent Journey: The Life of William O. Douglas*. New York: Harper & Row, 1980.

Snowiss, Sylvia. *Judicial Review and the Law of the Constitution*. New Haven: Yale Univ. Press, 1990.

——. "The Legacy of Justice Black." *Supreme Court Review* 1973: 187–252.

Strossen, Nadine. "The Religion Clause Writings of Justice William O. Douglas." In *"He Shall Not Pass This Way Again": The Legacy of Justice William O. Douglas*, ed. Stephen L. Wasby, pp. 91–107. Pittsburgh: Univ. of Pittsburgh Press, 1990.

Tigar, Michael. "Book Review." *Michigan Law Review* 67 (1969): 612–22.

——. "The Supreme Court, 1969 Term--Foreword: Waiver of Constitutional Rights: Disquiet in the Citadel." *Harvard Law Review* 84 (1970): 1–28.

Tocqueville, Alexis de. *Democracy in America*. Vintage Books ed. New York: Knopf, 1945.

Tribe, Laurence. *American Constitutional Law*. 2d ed. Mineola, N.Y.: Foundation Press, 1988.

Tushnet, Mark. "Book Review." *Law and History Review* 8 (1990): 310–17.

——. *Making Civil Rights Law: Thurgood Marshall and the Supreme Court*. Forthcoming, 1993.

——. "The Optimist's Tale (Book Review)." *University of Pennsylvania Law Review* 132 (1984): 1257–73.

——. "Toward a Revisionist History of the Supreme Court." *Cleveland State Law Review* 36 (1988): 319–54.

——. with Katya Lezin. "What Really Happened in *Brown v. Board of Education*." *Columbia Law Review* 92 (1992): 1867–930.

Urofsky, Melvin I. "Conflict among the Brethren: Felix Frankfurter, William O. Douglas, and the Clash of Personalities and Philosophies on the United States Supreme Court." *Duke Law Journal* (1988): 71–113.

——. *Felix Frankfurter: Judicial Restraint and Individual Liberties*. Boston: Twayne, 1991.

——. "Getting the Job Done." In *"He Shall Not Pass This Way Again": The Legacy of Justice William O. Douglas*, ed. Stephen L. Wasby, pp. 33–49. Pittsburgh: Univ. of Pittsburgh Press, 1990.

——. ed. *The Douglas Letters*. Bethesda, Md.: Adler & Adler, 1987.

Varat, Jonathan D. "Justice White and the Breadth and Allocation of Federal Authority." *University of Colorado Law Review* 58 (1987): 371–427.

Warren, Earl. *The Memoirs of Earl Warren*. Garden City, N.Y.: Doubleday, 1977.

——. "Mr. Justice Brennan." *Harvard Law Review* 80 (1966): 1–2.

——. "Mr. Justice Harlan, as Seen by a Colleague." *Harvard Law Review* 85 (1971): 369–71.

Warren, Samuel, and Louis D. Brandeis. "The Right to Privacy." *Harvard Law Review* 4 (1890): 193–220.

Wechsler, Herbert. *Principles, Politics, and Fundamental Law*. Cambridge: Harvard Univ. Press, 1961.

White, G. Edward. *The American Judicial Tradition*. 2d ed. New York: Oxford Univ. Press, 1988.

——. "The Anti-Judge: William O. Douglas and the Ambiguities of Individuality." *Virginia Law Review* 74 (1988): 17–86.

——. *Earl Warren: A Public Life*. New York: Oxford Univ. Press, 1982.

——. "Earl Warren as Jurist." *Virginia Law Review* 67 (1981): 461–551.

——. *The Marshall Court and Cultural Change*. New York: Macmillan, 1988.

White, Morton. *Social Thought in America: The Revolt Against Formalism*. Boston: Viking Press, 1949.

Wilkinson, J. Harvie. "Justice John Marshall Harlan and the Values of Federalism." *Virginia Law Review* 57 (1971): 1185–221.

Wolfman, Bernard, Jonathan L. F. Silver, and Marjorie Silver. *Dissent without Opinion: The Behavior of Justice William O. Douglas in Federal Tax Cases*. Philadelphia: Univ. of Pennsylvania Press, 1975.

Wood, John. "John M. Harlan, as Seen by a Colleague in the Practice of Law." *Harvard Law Review* 85 (1971): 377–81.

Woodward, Bob, and Scott Armstrong. *The Brethren: Inside the Supreme Court*. New York: Simon & Schuster, 1979.

Wright, Charles Alan. "Hugo L. Black: A Great Man and a Great American." *Texas Law Review* 50 (1971): 1–5.

Yarbrough, Tinsley E. *John Marshall Harlan: Great Dissenter of the Supreme Court.* New York: Oxford Univ. Press, 1992.

——. *Mr. Justice Black and His Critics.* Durham: Duke Univ. Press, 1988.

Zinn, Howard. *Disobedience and Democracy.* New York: Random House, 1968.

CONTRIBUTORS

MARK TUSHNET is Professor of Law, Georgetown University Law Center.

G. EDWARD WHITE is John B. Minor Professor Law and Sullivan & Cromwell Professor of Law and History, University of Virginia.

MICHAEL E. PARRISH is Professor of History, University of California, San Diego.

MELVIN I. UROFSKY is Professor of History, Virginia Commonwealth University.

TONY FREYER is Professor of History and Law, University of Alabama.

NORMAN DORSEN is Frederick I. & Grace A. Stokes Professor and Director, Arthur Garfield Hays Civil Liberties Memorial Program, New York University Law School.

ROBERT C. POST is Professor of Law, University of California, Berkeley.

WILLIAM E. NELSON is Professor of Law, New York University Law School.

LAURA KALMAN is Professor of History, University of California, Santa Barbara.

NOTE: Case names are given only for cases receiving textual treatment.